THE

Wine Maker®
GUIDE TO
HOME WINEMAKING

Quarto.com

© 2024 Quarto Publishing Group USA Inc.
Text © 2024 Battenkill Communications, Inc.

First Published in 2024 by The Harvard Common Press, an imprint of The Quarto Group, 100 Cummings Center, Suite 265-D, Beverly, MA 01915, USA.
T (978) 282-9590
F (978) 283-2742

The Harvard Common Press titles are also available at discount for retail, wholesale, promotional, and bulk purchase. For details, contact the Special Sales Manager by email at specialsales@quarto.com or by mail at The Quarto Group, Attn: Special Sales Manager, 100 Cummings Center, Suite 265-D, Beverly, MA 01915, USA.

28 27 26 25 24   1 2 3 4 5

ISBN: 978-0-7603-8504-3

Digital edition published in 2024

eISBN: 978-0-7603-8505-0

Library of Congress Cataloging-in-Publication Data

Title: The WineMaker guide to home winemaking : craft your own great wine : beginner to advanced techniques and tips : 30+ recipes for classic grape and fruit wines.
Other titles: Wine maker guide to home winemaking | Winemaker.
Description: Beverly, MA, USA : The Harvard Common Press, an imprint of the Quarto Group, 2024. | Includes index.
Identifiers: LCCN 2023038536 (print) | LCCN 2023038537 (ebook) | ISBN 9780760385043 (trade paperback) | ISBN 9780760385050 (ebook)
Subjects: LCSH: Wine and wine making--Amateurs' manuals.
Classification: LCC TP548.2 .W56 2024 (print) | LCC TP548.2 (ebook) | DDC 641.2/2--dc23/eng/20230907
LC record available at https://lccn.loc.gov/2023038536
LC ebook record available at https://lccn.loc.gov/2023038537

Design and layout: Burge Agency
Cover Images: Shutterstock (front) and Charles A. Parker (back)
Photography: Charles A. Parker except *WineMaker* on pages 103 and 124, and Shutterstock on pages 39, 47, 49 (both), 88, 94, 99, 111, 131, 154, 155, 159, 162, 166, 172, 173, 177, and 179

Printed in China

THE

WineMaker®
GUIDE TO
HOME WINEMAKING

CRAFT YOUR OWN
GREAT WINE

BEGINNER
TO ADVANCED
TECHNIQUES
AND TIPS:
RECIPES FOR
CLASSIC GRAPE
AND FRUIT
WINES

HARVARD
COMMON
PRESS

Contents

Introduction

As a home winemaker twenty-five years ago, there was very little accessible information on the hobby. If you were fortunate when you first started out, you knew someone who made wine and could give you pointers on what they did. Or maybe winemaking was a family tradition passed down for generations so your techniques and recipes followed those relayed to you by your father, and father's father, or mother and her mother. . . . There were many amateur winemakers at the time, but the problem was that the advice being passed on to new home winemakers wasn't always accurate. This information void was the motivation for *WineMaker* magazine's inception in 1998. And even though the internet has improved the accessibility of information, the reliability for accurate information remains the reason *WineMaker* is the most trusted source for hobby winemakers worldwide.

Over the last quarter century, *WineMaker* authors, technical editors, and review board members have included professional winemakers, oenology professors, industry leaders, and passionate home winemakers who all share the common goal of passing on a love for making and enjoying great wine. We've strived to provide science-based information in a fun and approachable way to winemakers of all experience levels. Although helping readers make the best wine possible has always been our first goal, keeping the hobby enjoyable for everyone—from first-time vintners to longtime cellar rats—is a close second.

Winemaking is a hobby that combines science and art, striking a balance between the two in a way that any wine lover can be drawn in to and bring to it their own finesse to be displayed in the finished bottle. It brings friends and family together in fields at harvest, at the crusher as lugs of grapes are added one by one, while conducting trials to find the perfect blend, and, of course, around the table when the bottle that so much work went into creating fills the glasses of those gathered. It's a hobby we winemakers take a great deal of pride in and wish to share with others.

Our dedication to the growth of home winemakers for over a quarter century—through our bi-monthly magazine, in-person and online conferences and educational seminars, organizing the world's largest amateur wine competition each year, and other outlets—means we've compiled a tremendous archive of information. This book that you've just picked up is our attempt to pass the very best of that information on to an even wider audience of winemakers in a concise fashion. We believe this book includes something for everyone—from starting with the basics for those considering the hobby but unsure where to begin to advanced topics for hobbyists who have a cellar full of homemade wines dating back many vintages. The primary focus is on making still red and white table wines from grapes, but we also cover making wines from kits, juice, and fruits other than grapes, and explain the process and techniques home winemakers may employ to make sparkling, rosé, and sweet wines. Recipes include using the most common *Vitis vinifera* grapes as well as numerous hybrid grapes and country wines.

The hobby has come a long way over the past twenty-five years and it's been a pleasure meeting, speaking with, and getting to know so many of you over that time. Let's make the next vintage our best one yet.

Dawson Raspuzzi, editor

Chapter 1:
The Basics

Buy a kit or plant a vineyard? This is an extreme example of the decisions you will make when you set out to become a home winemaker. The scope is broad, but many steps along the way overlap or echo one another, whether using the most basic gear to make a few bottles of raspberry wine from bushes in your garden or producing barrels of wine from fresh grapes. This chapter begins with the winemaking basics that need to be understood before going into greater detail about the equipment, process, techniques, ingredients, and science of making wonderful wines at home.

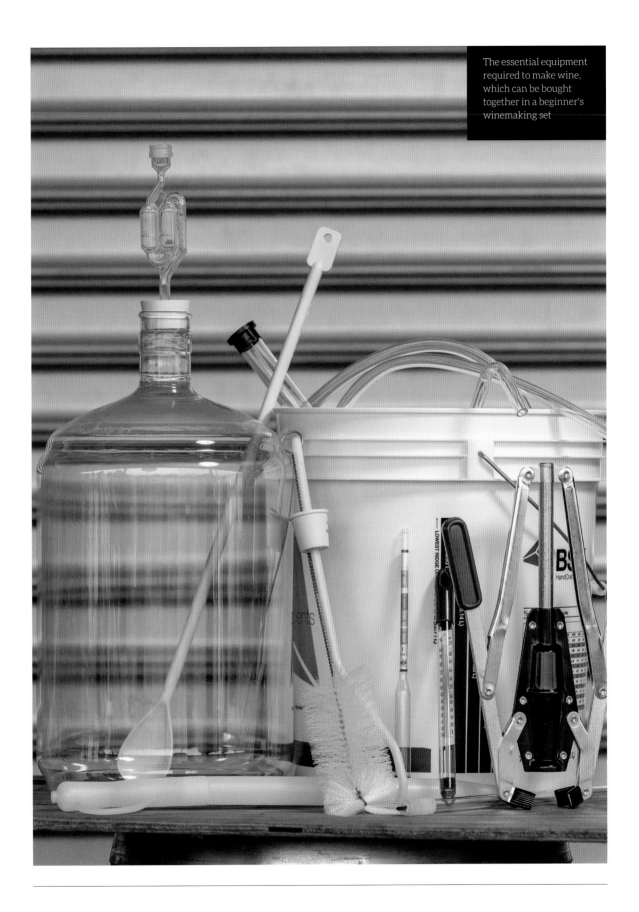

The essential equipment required to make wine, which can be bought together in a beginner's winemaking set

Necessary Basic Equipment

To make homemade wine from kits or fresh fruit, the first thing you need to do is acquire the appropriate equipment. The simplest way to accumulate your gear is to buy a complete winemaking equipment set from your favorite home winemaking retail shop. How elaborate of a winemaking operation you want will determine just how much equipment you will possess and may include grape processing equipment, barrels or stainless-steel aging vessels, an entire wine lab of testing equipment, and more. But let's start with the basics. Here's a piece-by-piece overview of the essential equipment you need, no matter the type or style of wine you plan to make.

Food-Grade HDPE Plastic Bucket

This is the most cost-effective fermenter that every beginner winemaker should start with. Winemakers can perform punchdowns during fermentation on grape skins; they are lightweight, easy to clean, and easy to pour when handling large bags of juice or concentrate. We recommend a 7.9-gallon (30-L) bucket if you plan to produce standard 6-gallon (23-L) wine kits. HDPE buckets are not meant for longer-term storage of wine. Usually you want your wine to be in a bucket for about 2 weeks, maximum.

Carboys

These can be purchased as either glass or plastic (PET) and are used as vessels for storing wine after primary fermentation is complete. Both types have pros and cons. Glass is heavier and more dangerous if dropped so special care is required when handling glass carboys. But glass is impermeable to oxygen, which can be either a pro or a con. Plastic carboys are a much safer option, but there is a minimal exchange of oxygen through their surface, and you need to be more careful not to scratch the interior, as scratches are good places for bad microbes to survive. No matter which carboy you have, always keep your aging wines above the shoulder. A typical carboy size is 6 gallons (23 L) for those who plan to produce 6-gallon (23-L) wine kits, supplemented with 5-gallon (19-L), 3-gallon (11-L), and 1-gallon (3.8-L) sizes if working with fresh grapes.

Rubber Bung and Airlock

A bung is a slightly tapered rubber stopper with a hole in it. The airlock fits into it and helps form a valve that seals the carboy. The airlock prevents oxygen and spoilage organisms from entering, while allowing fermentation gas to escape. For the most part, glass carboys take a #6.5 bung whereas plastic fermenters use a #11. Before purchasing a bung, make sure it will fit your fermenter. The airlock must be half filled with water and attached to the carboy. As an alternative, for added peace of mind, some people like to fill the airlock with a high-alcohol solution such as a cheap vodka.

Siphon Hose

A siphon hose is 6 feet (1.8 m) of food-grade tubing attached to a rigid acrylic rod, with a spacing tip on the end. The siphon hose is used for transferring wine from one container to another, leaving the sediment behind. The rigid rod prevents the tubing from collapsing when draped over the edge of a pail or carboy. The spacing tip on the end of the rod prevents the siphon action from sucking up sediment off the bottom of the pail or carboy. When the hose gets stained from repeated use, throw it away and get a new one. The soft vinyl is difficult to clean properly and hoses are inexpensive to replace.

Siphon Bottle Filler

Although it's possible to fill bottles by pinching the end of the hose to stop the flow, a siphon filler makes this a much neater, faster operation. A siphon filler is an acrylic tube with a needle valve on one end; this slips over the end of the siphon hose. The wine will only flow when the valve is pressed against the bottom of the bottle. You can then withdraw the filler and spill only a few drops of wine before moving on to fill the next bottle.

Thermometer

Good thermometers are essential for ensuring that your must (crushed fruit and juice) is at the right temperature for fermentation. They're also useful for checking the temperature of your fermentation room. Floating thermometers feature a plastic cap with a ring on top. This allows you to tie a string to the thermometer and drop it into the carboy to check the temperature of the fermenting must. The thermometer can then be hauled out by the string. Winemaking thermometers don't contain mercury, but they do contain volatile chemicals, like toluene. If you break one into your must, discard the batch immediately. Probe-type metallic thermometers don't break easily and are another good option.

Hydrometer

Looking much like a glass thermometer, a hydrometer measures specific gravity and is used to monitor the progress of fermentation. A hydrometer consists of a glass tube with some steel shot sealed in the base, and a strip of marked paper on the inside. As the yeast eats the sugar and makes alcohol, the hydrometer will sink lower and lower. By measuring the progression of this sinking, you can accurately track your fermentation. The test jar is a clear, tall, footed tube. Fill it with a wine sample, drop in your hydrometer, and read the results.

Wine Thief

No, a wine thief is not your thirsty brother- or sister-in-law. A wine thief is a hollow glass or plastic tube with a hole in each end. It is used for removing samples from the carboy. Poke the pointy end below the surface of the wine, and allow the tube to fill. Once the wine reaches the desired level, place your finger over the top and keep the thief upright as you transfer its contents.

Spoon

Your winemaking spoon should be stainless steel or food-grade plastic, approximately 28 inches (70 cm) long so it can reach all the way to the bottom of the carboy and the fermenter.

Brushes

Carboy and bottle brushes are good for scrubbing goo out of narrow-necked vessels. Sturdy brushes are essential for cleaning chores.

Corker

There are a few types of corkers available to home winemakers. The twin-handled, hand-operated units work for smaller batches, but the larger floor corkers are better. They have interlocking jaws that "iris" shut to compress the corks and insert them. We'll share much more on corkers in the section on bottling (see page 116) later in the book.

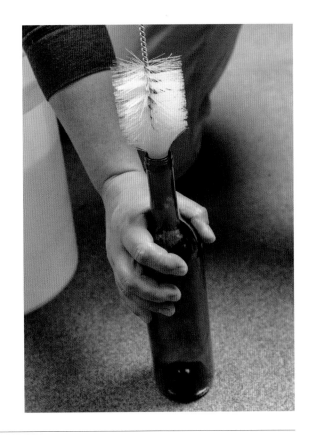

Cleaning and Sanitation

Cleaning and sanitizing are the boring, dull parts of the winemaking process. For that reason, the subject doesn't come up in conversations with friends and neighbors who are excited to learn about your winemaking hobby, and it doesn't grace the label with all of the elegant descriptors you may choose to include about the process of turning grapes into wine. It is, however, one of—if not the—most important parts of winemaking. It is a lot like work, and this hobby is all about having fun—but that doesn't mean we can pretend it isn't necessary.

Although cleaning and sanitation are usually lumped together, it is critical that the home winemaker understand the two are not synonymous, and home winemakers take serious risks if they do not pay attention to these critical areas. *Cleaning* means to remove soil, grease, and other residues from the surface of utensils or equipment. That serves two beneficial purposes: removing contaminants that might directly affect the quality of your wine and clearing the surface for effective contact with a sanitizer. *Sanitizers* kill or inactivate most remaining microorganisms on the surface. You must clean your equipment before sanitizing it because you cannot properly sanitize equipment that has visible residue on it. It is also important to clean all your equipment after you are done using it, which will make repeating these steps before using the equipment next that much quicker and easier as there will not be any hard-to-remove residue.

One last clarification: Sterilization and sanitization are two different things. *Sterilization* is a laboratory term for a complete lack of organisms, something that can be performed in a pressure cooker at home, but for winemaking purposes is often overkill. Sanitation is the next best thing, killing nearly all microorganisms that pose a threat to wine.

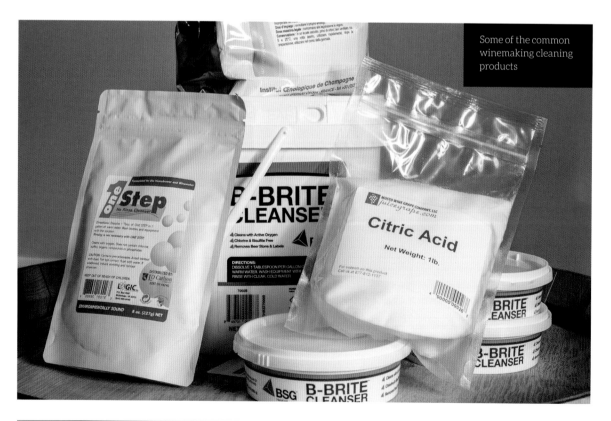

Some of the common winemaking cleaning products

First Things First: Cleaning

First you need to clean your fermenter, airlock, bungs, hoses, siphon, and any other pieces of equipment that will come in contact with your wine. This can also include things such as spoons and funnels that are easy to overlook. It is tempting to just hose them out and start making wine, but that will expose your wine to bacterial infections. You would hate to have a ruined batch after all the time and effort it takes to make it!

There are two methods of cleaning your equipment: either using a cleaning solution and scrubbing your equipment—which takes less time but more elbow grease—or using a cleaning solution and allowing the equipment to soak clean. A combination of the two, with something like a 20-minute soak and then light scrubbing, works great.

You should avoid household cleaners because they are either unsafe for human consumption (like bathroom and oven cleaners) or are too mild for use in your home winery (like Ivory liquid detergent), not to mention those products are often scented, and the perfume may linger or leave a film or other residues when used on plastic containers, tanks, or hoses.

Fill carboys and fermenters to the very top with your cleaning solution, and immerse all of your small equipment in a sink or bucket.

For hoses, airlocks, and siphons that you can't scrub, a good cleaning chemical and patience is the best bet. These pieces of equipment are inexpensive and, eventually, will need to be replaced when they don't clean easily.

When scrubbing plastic equipment, use a sponge or cloth towels to avoid scratching them. For glass and stainless steel, scratches are not much of a problem so more abrasive scrubbers are acceptable, but avoid steel wool or the most abrasive items that may cause scratches.

Cleaning Products

These are manufactured to help soften, dissolve, and lift off dirt, grease, and other contaminants. With a single exception (discussed later), all are intended to be rinsed off. To help with that, they are formulated for easy rinsing to avoid leaving material behind. There are many other products available; these are just the most common. Whatever you use, read the manufacturer's instructions and observe safety guidelines.

TDC Liquid Cleaner

This product resembles dishwashing liquid, but differs in several respects. It is unscented so does not impart a perfume-y aroma. Marketed by National Chemicals Inc., primarily to the bar and restaurant trade, TDC liquid cleaner is a highly concentrated mixture of nonionic surfactants, glycolic acid, and other proprietary components. "Surfactants," a word derived from "surface-active agents," are large molecules that have one end soluble in water and the other end soluble in oil. When used in a water solution to clean a greasy surface, the oil-friendly end helps lift any film and the water-friendly end keeps it suspended in water to be rinsed away. The glycolic acid in TDC helps keep the pH low to assist in dissolving mineral residues and promote easy rinsing. It is suitable for glass, plastic, and metal surfaces. Use rate is $1/4$ ounce or $1^1/2$ teaspoons (about 7 ml) in 3 to 5 gallons (11 to 19 L) of clean water. Rinse thoroughly after use.

Sodium Percarbonate

This simple mineral compound is a remarkably effective cleaner and oxygen bleach that is particularly effective at removing stains or color residues from equipment. It is a combination of sodium carbonate (soda ash) and hydrogen peroxide, which releases oxygen in the water, leaving just the soda ash residue to be rinsed away. Also known as sodium carbonate peroxyhydrate, it is sold under brand names like OxiClean and Proxycarb. The high pH provided by the carbonate helps remove greasy materials through the process of saponification, where the fat is converted to a water-soluble soap and rinsed away. Meanwhile, the hydrogen peroxide provides an oxygen bleaching action. The hydrogen peroxide is also antimicrobial and can kill organisms that may be on the surface. This is especially useful

Brushes of various sizes come in handy for scrubbing hard-to-reach areas.

with porous materials such as wood or plastic. Use rate is from $1/8$ to $1/2$ ounce (3.5 to 14 g) per gallon (3.8 L) of cold or warm water. Do not use hot water as it tends to generate the oxygen too quickly and the bleaching action is lost. With its high pH, wear eye protection and consider rubber gloves for extended contact or when working with high concentrations. Rinse thoroughly, apply a citric acid rinse (to neutralize the carbonate), and rinse again.

PBW

Though PBW stands for "powdered brewery wash," do not let that stop you from using it just because you are a winemaker. Straight A is another proprietary product with a similar formulation. These granular cleaners resemble sodium percarbonate in a number of ways and may include some of it in their formulas. PBW also contains the strongly alkaline compound sodium metasilicate but is buffered to make it safer in use and milder on materials. The formula also includes surfactants so, in some ways, you are getting the effects of a detergent, like TDC, and a cleaner, like sodium percarbonate, at the same time. It can be used in cold, warm, or hot water. PBW is considered particularly effective at removing protein residues. Use rate is about $3/4$ to 2 ounces (21 to 56 g) per 1 gallon (3.8 L) of water. As with percarbonate, use eye protection and consider gloves for extended contact. Rinse thoroughly, apply a citric acid rinse, and rinse again.

One Step No-Rinse Cleanser

This is another white, granular proprietary product. It contains sodium percarbonate and sodium carbonate, which will provide an alkaline cleaning condition to remove oils and generate oxygen to disrupt proteins. It also contains sodium citrate to buffer the pH and make it safer to use, plus sodium chloride. As with the other brand-name cleaners described earlier, its exact formula is a trade secret. The chief difference with One Step as compared to these other cleaners is in its "no rinse" instruction. Some winemakers prefer to clean and rinse winery equipment and utensils, then separately sanitize them with a certified no-rinse sanitizer. However,

many users are satisfied that One Step can both clean and sanitize, saving some time and effort. On their website, One Step's maker, Logic, Inc., notes that the peroxide action is highly antimicrobial and should adequately sanitize surfaces.

Sanitation

Sanitizing should be done immediately before using equipment that will come in contact with must or wine so there is no time allowed for spoilage organisms to return. Just as with cleaning, there are a number of products and methods to sanitize winemaking equipment. Whichever products you choose, use them according to the manufacturer's instructions, which will tell you how much to use and how much contact time is required to effectively sanitize the surfaces. Here are the most common sanitation products and methods.

Boiling

Although effective, this technique is limited to objects that are small enough to fit in a pot and are sufficiently heat resistant to be boiled. Boil for at least 15 minutes. There's no need to rinse; just drain and allow to cool.

Sulfites

For sanitizing utensils and equipment with sulfite, use a 1 percent effective solution of sulfite, keeping it in contact with surfaces for 10 minutes. Citric acid can be added to improve effectiveness. Because sulfite needs to be rinsed off before proceeding, using it includes a small risk of re-contaminating the sanitized surface with nonsterile tap water.

Iodophor

BTF and IO Star are brands of iodine-complex sanitizers. Using $1/2$ to 1 ounce (15 to 30 ml) in 5 gallons (19 L) of water provides active iodine at 12.5 to 25 ppm (mg/L). With a 1- to 2-minute contact time with clean surfaces, most organisms are effectively killed or disabled. For some applications, air-drying is recommended. In many cases, you can just drain out the sanitizer and proceed without worrying about a small amount of residue that will not introduce any odor or flavor into the wine. Some users prefer to rinse when they have confidence that the rinse water is fresh and clean. The characteristic amber iodine color may stain soft plastics, like vinyl hoses, but does not damage them otherwise. It is not recommended for use on elastomers. As the color of a batch fades over a period of a few days, you will need to add more iodophor or prepare a new batch.

Star San

This sanitizer uses phosphoric acid and surfactants to kill microorganisms on clean surfaces. The surfactants in diluted sanitizer may leave foam or bubbles when it is poured out, but that small residue represents no significant risk to your wine. Use 1 ounce (30 ml) in 5 gallons (19 L) of water with a 1- to 2-minute contact time. As with iodophor, you may want to air-dry, but a damp surface will not generally harm the wine in any way. Because of the strong acid, do not use it on steel (other than stainless).

Chlorine Bleach

Although bleach has been used in a pinch for ages, it is not recommended for sanitizing. Chlorine is effective at killing microbes, but it has two serious deficits for use in a winery: The odor is so strong that it must be completely rinsed off to avoid off-odors in your wine, and, most important, chlorine is often a critical player in the development of TCA (trichloroanisole) contamination in wine. TCA is the bad actor in the "cork taint" odor of spoiled wine. Given the opportunity to interact with porous surfaces such as wood or cardboard, particularly if mold is present, it can contaminate an entire winery.

Citric Acid

Although not an aggressive sanitizer, citric acid introduces a low pH and helps retard spoilage organisms. It is especially useful on porous surfaces, like inside an oak barrel, where you should never use any kind of sanitizer (except steam or sulfite). Use percarbonate to clean a problem barrel and follow with a citric acid rinse. Use about 1 tablespoon (14 g) per gallon (3.8 L) of water and rinse off after use.

Ethanol

A 70 percent solution of ethanol is a quick and effective sanitizer. Using the Pearson square (described on page 107) is an easy way to calculate the Everclear-to-water ratio needed for this. Since your wine will contain ethanol anyway, you can just spray a utensil, shake it off, and use it. Depending on where you live, you may find Everclear in your local liquor store at either 151 proof (75.5 percent ABV) or 190 proof (95 percent ABV). Dilute it with distilled water to 70 percent and store in a plastic pump spray bottle for quick use. No rinsing is required.

When to Clean and When to Sanitize

Harvest and Crush

Grapes are not washed at harvest. All your winemaking equipment should be washed, but when to sanitize is a winemaker's decision. Most winemakers will tell you to wash picking bins and the crusher/destemmer, but do not sanitize them. Sanitizing the food-grade plastic fermenters grapes are crushed into isn't a bad idea.

Fermenting

Besides the fermenters, punchdown or stirring tools should be washed after each use and sanitized just before using again. Keeping a spray bottle of ethanol or a bucket of iodophor or Star San in the winery is useful for these types of tools, as they can quickly be sprayed or dipped into the bucket before use, or just kept in the sanitizer between uses. Although brief contact is not a problem, Star San may corrode stainless steel if left in contact with it.

A spray bottle filled with sanitizer solution makes sanitizing larger items easy and saves money compared to filling an entire pail to soak equipment.

Pressing

After washing the press with percarbonate and rinsing it off, drenching it with citric acid solution is a good idea. Let stand for a few minutes, then rinse with clean water.

Bulk Aging

TDC or percarbonate does a great job cleaning glass or plastic carboys and stainless-steel tanks. Sanitize with iodophor or Star San. For oak barrels, simply rinse with hot water. If you suspect a problem with a barrel, use a soaking technique of up to 1 pound (454 g) of sodium percarbonate in a 60-gallon (227-L) barrel. Dissolve the percarbonate in a few gallons (about 10 L) of water first and funnel it into the barrel. Fill with clean water and let soak for several hours or overnight. Pour out, rinse, and then swirl with a few gallons (about 10 L) of citric acid solution to neutralize alkaline residue from the percarbonate. Rinse again, drain, and fill with wine.

Racking

Clean and sanitize the hoses and receiving vessels with your products of choice. For pumps and hoses, prepare buckets filled with cleaner, water, and sanitizer. Recirculate one after another for 2 minutes at a time.

Bottling

Spray the jaws of your corker with ethanol just before using. Wash and sanitize used bottles as you do carboys. New bottles are sanitary as received and should not require any treatment before filling. Always sanitize the racking cane or pump and hoses, as well as the bottle filler. Corks sealed in their original bags should be packed in sulfur dioxide gas and do not need to be sanitized. If the pack has been opened, dip corks in a sulfite solution just before use.

Grab a Pencil and Take Notes

Keeping a detailed log of each wine you make will allow you to track your wine's daily progress from the vineyard to the bottle, and it is a great reference tool for the next time you make a similar wine. In a couple of years from now, when you want to replicate that fantastic vintage from a previous fall that has continued to evolve into a fantastic wine in the bottle, you will be thrilled you kept those notes. Which yeast did you use? Did you add malolactic bacteria? Did you adjust the acid? What were the fermentation temperatures?

What Information to Record

A well-kept winemaking log can help you to arrive at smarter decisions and save tons of time. As the saying goes: if it's not recorded, it didn't happen. There is no such thing as the one perfect log that suits all types of winemakers. To make your logs efficient, you must choose what's important *for you* to record.

As with most activities you set out to do, it is vital to answer the four Ws (and the one H):

What: If you are getting ready to make your first wine, be aware that, down the line, you'll wish you had everything nicely labeled with proper traceability. Come up with names for your batches/lots and make them comprehensive and easily recognizable. As an example, kit winemakers should be recording the make, model, and year of the kit and develop a tracking system for their carboys.

When: In winemaking, timing is crucial and keeping a close eye on when things happen will give you the right perspective for making decisions. Always record dates.

Who: When you are a one-member crew, this is less important, but as teams start growing in number, it is essential to know who did what. In case something goes awry, you can track it back quickly, understand why, and take preventive actions to avoid repeating mistakes.

Where: If you have different sizes, shapes, or types of vessels, it is crucial to know where each batch/lot is at a given time. If you have to scatter your winemaking to a few areas in your house, those locations go here too.

How much: Quantifying is key! When talking about additions, write down the units: 4 g/L are not the same as 4 lb./g so just writing down "4" won't get you anywhere when it's time to refer back to old vintage notes.

Here is a list of the chemical analyses that should always be recorded whenever possible (more on several of these in the advanced winemaking chapter, starting on page 133):

Brix/sugars

Free sulfur dioxide (FSO_2)

Lactic acid

Malic acid

pH

Residual sugar (RS)

Titratable acidity (TA)

Total sulfur dioxide (TSO_2)

Volatile acidity (VA)

Chemistry is essential, but temperature is one of the most critical physical variables in winemaking. In addition to paying close attention to fermentation temperatures, keep an eye on the ambient temperature where you store your wine. It will give you the right frame to understand at what temperature the wine will settle down. If working in a rather cold cellar, all chemical and biological processes slow, and might even stop. Likewise, if your cellar gets too warm, your fermentations will most likely speed up, bringing some negative consequences, such as yeast dying or getting a jammy fruit in your wine.

On your sheet, leave space for "comments," where you can include some more sensory observations. Take notes, including the date, on what the juice looks, smells, or tastes like each time you are working on your wine (like inoculating, racking, filtering, clarifying). Observe how it behaves before and after working on it. This way, you'll gain a better sense of how a wine develops from start to finish.

Did something unexpected happen? Did you punchdown more often than usual? Write it down, it's all valuable information.

Log your dry supplies as well. On a different sheet, write down all the products you use, such as yeast, tartaric acid, enzymes, tannins, oak, etc. As you receive the supplies, write down the providers, lot numbers, and expiration dates. If you have any problems with a specific product, you will be able to track it down.

Traceability

Traceability is the ability to ensure the tracking, if possible, in real time, of activities and information flow linking activities. To be able to check where your Amazon package is located in real time, somebody has to log the information at every step of the process. By the same logic, you will have to link the information flow during the winemaking process. Naming your wines with a unique code is the same as having a proper tracking number for your parcel.

A rather logical and well-accepted naming system among commercial winemakers worldwide is as follows:

YY-VAR-#

Where:

YY equals the year of vintage (e.g., 22 for 2022).

VAR is the two- to three-letter code for your grape variety (e.g., VIO-CS-PN-MAL). In case you work with blends, you can use other three-letter codes.

is sometimes a number used to indicate the stage of the process, for instance:

1. Alcoholic fermentation complete

2. Malolactic fermentation (MLF) complete

3. Racking out of fine lees

4. Clarified

5. Filtered

So if a vessel is labeled 20-MAL-2, it means that it is a 2020 vintage Malbec that is MLF complete. The concept is rather simple, but it helps a lot when working with multiple and different batches.

This naming system is the wine's ID/tracking number—if you use this system, refer to it identically throughout the whole process.

How you record this information is up to you. Handheld devices allow for easy on-the-go updated records. Shared documents and the sharing of files can significantly improve communication within bigger teams and even with those you share the wine with. Even with the benefits of electronic records, there's still romance in scratching notes on a pad of paper. Some "paper" options include a pocket journal (or the modern version being the Notes app, or other app on your phone computer, or tablet), a binder, or electronic spreadsheet.

Kit and Juice Winemaking

S tarting with a kit is the simplest way to make wine and a great way for those new to the hobby to become familiarized with the winemaking process without a significant investment in time and money. There is no need for crushing and pressing, or even running tests on the juice, as you know exactly what you are working with from the start. With a kit, water, the basic equipment outlined in chapter 1, and a firm understanding of proper cleaning and sanitation protocols, you have everything you'll need to make your first batch of wine. As an added bonus, kit wines are generally ready to drink in 6 to 8 weeks so the time you need to wait to taste your wine is never too far off.

But wine kits aren't just for novice winemakers. They offer even the most experienced winemakers opportunities not available with fresh grapes—from exploring unique varietals from regions around the world to the ability to make wine year-round. With a kit, the science behind making a great wine is taken care of, while the art of making a great wine is in your hands.

The foundation of a wine kit is a combination of juice and juice concentrate, with concentrate being made from juice that has had some of its water removed. This means water will need to be added when making wine; as long as the water tastes good to drink, it should be good to add to your wine.

Today's kits contain a juice base that is pre-balanced, which means no need for pH/TA testing or adding nutrient or energizer to ensure full fermentation, and the Brix is predetermined to ensure a balanced wine with an appropriate final alcohol content. In addition to the juice base, the contents of a wine kit will vary slightly depending on the wine style you choose, but will generally include:

❖ Bentonite, a clay that helps disperse yeast throughout the must, remove proteins that can impact the flavor of wine, and aid in the clearing process

❖ Chitosan (ky-toe-zan), a fining agent that binds with suspended particles in wine to aid in clearing it; used in tandem with kieselsol

❖ Isinglass (eye-sing-las), a form of collagen used as a fining agent to aid in clearing

❖ Kieselsol (key-sel-sol), a fining agent that binds with suspended particles in wine to aid in clearing it; used in tandem with chitosan

❖ Potassium metabisulfite, a stabilizer that prevents spoilage and stops fermentation

❖ Potassium sorbate, a stabilizer used in tandem with potassium metabisulfite to inhibit further yeast growth

❖ Yeast to ferment the juice

Select wine style kits may also include:

❖ Chaptalization pack, to be added at an exact point in the winemaking process to increase the final alcohol content for dessert wines

❖ F-pack (flavor pack), included mostly in fruit wine kits to add sweetness and each style's unique flavor

❖ Grape skin packs, which may be dried or crushed grapes, to add tannin and structure to the finished wine; usually found in ultra-premium kits

❖ Oak chips, powder, or cubes to add flavor, tannin, structure, and aromatics to certain wine kits, usually red wines

❖ Reserve pack, used to sweeten and balance a finished off-dry wine; may contain juice and sweetener, or sweetener only

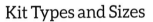
After pouring the juice concentrate into your fermenter, top it up to the level called for in the instructions with a good-quality drinking water.

Kit Types and Sizes

For today's home winemaker, there are so many wines to choose from, including the most popular varietals from all around the world to lesser known grapes grown only in specific regions, and blends. There is also a wide selection of fruit wine kits that are lower in alcohol, sparkling wines, and dessert wines.

Most kits will make 6 gallons (23 L) of finished wine so "kit size" is the amount of juice base that comes in the kit. The larger the kit, the higher the juice-to-concentrate ratio. Some of the varietal characteristics are sacrificed in the concentration process, so the top tier kits are the largest size that contains the highest juice-to-concentrate ratio. Kits use a "Good, Better, Best" model when describing sizes, similar to commercial wines. All kits make great wine—picking the right one depends on your expectations, palate, and budget.

The largest (Best) of the kit offerings will contain region-specific juice and more varied oaks, depending on the kit, to create a more structured, rich wine, often with higher alcohol content. Medium-size kits (Better) generally contain country-specific juice and concentrate, more limited oaking styles, and no grape skins. Smaller kits (Good) make budget-friendly wine meant to be approachable and easy to drink.

In addition to 6-gallon (23-L) table wines, kit companies offer dessert wines that generally make 3 gallons (11 L) of finished wine. These wines are often limited releases with flavors like chocolate, raspberry, and mocha. Ice wine–style kits are also seasonally available. Some manufacturers also produce 1-gallon (3.8-L) kits made using the same methods as larger kits, but everything is done in 1-gallon (3.8-L) jugs. These kits are available in the most popular wine styles and are a great way to familiarize yourself with new styles or varieties, diversify your wine cellar, or gain experience without investing in a full-size kit.

Follow Directions or Try Something New

Wine kits are manufactured in a way that eliminates the chance of failure and ensures the resulting wine will be consistent repeatedly when directions are followed. As such, we recommend following those directions exactly until you are comfortable with the process and know what to expect from the resulting wine. However, part of the fun of the winemaking hobby is putting a personal twist on things. If you are going to stray from the directions, the first question to ask yourself is, "Why?" There are two acceptable answers to that question:

1. To improve the wine: Maybe the last time you made that Cabernet Sauvignon kit you felt it was lacking in mouthfeel, or the addition of medium-plus toasted American oak chips was a little too aggressive and you desire softer oak flavors of vanilla; this time, try medium-toast French oak.

2. Experimentation: You may decide to experiment to learn what various tweaks do to the flavor, aroma, structure, or body of a wine kit. Due to their year-round availability and consistent results, kit wines are a great base for experimenting with various methods and ingredients.

No matter the reason, if you are going to stray from the directions, we highly recommend making just one change at a time. If many tweaks are made at once, how will you know which benefitted the wine and which did not? This is also why we advise following the directions the first time you make wine from a particular kit, which will be your base to compare adjusted wines to. Assuming you've taken our advice up to this point, let's now look at the most common adjustments winemakers may consider.

1. Yeast choice: All wine kits on the market today use dry yeast, with the most common being Lalvin EC-1118. Dry yeast is used because it offers better shelf stability than liquid yeast, and EC-1118 is the most popular choice because it is dependable and predictable for the majority of kit winemakers. If minor process errors occur, kit companies want

a yeast that will still get the job done. If you have made many kit wines and understand the process of fermentation based on this experience, you may want to experiment with different strains to influence the characteristics of the finished wine more toward your liking. We'll get more into yeast selection on page 60.

2. Oak: Oak adds tannins to wine and gives it more body, aroma, and flavor. Oak is often included with red and certain white kits; however, if used sparingly, oak can firm up any wine. For example, if you feel that a particular kit wine is "thin," adding a little oak, even to white wines, will give the wine a little more body and improve the mouthfeel. When it comes to oak alternative products, three factors to consider are the form of the product, origin, and char level. We'll dive deeper into the subject of oak in chapter 5.

3. Adding sugar: Sugar can be added to accomplish two goals—raising the alcohol level of your wine (when added before or during fermentation) or sweetening your wine (when added post-fermentation). Refer to the sections of chaptalization (page 43) and backsweetening (page 112) for more on these techniques.

4. Fortification: You may decide to fortify your dessert wine with brandy, Everclear, or even a flavored spirit to increase alcohol and give the wine more depth of flavor. Bench trials to find the right amount are important here. Remember, you can always add more of your fortifier so starting with less than you believe is needed is a good strategy. When a wine is fortified, it will likely improve after being cellared at least a year to allow the flavors to better blend together. Read more about fortification on page 78.

5. Fermentation temperature: Every wine yeast has a recommended temperature range, and fermenting at one end of the range compared to the other can have a significant effect on the final wine. Wine kit instructions usually recommend warmer fermentation temperatures. Part of the reason for this is that the warmer the fermentation, the quicker it will finish, which is often viewed as a positive for kit manufacturers who advertise a kit's ability to produce wine in a matter of weeks. However, if time isn't an issue, you may wish to try fermenting at the lower end of your yeast strain's recommended range. Learn more about the impact of temperature on fermentation on page 26.

6. Aging: This isn't necessarily a tweak to the process; however, it is worthy of consideration, even for first-time kit winemakers. Although wine kits are ready to drink in weeks, many styles will improve with age, including bold red wines and dessert wines. Hold on to some bottles for an extended time and evaluate how the wine has changed with each one you open.

Frozen Must/ Juice

F rozen musts are becoming more and more common with a growing list of available grape varietals that includes *vinifera*, hybrid, and native varieties. A container of frozen must is exactly what it sounds like—crushed and destemmed grapes in their own juice. Someone else has done the crushing and destemming for you. For red wines, whatever comes out of the crusher/ destemmer goes directly into the tub: crushed grapes, seeds, and a few stems. For white wines, it is normally settled juice. Either way, it is flash frozen solid and is maintained in this state until it is sold to someone who will make wine from it.

Some of the same advantages of working with wine kits are also true when starting with frozen must—availability is year-round, your investment in winemaking equipment is minimized, and the timing is in your hands, as opposed to using fresh fruit, which dictates when it must be processed. You do not need a crusher/destemmer, but you will need a wine press for the red grapes to separate the liquid from the solids. Whites are usually already in juice form. Further, frozen musts eliminate the lifting effort of loading the fresh grape lugs into the crusher/destemmer. One area where these two winemaking styles diverge is the guarantee of success: kits come balanced and set up for success whereas making wine from frozen juice is similar to making wine from fresh grapes in that it requires more intervention.

Wines produced from frozen musts rival those made directly from fresh fruit. And why wouldn't they? When you start with good quality berries and flash freeze them as they are crushed or pressed, all you are doing is interrupting the fresh winemaking process with a deep freeze and restarting it when it is convenient. There is no appreciable difference between the resulting wines made from fresh grapes and those made from frozen must or juice. Several studies have shown a small increase in total phenolics from frozen grapes, but so far none has demonstrated a sensory impact.

Producers of frozen must often identify specific source vineyards on their container labeling. Depending on the producer, some frozen musts may even contain additives, such as sulfites or enzymes added at the time of crushing and freezing, which will be indicated, if added. Some local grape purveyors provide custom freezing at the specific request of individual customers to crush/destem, add sulfites, enzymes, and any other additive desired. Note, however, specific pail metrics such as sugar, pH, and titratable acidity should still be confirmed by the winemaker when the juice is thawed since these numbers frequently are measured for an entire lot and may vary pail to pail, most notably among red pails.

Take your own readings—sugar, titratable acidity, and pH—regardless of what the label says. Readings should be measured at room temperature or after the pail is completely thawed and accounting for the cold temperature of the must (most measuring protocols are based on room temperature). It is also important to mix the juice before taking samples. The ice that forms and floats during the juice thawing is water. An undisturbed pail of thawed juice may be 6°Brix on top and 40+°Brix on the bottom. Potassium combined with the tartaric acid will create cream of tartar on the floor of the pail. This natural separation makes accurate analysis of the juice or grapes difficult initially; however, it also allows for the production of ice wine or natural acid reduction, if you desire. One juice—many possibilities.

Once received, thaw the buckets at 65°F to 75°F (18°C to 24°C). At this temperature, it should take 1 to 2 days to completely thaw and reach a temperature suitable for fermentation (the buckets will most likely already be partially thawed by the time they arrive, if being shipped). Thawing at colder temperatures will take longer, which gives wild microbes a better chance at corrupting the juice. Thawing or fermenting at warmer temperatures can risk cooking off some of the flavors.

When it gets to the actual winemaking process, there is an interesting benefit for red varieties. As the frozen must thaws over the course of several days, a cold soak is achieved (learn more about cold soaking in chapter 3). As the must is allowed to thaw slowly and so stays in a low temperature liquid state for at least 4 days (perhaps fewer in some conditions), maximum color extraction can be achieved. In addition, the tannins extracted during this time are water-soluble and will be of the softer variety, as opposed to the harsher, alcohol-soluble variety imparted during primary and, possibly, post-fermentation maceration.

Once the must reaches ambient temperature, the winemaking process used should be no different than when working with fresh grapes.

Chapter 2:
Making Wine from Grapes

Anybody can make wine from grapes, even without the space or time to maintain their own backyard vineyard. Growing your own grapes to make wine from is extremely rewarding for those who have the time, energy, and dedication to do it. But as with any agricultural product, grape growing relies on factors outside of your control and takes a tremendous amount of time so this book does not dig into the extensive topic of grape growing as entire books are written on the subject.

Sourcing Wine Grapes

So what are other ways home winemakers can get their hands on fresh grapes?

It will be easier if you live in or near a winegrowing region, and since every US state has at least one bonded winery, that may not be as difficult as it sounds. Getting grapes straight from the source is a great option for home winemakers who want to see, touch, and taste their grapes before bringing them home. Each vineyard is different (and many don't make grapes available to home winemakers looking to buy smaller quantities), so the best thing to do is plan ahead. Look for grapes grown in your area and make your variety selection from those. Some growers pack wine grapes in 18- or 36-pound (8- or 16-kg) plastic or cardboard crates that you can pick up at the vineyard or from a wine supply store that distributes for the vineyard. Vineyards often have their fruit contracted in the spring, so contact the vineyard manager before bud break and tell them what you are looking for. It also pays to follow up and visit throughout the growing year, as small-quantity orders are likely not high on their priority list, and it's good to let them know your expectations. If there are minimum purchase requirements, a great way to meet them is to find other home winemakers in the market for grapes. In years when crops are larger than expected, there may be good deals to be had at harvest, but banking on that is a roll of the dice.

If you are traveling less than an hour to pick up the grapes, transporting them shouldn't be too difficult, but any longer than that means transporting in a refrigerated vehicle. This requires renting a vehicle, which is also easier to accomplish if you can split the cost with other members of a home winemaking club.

Also don't be afraid to approach other home winemakers who may have hobby vineyards. If they grow more than they need, they may be willing to part with a couple hundred pounds for a fellow hobbyist—especially if you are willing to harvest the grapes yourself.

Grapes can often be bought in 18- or 36-pound (8- or 16-kg) crates.

Inspect grapes before buying them to make sure the quality is what you expect.

With so many wine grapes originating on the West Coast, vendors elsewhere in North America have arranged to receive and distribute fresh grapes from there during harvest time. Some also import South American or South African grapes during North American springtime. If you find a wholesaler, check in frequently with them, or get on their email list to receive periodic updates on what grape varietals will become available and when.

In addition to the ease, a benefit of buying grapes this way is that they receive grapes over a window of time (September through November for North American grapes, or April and May for Southern Hemisphere grapes), and reputable suppliers will store the grapes in coolers to keep them fresh so your opportunity to buy grapes isn't missed if one day doesn't work for you. That may not be the case when buying grapes from a vineyard.

Another benefit is that many of these sources provide custom crushing services and pressing for whites, which can reduce transportation costs and save you from the necessity of buying the equipment yourself.

Do your research and talk with these wholesalers to ensure they have what you are looking for at a price you are willing to pay. Don't be afraid to ask questions about the grapes—what region, and even vineyard, they come from, what climate they were grown in, when they are harvested, how they are shipped, etc. If possible, inspect the grapes before purchase to make sure they are what you expect.

Once again, your local home winemaking shop is a good place to start. Some supply shops offer equipment for use or rent. They may sell fresh grapes and may be aware of local growers who sell in small quantities, or maintain listings of local grapes for sale. Home winemakers typically pay about a dollar a pound ($2 per kg) for locally grown grapes. Local wineries that make white wine will sometimes sell pressed and chilled white wine juice to home winemakers. If you find one of those wineries, verify the type of containers you should supply or whether the juice is already packed in sealed plastic buckets for you to take away.

Whatever your source, plan on about 100 pounds (45 kg) of fresh grapes for 5 gallons (19 L) of finished wine—that's about two cases of standard 750-milliliter bottles.

Grape Winemaking Equipment

You have your grapes lined up for harvest time. Fresh grapes will need to be processed as quickly as possible upon receipt. For those who either need to or want to process their freshly procured fruit at home, more equipment is required than those items listed in chapter 1. The basic tasks you need to complete are crushing (possibly with destemming) and pressing the grapes. Also those fermenting red wines may need much larger fermentation vessels since the juice will ferment on the grapes (more on this in chapter 3). As with other aspects of home winemaking, your choices can range from small basic equipment to sophisticated machinery that mimics that of a commercial winery.

Crusher/Destemmer

You will need a crusher or a crusher/destemmer if processing anything more than you are willing to do by hand. A basic crusher has a hopper and two rollers mounted with a hand crank. You place the crusher over a bin or bucket, put grapes in the hopper, turn the crank, and crushed fruit—with the stems—comes out the bottom. A crusher/destemmer is similar at the top but has another sheet-metal box below the hopper with another shaft fitted with mounted helical paddles. As the crushed fruit, called "must" at this stage, falls into the lower box, the paddles beat the stems toward an opening at the end of the box. Stems fall out that end and destemmed must falls straight through. For larger production, you can get a crusher/destemmer with an electric motor instead of a hand crank. Your local winemaking store may rent equipment for harvest. If not, purchase prices range from a couple hundred dollars to a couple thousand dollars.

Most times, grapes should be removed from the stems and crushed, though this will vary by the winemaker's technique and style of wine they are after. Stems can add excess bitter tannins and herbaceous notes to a wine during fermentation, especially if the stems are still somewhat green and not lignified (lignification is part of the process of maturation of the grapevine). You will notice that the grapes' flexible green stems will start to turn brown and woody. By crushing the grapes, the juice is more easily released and the skin is more accessible to the yeast during fermentation. For red wines, this can aid color extraction, flavor, aroma, and tannins in the wine. For white grapes, along with the same concerns with the stems, crushing can enhance juice yield during pressing as it is easier to press a grape that has already been broken than one that is still solid. We'll discuss pressing in greater detail in a bit.

Crushers are available in a powder-coated painted finish, in stainless steel, or in a combination of the two. Stainless-steel equipment has the potential for a much longer useful life than the painted options, but proper care and maintenance will allow a painted unit to last many harvests without any paint chipping.

Which brings us to the subject of cleaning and maintaining this large piece of equipment after the grapes have been processed and before putting it away until the next harvest. This is a very messy process, so put on some old work clothes and get ready. If there is a lid on the destemmer body, take it off (but put the wing nut in your pocket—they are tricky little devils). Remove the stemmer grate from the body, standing back as grape pulp is launched from both sides as it springs out. Fill a bucket with water, warm if available, and a good winery cleaning product, like sodium percarbonate or Straight-A. If the crusher/destemmer is electric, protect the motor from getting wet by wrapping it in a plastic bag.

Hose off all visible grape residue from the hopper, the body, and the grate and lid that you removed. Using a long-handled brush, brush down all grape-contact surfaces with cleaner. Rinse again. Manually turn the stemmer shaft and hose out the grapes that

Grapes are loaded into the hopper of the crusher/destemmer, and an auger pushes them to the rollers where they are crushed.

are now visible that you did not see before. Be aware as you clean that most pieces of equipment have blind spots; inspect it all very carefully to find places debris may be hiding. Rinse again. Before storing the machine, let it air-dry completely: place it on a table, bench, or saw horses in a clean, dry area. If it must be outdoors, cover it with an old bed sheet to keep dust and debris off while allowing it to dry.

After a couple of days of drying, lubricate the chain and gears with a food-grade grease like Petrol-Gel or Sprayon LU210. Turn the gears manually, or briefly run an electric machine, to make sure grease is worked into the moving parts and everything is operating correctly. Not only will lubrication protect against corrosion while your machine is stored, but it will also help assure that small amounts of leftover sugars will not dry on the gears and make them seize up.

To store this fairly large piece of equipment, consider standing it on end to reduce the amount of floor space needed. Wherever you put it, make sure the surroundings are clean and dry so it will be in perfect condition months later. If it is in a dusty space, like a garage, keep that bed sheet over it.

Presses

For white wine, the next step is pressing. For red, it is bulk fermentation and then pressing. One can theoretically make do without a press for red wine production, utilizing only free-run juice (which some winemakers prefer), losing about 15 percent of the year's yield and sacrificing the extra tannin and color that come from press run wine. When working with white grapes, however, there's pretty much no way around it: You need a press.

Presses come in a couple of forms for the home winemaker. *Basket presses* are the most common for home use. Vertical hardwood slats held together by metal bands make two halves of the press basket. The basket rests on a metal base and the two halves come apart to empty the basket after pressing. You assemble the unit, place a bucket under the spout, and pour in the crushed white must or fermented red wine and must. Wine or juice runs into the bucket (have two on hand) and is then poured into the next container. A cast-iron ratcheting head is hand-cranked down a threaded shaft to apply pressure to the must. Common press sizes are numbered by the diameter of the basket measured in centimeters, ranging from 20 to 55. The smaller ones work well for a few gallons (liters) of wine and the larger sizes can work in the ton range. If you are normally pressing fermented or even just crushed grapes to make batches of 6 to 12 gallons (23 to 46 L), then a size 30 press should offer plenty of flexibility.

You can process smaller batches in a larger press, but you will lose some efficiency, and you may have to add additional wood blocks to reach your pressings so sizing your press to your usual batch size is a better option than going bigger for the occasional larger-production batch. Prices range from a couple hundred dollars to over one thousand.

At the larger sizes, additional press types are available. Hydraulic presses use an electric pump or a hand pump to push a piston plate down on the must, with a basket similar to that in the ratcheting presses.

The other press option is called a *bladder press*. This type of press typically has a stainless-steel basket with small perforations in it that is filled with the grapes as well as a rubber bladder inside the basket. Once the press is filled with grapes, a cover is bolted down to seal the basket. A garden hose is attached to the unit and water fills the bladder to apply pressure outwardly against the grapes, toward the basket wall.

Crushed grapes fall from the crusher/destemmer into a large bin.

The size of bladder press to be used, just like the basket press, should be based on your typical batch size. Bladder presses require the bladder to be filled completely, as such they are only intended for bigger batches.

Let's compare these two main options. There is no good way to gauge the amount of pressure pushing down on grapes in a basket press. The more pressure that is applied to the grapes, the more tearing and grape skins and crushing of seeds that may occur, releasing phenolics and excessive tannins that may be unwanted, depending on the style of wine being made (though, applying this much pressure with a home basket press is not a big concern, as it takes a tremendous amount of pressure).

In contrast, with a home bladder press, you attach a garden hose, turn on the water and then shut it off once you've reached your desired pressure, which

Pressure is applied from the center outward to squeeze juice from the grapes in a bladder press.

you can read on a pressure gauge. The more water that is added, the greater the pressure. You can do a quick pressing, moving the pressure up rapidly, or drag it out as long as you like.

As basket presses exert pressure on the must downward, perpendicular to the direction the wine travels (outward), and as the radius of the press cake (the compressed mass of skins and seeds) produced is large, some wine can get locked up closer to the center of the cake; if you want to get out every drop, you'll likely have to break up the cake and re-press it to do so, adding lots of time (and, to the second pressing, solids). A technique some home winemakers employ is to make a "second run" wine to get the most bang for their buck and extract even more juice, color, and flavor trapped in the skins. This can be done after the initial pressing by adding water, sugar, tartaric acid, and yeast energizer to the pomace (grape pulp), mixing it, and then pressing again. It is recommended to keep this juice separate and consider blending it with another wine after fermentation as it will differ greatly from the first run.

As the bladder press design has a bladder inflating in the center pressing outward in the same direction the wine must travel, there is a shorter distance for the deepest wine to travel, and a full pressing is possible in a single pressing.

In the cleaning department, the bladder press has an edge over the basket type as well. First, the basket on bladder presses is stainless steel. The wooden slats on a basket press may look much more romantic than cold steel, but porous wood can harbor spoilage bacteria and yeasts in the same way a barrel can. To clean a basket press, remove the basket and clean it separately. Remove the cage pins and put them in a safe place. Take the basket apart completely. Take off the press head and remove the ratchet handle. Carefully wash and dry the pins or pawls that make the ratchet work. These are usually non-stainless steel and will rust if left wet. Hose off the big parts, and brush them with cleaner just as for the crusher/destemmer.

For a wooden basket, you can remove wine stains and freshen the slats by making a solution of sodium percarbonate cleaner, such as Proxy-Clean, in a plastic trash can or a fermenter large enough to sink the basket in. Put both halves in and let soak for several hours, up to 24. Rinse again and air-dry in a clean area. Be sure to properly lubricate the screw shaft, the moving parts of the head, and the sliding ends of the pawls. Reassemble the press completely before putting it away; misplaced parts can be a real problem when you return to it a few months later. If you have a room or area that you use for winemaking, consider installing shelves just above your crusher. That way, you will have a secure place off the floor to store the press, while taking advantage of the fact that presses are not very tall.

The main difference between basket and bladder presses for the home winemaker is one of cost versus convenience. Bladder presses will cost significantly more but, due to the more evenly distributed pressure, are also more efficient and easier to use as the water pressure does all the work, versus your muscles as is the case when using a ratchet press.

Early Sulfite Additions

S ometimes seen as a personal choice, the use of sulfites in winemaking requires a delicate sense of balance and a light (though judicious) hand. Wine can be made without the addition of sulfite; however, the chances of it turning out palatable take a tremendous hit if you choose this route.

The target many winemakers use is to maintain 0.5 mg/L (parts per million [ppm]) of molecular sulfur dioxide in red wines and 0.8 ppm in white and rosé wines. At those levels, the added sulfite helps protect the wine against oxidation and browning while also inhibiting the growth of harmful microorganisms. One drawback to these cited levels is that we do not have a practical means of analysis for molecular sulfur dioxide in wine. However, there is a well-understood relationship between the amount of molecular sulfur dioxide and the sum of sulfite and bisulfite ions at a given pH. That sum is referenced as "free" SO_2, and we do have reliable analytical methods for this. Since the ratio is pH dependent, there are various calculator tools and charts to help interpret it. Here is a brief table that illustrates some of the ratios at the 0.5 and 0.8 ppm levels:

Free SO_2 Needed at Various pH Levels

pH	White Wine (0.8)	Red Wine (0.5)
2.9	11 ppm	7 ppm
3.1	16	10
3.3	26	16
3.5	40	25
3.7	63	39

Most winemakers choose to add sulfite at numerous stages of the winemaking process as its effects wear off with time. The first addition of sulfite is often around 50 ppm to freshly crushed must (or more, if the fruit is damaged or has signs of mold) to protect the wine until fermentation takes off. Later additions take place after fermentation is complete, during aging, and just before bottling. We'll dive much deeper into the reasons sulfite additions are necessary, how to do them, and how to test SO_2 levels in chapter 7.

Press Cuts

Press cuts, also called press fractions, are created by separating the juice during pressing. Free-run juice (collected without applying pressure) is sometimes kept separate from juice collected with little pressure, and some winemakers continue separating fractions as more pressure is applied. Determining when or if to make press cuts is often left to taste rather than the amount of pressure on the home winemaking scale. When pressing grapes, the free-run juice is considered the premium juice. To understand why, we need to look at the fundamental aspects of the grape berry, which come into play during pressing.

The berry's skin contains color molecules (anthocyanins), as well as some tannins and tannin building blocks (proanthocyanidins), and aroma compounds. The skin, and the pulp near it, also contain potassium ions that can buffer the weak acids found in grape juice and so raise the pH of the juice. The pulp contains nearly all the juice (water, acids, sugar) and the aroma compounds. Finally, the extractable part of the seeds contains tannin and tannin building blocks and, perhaps, some aroma compounds.

When pressing raw grapes, the juice from the pulp is the most easily extracted and so the juice collected at the beginning of pressing is high in sugars, acids, and aroma compounds. As pressing continues, the amount of sugar and acid in the juice drops, and the levels of potassium ions and phenolic compounds increase.

The drop in sugar can be as much as 1°Brix over the course of a press run, which may not have a significant effect on wine quality given the lower quantity of highly pressed juice to the total volume. Juice pH increases over the course of pressing as easily extracted acids are depleted and the potassium ion concentration in the juice increases due to skin maceration. The difference between free-run and press fractions may be 0.2 to 0.4 pH units; so pH could be an important consideration for some juices/wines already on the high end of the pH goal for that style.

Skin maceration during pressing also causes the phenolic content of the juice to increase. Limiting phenolic compound extraction is, perhaps, the most important justification for press cuts, as the phenolic concentration in the juice may more than double over the course of the press run. Phenolic compounds may consist of small bitter phenolics and color compounds or color precursors in white juice and red wine, and larger polymeric phenolic compounds (tannin) in red wines.

Basket presses common in home wine production are a relatively gentle method of pressing. This means basket pressing produces relatively low yields, and press cuts, likely, are not typically necessary. A bladder press applying more pressure to the grapes during pressing may give reason to separate press cuts. Tasting the juice coming from the press is the best way to recognize if a cut should be separated (and it can then be blended in later, if desired). With red wines, the important things to taste for are tannins and increased astringency. With white juices, the acid and sugar level of the juice are the easiest to taste (or these can be monitored using a refractometer and a pH meter).

Another option besides simply separating and blending back some portion of the press cut is to treat the press cut with a fining agent to remove undesirable components before blending it back into the higher quality juice or wine—which leads us to a discussion on fining at the juice stage.

Fining Juice

Most fining will be done closer to bottling, but there are other times when fining juice is appropriate. White wines, and sometimes rosés, may be fined at the juice stage for a couple of reasons. Some varieties are subject to a condition called "pinking" where the colorless-to-pale-straw juice takes on a pink or bronze hue. The phenomenon can occur at several stages of wine production, beginning with the must. It is caused by slight oxidation of certain colorless precursor compounds that, when exposed to air, can transform into their pink oxidized counterparts.

Since the color formed by "pinking" can persist into the finished wine, commercial winemakers with this problem usually address it in the juice stage to avoid further problems. Your first line of defense here is to sulfite the must at the crush. Nonetheless, when pressed, the white juice may appear brown and pink juice may appear amber. Both pinking and browning can be fined out with polyvinylpolypyrrolidone (PVPP).

For treating white wine to prevent browning, a simple mid-range dose can usually be applied without much complication. For improving the color in a pink juice, however, a trial is essential. A low but effective dose will brighten the color and remove browning, but too much can strip out the anthocyanins that are responsible for the reddish hue.

The next important juice stage treatment for white wines is removal of proteins to assist with later clarity and help avoid problems with heat instability. Bentonite is the most popular agent for this purpose. However, since a wide range of protein components may be removed by bentonite, dose control is

Bentonite may be added during the juice stage to remove proteins.

extremely important. Overfining with too much bentonite may lower the juice's amino nitrogen content, leading to the production of hydrogen sulfide and its associated stink. Settling and racking the freshly pressed white juice is probably a safer route to clearer white wine than a bentonite addition to the juice.

For red wines, a common juice stage fining if excessive browning occurs is with PVPP, exactly as for white wines. Furthermore, during fermentation, bentonite can be applied if nitrogen management is needed. We'll dig deeper into fining during the later stages of winemaking, when it is most common, in chapter 4.

Must Adjustment

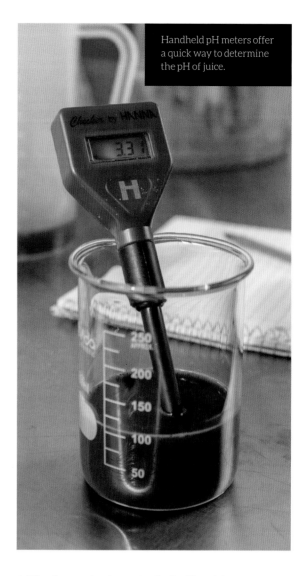

Handheld pH meters offer a quick way to determine the pH of juice.

Y our wine undergoes many changes on its way to the bottle. One process that is sometimes given little attention is adjusting the must before fermentation. Of course, there will be time for more adjustments later in the process, right up to bottling, but early intervention is often the easiest and best way to integrate the changes. Your first opportunity to make these adjustments is immediately after pressing.

By the time you have crushed and pressed your grapes, you should have a vision of the wine you intend to make. A good concept of where you want to go with your wine can inform many of your later decisions as you bring it along. Red, white, or pink? Big and bold, or elegant and refined? Easy drinking with a moderate alcohol level or a high-octane fruit bomb? These and many other characteristics can be influenced by must adjustment, but you need to know where you are going to apply them successfully.

What Can Be Adjusted at This Time?

The features amenable to adjustment at the must stage of winemaking cover a wide range. The most important should be considered for every wine. Other, lesser, influences are entirely optional depending on your vision for your wine and your desire to optimize it.

❖ The first major factor is **alcohol level** (ABV, or percent alcohol by volume). Since that is directly produced from the sugar concentration in the must, that is where the adjustment begins.

❖ The next major factor is the **titratable acidity**, or TA. Since that goes hand in hand with **pH**, the hydrogen ion concentration, they should be addressed together.

❖ Beyond these major factors, you have the opportunity to influence **tannin level**, **fruit aroma**, **body**, and **mouthfeel**.

If you grow your own grapes, some of your conceptual targets can start even before the crush. Measuring sugar, acid, and pH in the vineyard before harvest can help you begin close to your ideal objective. If you purchase grapes from a grower, you may have some influence over the harvest date and the corresponding harvest parameters. If you buy grapes already picked, or juice, you will begin your work at the must assessment stage.

Before you can make any adjustments, though, you need to know where you stand with your must. It's time to assess!

Sugar measurement is the critical first step in assessing your must. If you are working with fresh grapes for your initial evaluation, you can put 20 or 30 grapes in a small plastic zip-top bag and pop them with your fingers. Mix the juice well and check it with a refractometer. If your goal is a lower-alcohol wine, you will be looking for a number between about 19 and 21°Brix. Applying a common

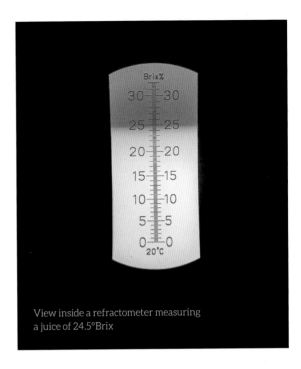

View inside a refractometer measuring a juice of 24.5°Brix

Refractometers require just a drop of juice for a Brix reading.

rule, multiply the starting Brix number by 0.55 to estimate your final ABV. This range would predict 10.5 to 11.6 percent ABV.

On the other hand, if you are looking to make a blockbuster wine, you will want a Brix level of 24 to 26 to produce an estimated 13.2 to 14.3 percent ABV.

After crushing and soaking, the Brix level may change. Since the refractometer cannot be used reliably once alcohol is present, you will monitor fermentation with a hydrometer. Begin using that as soon as you have crushed (or crushed and pressed for white wine). Because the refractometer and hydrometer measure sugar by completely different technologies, they may not agree exactly. Since you need to use the hydrometer later, anyway, just switch to that technique and move on.

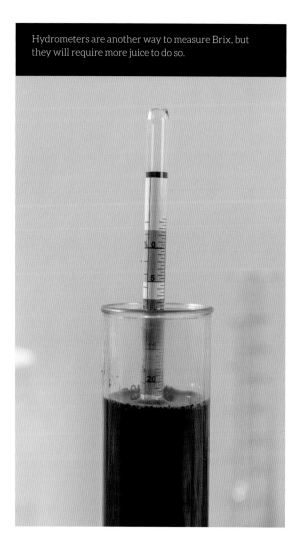

Hydrometers are another way to measure Brix, but they will require more juice to do so.

The next critical measurements are the linked values of TA and pH. For the at-home TA titration testing, you can use a simple kit that employs a phenolphthalein visual end point, a sophisticated titration setup with a burette and a pH meter, or a special-purpose meter from companies such as Vinmetrica or Hanna. If you have a meter system, it probably includes a pH meter already. If not, you will want to get that separately. For most red wine musts, you will want a TA range from about 6 g/L (equivalent to percent, also expressed as 0.6 g/100 ml) to about 8 g/L. Much lower than this range and the wine will likely be perceived as "flabby;" and much higher, it will be too tart. Since we like a brighter flavor profile in most white wines, the range in the juice will be more like 7 to 9 g/L. These values are slightly higher than the levels desired in the finished wine because TA is known to decline during fermentation (both alcoholic and malolactic, if done), cold stabilization, and aging. The pH has more to do with the ultimate stability of the wine, whereas the TA is critical to the flavor. Desirable pH ranges for red and white wines are 3.3 to 3.6 and 3.1 to 3.4, respectively (for a deeper dive into pH and TA, see chapter 7).

To assess other characteristics amenable to must adjustment, you will need to rely on tasting the juice, since numeric targets for these parameters are not readily available. For this exercise, get a helper (or two) with a good palate so you can talk over your perceptions and get another point of view. Taste the juice for its tannic profile or astringency, trying to mentally subtract the very high sweetness. You may also be able to gain some perception of mouthfeel from the juice as well as evaluate the aroma.

If you are fortunate enough to make wine from the same source of grapes every year, use the results and winemaking notes from previous vintages to guide your choices about tannins, mouthfeel, aromas, and any benefits of oak addition.

With knowledge about where your numbers align to your goals, it may be time to make adjustments.

Chaptalization may be required if the measured Brix of your fruit is low.

Sugar: If your Brix measurement on the crushed must came in lower than your target, you can add sugar, a process known as *chaptalization*. It's a process not allowed for commercial wineries in many locations, but when making wine with certain types of grapes or country wines, it's basically required. Strawberry must, for instance, may be as low as 5°Brix when fully ripe.

There are numerous benefits of chaptalization when the sugar level of the fruit you are fermenting is less than ideal. Higher-alcohol wines are more shelf stable as the elevated ethyl alcohol concentration is lethal to many spoilage organisms. The higher alcohol levels are one reason that wine can be safely stored for years when properly managed. Another reason winemakers may chaptalize their wine is called "amelioration"—when overly acidic juice is watered down, sugar is added to bring the sugar levels back up. This technique is more common with cold-climate hybrid wine grapes that can come in with titratable acid levels well over 10 g/L—in other words, very sour.

Using the Brix scale is an easy way to determine how much sugar is needed since it's a measure of the percentage of sugar. For practical purposes, we can say 10 grams of sugar per liter will add 1°Brix. So if your juice is 18°Brix and you want to raise it to 22°Brix, and you have 25 liters, you will want to add 2.2 pounds (1 kg) of sugar:

4°Brix × 10 g/L × 25 L = 1 kg or 2.2 lb. of sugar

Although this calculation is a bit simplified, it will get you in the ballpark for our winemaking purposes.

The most common way winemakers chaptalize their wine is using common table (granulated) sugar. Weigh the amount of sugar needed and dissolve it in a minimum amount of warm juice you are chaptalizing. Then mix the resulting syrup into the whole mass.

Using concentrates, grape or otherwise, is another way a wine or must can be chaptalized.

Dissolve a measured amount of tartaric acid into a small amount of distilled water and add it to the must to increase TA.

Most of these come in around 68°Brix, are often fruit-specific or varietal-specific (although not always), and vary widely in volume. In this case, the sugar is already dissolved and the concentrate can be added directly to the must and mixed in. One way to calculate how much to add to reach your target Brix is using the Pearson square (learn more about these calculations on page 107).

Water: If your Brix number is higher than your target, add water (preferably distilled or reverse-osmosis treated, to avoid adding minerals). In this case, estimate the gallons (liters) of juice as described previously for red wine, or measure it directly for white juice. Then set up the following equations to determine the amount of water to add:

(volume of juice) × °Brix of juice)/desired Brix = needed volume after adjustment

then,

Needed volume after adjustment – volume of juice = water to add

As an example, suppose you have 6 gallons (23 L) of juice at 26°Brix and you want it at 24°Brix:

(6 gallons × 26°Brix)/24°Brix = 6.5 gallons (25 L)

(23 L × 26/24 = 25 L) and, 6.5 gallons – 6 gallons = 0.5 gallon of water to add (25 L – 23 L = 2 L)

Match your water temperature to the must and stir in the water. Make sure the water you use is free of chlorine (carbon block filtration or a metabisulfite addition can treat chlorinated water).

A note of caution with red wine must: Very high Brix musts are often found to contain shriveled grapes and raisins. As these soak over a period of a day or two, additional sugar may soak out of them. So measure your initial Brix, add needed water, and measure again. The next day, measure again to make sure the must has not "soaked up" to a higher Brix level, requiring a second water addition.

Acid: If the TA is lower than your target, the adjustment is simple. Since TA is measured as tartaric acid and that is the acid you want to use, you just need to estimate your volume and weigh the acid for addition. Because TA results are in metric units, it is easiest to go with those for the addition calculation. For example, suppose you have juice at 4 g/L and you want 6 g/L. Plan your addition in grams per liter:

6 g/L – 4 g/L = 2 g/L to add

Estimate your juice yield, and convert to liters:

6 gallons = 23 L

Calculate the tartaric acid addition:

23 L × 2 g/L = 46 g to add

Dissolve the tartaric acid in a small amount of distilled water and stir it into the must.

A word of caution: We specify tartaric acid because citric acid is strongly discouraged in winemaking from grapes, particularly red winemaking, as citric acid, is metabolized into acetic acid (vinegar/volatile acidity) by lactic acid bacteria. Tartaric acid has become quite expensive compared to citric, but that does not mean that citric acid is a good substitute for tartaric acid.

Lowering the acid level is a bit more complicated. You cannot simply take out the acid, so you need to neutralize it with a basic (alkaline) material. Potassium bicarbonate, available at home winemaking supply stores, works well for this. Adding it at 1 g/L will reduce TA by a corresponding 1 g/L. Do not try to adjust more than 2 g/L, as a salty or bitter taste may result. The calculation is the same as our example for addition, except you are adding potassium bicarbonate instead of tartaric acid.

Since you can further adjust the TA later in the winemaking process, you may wish to make only a half or two-thirds addition of your calculated acidification or deacidification, and wait to make a final adjustment after.

You can also expect a decrease in TA if you perform malolactic fermentation, and from cold stabilization. Note that to lower pH utilizes the same process as adding acid, and raising pH is the same process as adding potassium bicarbonate. The pH does not change linearly with the additions, so calculate for TA first, then make the needed adjustment. If a pH target would require going significantly outside of the TA target range, then it is safest to use TA as your primary guide (for taste) and deal with your pH concerns (for stability) later.

Tannins: If the juice seems in need of more tannic "grip," you can add tannins to the must in several forms. You can use oak chips or oak dust, which may also add oaky flavor components. You can add grape tannins or specialized fermentation tannin products like FT Rouge Soft and FT Blanc Soft from Scott Laboratories. Use rates vary from less than 1 g/gallon (3.8 L; 0.26 g/L) in white juice to as much as 4 g/gallon (3.8 L; 1 g/L) in red must. Follow the manufacturer's instructions for any product you choose. For any addition, calculate your total desired amount and weigh it. For white juice, add with mixing when you rack the settled juice off the fruit lees. For red must, sprinkle the product on top, then mix it in at the time of the first punchdown.

Mouthfeel: Although tannin and oak additions will have some positive effects on mouthfeel, you may be able to get further enhancements by adding specific inactivated yeast nutrient products to the must. Materials like OptiMUM White and Opti-Red from Lallemand are used at rates from 1 to 2 g/gallon (3.8 L; 0.26 to 0.52 g/L), and added at the same time as the tannin products just described.

Aroma: Enhancing aroma in your finished wine is more about liberating what is already in the grapes than about adding aromas themselves. Many aroma precursors in wine grapes are bound to sugar molecules in a nonaromatic form. Some of these compounds are also found in the skins of the grapes. To enter the wine, they need to be cleaved off by enzymes. Although this process occurs naturally with yeast enzymes during red wine fermentation, it can be enhanced. To have any chance with white wine, it requires enzymatic activity on the crushed grapes, before pressing and removal of the skins. Add enzymes such as Lallzyme EX or EnartisZym Color Plus to the crushed grapes about 15 minutes after your initial addition of sulfites. Use rate is about 1 g/100 lb. (1 g/45 kg) of grapes. Mix the weighed enzyme powder with a small amount of distilled water and stir it into the must. These enzyme additions can also improve color extraction in reds and mouthfeel in both reds and whites. We'll get into greater detail about enzymes in chapter 7.

When Grapes Throw You for a Curve

N ow that we've covered must adjustments that may be required if grapes don't give you everything you desire, we need to take it a step farther. Sometimes the wine you dreamed of making before picking up grapes just isn't feasible. Minor adjustments are one thing, but when grapes are more seriously flawed, or a characteristic is so far from what is needed for the desired style, a winemaker needs to be flexible enough to change their plans altogether.

Damaged Fruit/Quality Issues

Making a quality wine requires quality grapes. Mother Nature is probably the primary influencer of grape damage. The most severe cause of damage may be rains at the end of the growing season, which result in *Botrytis* bunch rot. Severe cases of bunch rot are visible and will, hopefully, be left in the vineyard by those harvesting the grapes. There may, however, be less visible bunch rot, in which case you may receive these as part of your allocation from the grower. To mitigate this, inspect your grapes at the crush pad. This might involve extensive and detailed inspection and removal of damaged fruit from the clusters that will be used to produce wine. To take extra precaution, if you suspect damaged fruit, add a stronger dose of SO_2 after the crush, which will help diminish mold effects on the juice. SO_2, however, will not "fix" the sensory and quality issues that bunch rot has already created.

Clusters impacted by *Botrytis* should be left on the vine during harvest (unless the intention is to make a Sauternes-style sweet wine).

Bird damage is another common quality issue. If the grower nets their vineyard, you can be better assured that bird damage will be minimized. A small amount of bird damage will not have a substantial impact on fruit quality and finished wine, but using pristine fruit is obviously preferred. If you find extensive damage, sort these clusters out of the batch or take the time to clip out the damaged areas. It is again advisable to give a stronger dose of SO_2 after the crush, if you suspect excessive damage, to eliminate bacterial issues within the juice.

Uneven ripening may also occur. Visible signs include some berries in the clusters appearing very dark—and therefore ripe—whereas other berries in the same cluster are a lighter shade of color or even green or underdeveloped (underripe). The underripe berries will impart a harshness to the finished wine. The resulting must will also be lower in sugar and higher in acidity than you may have expected. Uneven ripening is common with all harvests and a minimal amount does not necessarily require intervention, but if a lot of the grapes are affected you may consider sorting out those clusters.

With the exception of bunch rot, quality issues might be somewhat mitigated by pivoting to make a rosé out of your red grapes. Minimizing skin contact and eliminating fermentation on the skins limits contact with damaged areas and reduces off flavors and bacterial effects to the wine.

The message here is, don't pass damaged fruit into the winemaking process. If you are trying to "make your numbers" for wine volume, consider trying to purchase more grapes of the same variety, or get a second variety that can be processed and used later as a blend. Including bad grapes should never be the solution to meet an expected volume.

Not the Brix You Expected

With uneven ripening, your grapes will likely be at a lower sugar level than what you expected. To make the best wine possible out of this situation you might decide to increase sugar levels (see page 43). However, that is not the only option. Consider blending with another wine of a higher Brix or, as recommended if the fruit is damaged, create a dry rosé. A rosé wine will not have the skin and unripe seed contact through fermentation that would otherwise create a harsh and astringent red wine. With a rosé you will get all the aromatics of the varietal and a nice crisp wine for summer consumption.

If you find that your grapes are of good quality but not at the level of ripeness desired for your finished wine, perhaps you just do nothing. A small delta between harvest expectation of Brix and delivered grapes does not necessitate cause for action. Accept that you will have a lighter-style wine this vintage. A large delta between expected versus delivered Brix might have consequences that require remediation.

Smoke Taint Concerns

With the seemingly ever-present threat of wildfires across the globe, impacts on grape growing and wine production are occurring more often. Every vintage seems to be at risk in certain geographic areas and cause for concern is justified. The science behind smoke taint on wine is still evolving within the scientific community, with the Australian Wine Research Institute and University of California, Davis (UC-Davis), being at the forefront of this research. The information provided here comes from these researchers in relation to how it occurs and how to correct or minimize the impact on wine production and quality.

Sensory evaluations describe smoke taint as a distinctive lingering retro-nasal ashtray character. Addressing smoke taint in a wine after fermentation is expensive and only wineries with lots of resources and money can justify the work necessary to remove the smoke components from a finished wine. Research has determined a few things, however, that can be considered at the home winemaking level if you think your grapes might have been exposed.

Smoke taint takes place on the skin of the grapes, in which volatile phenols react with grape sugars. If you minimize skin contact with the wine juice, then the smoke components are less likely to transfer into the juice and finished wine.

Although the timing of wildfires more often occurs in the later stages of grape ripening, smoke taint can take place when grapes are pea size and effects may increase after veraison (the onset of ripening when the grapes change color). However, the fresher the smoke (less than 24 hours), the greater the risk of smoke tainting the finished wine. On the other hand, the density of the smoke does not necessarily equate to increased smoke taint risk.

Smoke in your source vineyard is not necessarily a cause for concern. Heavy smoke blown into the vineyard from a wildfire 50 miles (80 km) away that took more than a day to blow in is not likely to affect the grapes and wine quality. Even if smoke persists in the vineyard for several days, there is minimal impact. However, a wildfire that is very near the vineyard, where smoke and ash are coming directly from the fire, will likely have a significant impact on wine quality.

Rinsing off the grapes with water does not eliminate the smoke taint and only waters down the juice. However, if grapes have visible ash on their surface, the recommendation is to wash off the ash at the winery before the winemaking process starts.

So what can the home winemaker do? If you have red grapes, the best option, according to the research community, is to make a rosé wine. Rosé wine production minimizes or completely eliminates skin contact. If you suspect the worst-case exposure, it might be best to completely eliminate skin contact and make a vin gris–style rosé. The same considerations apply to white wines. Sensory evaluations by researchers note that there still may be subthreshold impacts to wine quality.

Uneven ripening may result in a lower Brix than expected.

Wildfires in recent years have made smoke taint in nearby vineyards a concern for winemakers.

Chapter 3:
Fermentation

The quality of wine starts in the vineyard with the health and ripeness of the grapes. The next important step in the quality of wine is fermentation, which is the sole responsibility of the winemaker. Fermentation is hard to visualize due to the fact that yeast are only 0.8 to 1.0 micron in size but perform complicated and critical pathways within the yeast cell. We rely on knowledge gained through research, each fermentation experience, and most important, our senses. No two fermentations are the same and there is something to learn from each to bring to your next fermentation. Whether you are new to winemaking or have years of experience, fermentation is a complicated process but so important to the consistency and quality of the wine. Just as in previous chapters, we'll begin this chapter focusing on fermentation with the equipment needed to turn grape juice into wine.

Fermentation Equipment

There are quite a few fermenter options, each with its pros and cons, and some specific to the style of wine you are making. A wine container must be sturdy enough for the purpose and not likely to introduce negative changes to the wine quality. Size is important, depending on the winemaker's capacity to move heavy containers. Other considerations include cost, convenience, inertness, cleaning, sanitation, and availability.

Oak Barrels

Oak barrels hold a special place among wine containers. They are the only option chosen to deliberately make changes in the beverage, as all other containers are valued for being inert.

Barrels are most commonly used as aging vessels, although white wine (where you don't have a cap that requires punching down during fermentation) can be fermented in them as well. The practice, common in some French regions, adds a rounder, creamier flavor and texture to the wine than aging in any other type of vessel and moving the wine to barrel afterward. To barrel-ferment a white wine like Chardonnay, leave about one-fourth of the barrel capacity as headspace for foaming and fit a fermentation lock in the bung hole.

For much more on barrels and the effect they have on wine, refer to the section on oak in chapter 4.

Glass

Glass has a long history in winemaking and remains the foremost container for finished wine. Like barrels, most glass containers have a narrow opening and are not suitable for red wine primary (alcoholic) fermentation. Fitted with a fermentation lock, a glass carboy or demijohn is very satisfactory for white wine fermentation and for aging red or white wine. Sizes range from 1-gallon (3.8-L) jugs up to 14-gallon (54-L) demijohns. Neck sizes vary, but rubber stoppers or silicone bungs can be found to fit any narrow-mouth container. For a 1-gallon (3.8-L) jug, expect to pay just a few dollars, with glass carboy and demijohn prices ranging up to about $70 USD. A good liquid detergent, like TDC, or a powdered cleaner, like PBW or sodium percarbonate, will do a good job of cleaning glass. Sanitize before use with iodophor (BTF or IO Star) or phosphoric acid (Star San). Glass is an excellent all-around choice in the home winery with just two significant limitations: glass containers are heavy and fragile. Handle carefully, avoid handling when wet, if you can, and consider setting carboys in plastic milk crates or using purpose-built carboy handles or harnesses to minimize the risk of breakage.

Plastic

"Plastic" refers to a wide variety of synthetic polymers. Those most commonly found in winemaking are high-density polyethylene (HDPE) and polyethylene terephthalate (PET). For winemaking, HDPE is most often found as buckets or open fermenters (food-grade trash cans). If the specific container has been submitted to the National Sanitation Foundation and approved for food contact, it will bear the NSF logo. The container may also display the resin identification code "2" with a recycling arrow logo. Choose fermenters with these marks to be sure that you will not introduce contaminants to your fermentation. HDPE, unlike vinyl (PVC) polymers, does not contain plasticizers that can leach out of the container; do not use PVC buckets or bins for wine.

HDPE primary fermenters are available in sizes ranging from 5-gallon (19-L) buckets up to 176-gallon (666-L) fork-liftable bins. Some home winemakers can successfully employ these large bins, about 4 feet × 4 feet and 2 feet deep (1.2 × 1.2 × 0.6 m), commonly referred to as a half-ton bin or by the trade name MacroBin. If the large size and weight are a challenge for your home winery, the middle-size bins, 32 to 44 gallons (121 to 167 L), may prove more suitable. The half-ton bin, as implied by the nickname, can be used to ferment about

1,000 pounds (454 kg) of red must. A 32-gallon (121-L) bin can accommodate about 225 pounds (102 kg) and the 44-gallon (167-L) bin about 330 pounds (150 kg). Three or four of these containers can approximate the capacity of a full-size bin, with the additional benefit being that they nest in a stack for off-season storage. Some narrow-mouth HDPE containers have also been introduced for fermentation. Although safe and inert, there is some concern that HDPE may be somewhat permeable to oxygen, allowing transfer from the air, like storage in an oak barrel. But many of these containers are thick-walled, meaning a slower transfer, and for shorter-term applications for winemaking, like for primary fermentation, are perfectly suitable.

More resistant to oxygen transfer is the other common winemaking plastic, PET. For the home winery, PET is generally in the form of carboys from 3 gallons (11 L) to 6.5 gallons (25 L). It has a resin identification code of 1 and will display the letters PET or PETE. With an extensive history of commercial alcoholic beverage containers and good oxygen transfer resistance, PET carboys offer very effective alternatives to glass carboys. Like HDPE, it is manufactured without plasticizers. There are both narrow- and wide-mouth versions of these PET carboys. Narrow-mouth versions should be heavily preferred for longer-term aging.

Many of the same cleaners and sanitizers used for glass may be used for plastic, but there are some exceptions. One additional caution is to be very careful about using brushes on these surfaces as they may scratch them. Scratches could allow for the trapping of spoilage organisms that would be difficult to eradicate with sanitizers. Prices for plastic containers range from around $10 USD for a food-grade bucket through $20 to $30 USD for PET carboys and up to $500 USD for a half-ton bin.

Stainless Steel

A cylindrical tank with an inset lid is the most common stainless-steel container in home wineries. The lid has a vinyl or rubber gasket and a dedicated air pump to inflate it. Because the lid can be positioned anywhere within the height of the tank, the capacity is variable up to the maximum volume. Most of these tanks are type 304 stainless steel (also known as 18/8), which is sufficiently corrosion-resistant for wine use (but avoid excessive exposure to sulfur dioxide as pitting may occur). Type 316 is also suitable, but generally more expensive. Tanks are marked in some way to indicate suitability for food use, such as Italian tanks that are marked "per alimenti." Sizes range from 13 gallons (49 L) to 260 gallons (984 L) or more. All include a valve near the bottom and some may include other features such as cooling jackets, sight gauges, secondary racking valves, and so forth. Most feature a rather tall and narrow profile, making them less than ideal for red wine primary fermentation where a ratio of about 1:1 height to width is preferred.

With the lid in place, they are suitable for white wine fermentation and for any wine cellaring purposes. Tank prices range from about $300 USD for the smaller sizes to well over $1,000 USD for large tanks.

Maceration Techniques

Maceration is the process of extracting chemical compounds from the solid parts of the grape berry into the juice. Maceration doesn't play a big role in white wine production, with the exception of some aromatic whites and orange wines, but is a critical component of red winemaking. Maceration time and temperature, as well as processing options, affect the color and tannic astringency of the resulting wine. Both color and tannin components are phenolic molecules. The location and the molecular size of the phenolic compound have a big impact on when and how much of a particular type of phenolic compound is extracted into wine. Anthocyanins, the phenolic compounds that contribute color to wines, are found predominantly in the skins of most grape varieties. Tannin compounds, a wide class of compounds that have similar base structure but differ in size and type, are found in the skins, seeds, and pulp of the grapes as well as the grape stems.

The rate of extraction of color and tannin molecules from the skin tissue into the juice is determined mostly by the size of the molecule. Anthocyanin molecules are relatively small and so are extracted into juice quickly. Most tannin molecules are polymers, and their larger molecular size means they are extracted more slowly into the juice. Grape seeds contain large quantities of tannin that are extracted the most slowly, unless the seed is damaged, so winemakers go to great lengths to ensure seeds are treated gently and never crushed in rollers that are too tight, or ground in pump internals or other processing equipment. Research has shown that most of the color is extracted in the first day or two of maceration, whereas tannin extraction is more gradual and continues as long as the skins and seeds are in contact with the juice.

Punchdowns and pumpovers are the two most common methods of maceration and should be employed during active fermentation. In commercial production, most winemakers believe punchdowns, despite the name, are gentler and less oxidative than pumpovers. However, the research regarding the impact of punchdowns versus pumpovers doesn't show a lot of difference between the two methods in terms of color and tannin extraction. The other big split between punchdowns and pumpovers is based on tank size. Very small lots are more convenient to punchdown than pumpover, and the opposite is true of very large tanks. For this reason most home wine producers favor punchdowns.

Foot treading, like Lucille Ball does in her famous grape-stomp scene in *I Love Lucy*, is a time-honored method of maceration still practiced by some traditionalists. Most modern winemakers, however, prefer to keep their shoes on and manually punchdown the cap using their arms or a punchdown tool. A sturdy and easy-to-clean punchdown tool is a good investment; you can find them at home winemaking shops and online, or you can make your own out of wood or stainless steel.

Pumpovers require a pump, of course, but also some method of keeping skins and seeds out of the pump internals. Commercial producers often use screens inside the tank that prevent solids from getting stuck in the tank valve, as well as a sump below the tank outlet with another screen to collect skins and seeds before the pump inlet. Home winemakers and small-lot producers often ferment in tanks, MacroBins, or food-grade trash cans, which don't have a screened bottom valve. In this case, using a perforated suction tube, with the inlet hose to the pump inside it, is a workable method for pumping over.

Pumpovers, and to a lesser extent punchdowns, can have the added benefit of adding a bit of oxygen to fermentation. Oxygen during alcoholic fermentation helps with both color stabilization and tannin integration. Oxygen can also be important for yeast health, preventing yeast from producing reductive, or stinky, aromas late in fermentation.

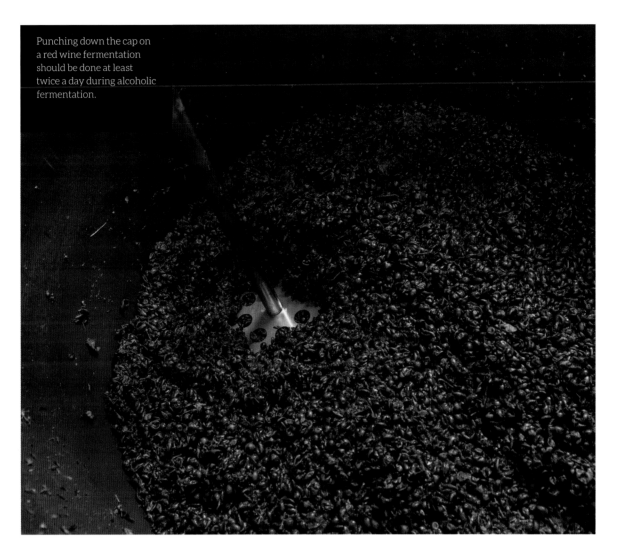

Punching down the cap on a red wine fermentation should be done at least twice a day during alcoholic fermentation.

To incorporate more oxygen into the fermenting must, a Venturi tube or sparging stone and oxygen tank are required.

Whether doing punchdowns or pumpovers, breaking up the cap should be employed at least once a day during active fermentation, and twice a day is generally recommended. Once fermentation is underway and the cap has formed, the juice beneath it contains an inhibitory level of alcohol and is saturated with carbon dioxide, limiting microbial growth. Getting the cap wet and keeping it in contact with the fermenting liquid beneath it helps with tannin extraction, but more important, it also limits microbial growth in and on the cap. Both acetic acid

bacteria and spoilage molds and fungi will grow in the cap if it is not periodically wetted with the fermenting juice.

Another benefit of mixing up the red fermentation is temperature dispersal. Your fermentation will be hottest just below the cap so punching down will cool the fermentation by allowing some heat to escape while also bringing the must to an even temperature throughout.

Doing this maceration step at least once per day also gives you the opportunity to assess the fermentation by taking a sample and measuring the Brix level. This daily sample should also be sniffed to check for off aromas and tasted to determine if tannin extraction is progressing according to your goal for the style and type of wine being produced.

Temperature is an important aspect of color and tannin extraction, with increasing temperature during maceration increasing the extraction. Some winemakers use this to their advantage in hot pressing, where the must is heated to between 150°F and 180°F (66.5°C and 82°C) for a short period of time before pressing, instead of waiting the 24 to 48 hours it usually takes to extract color. Color is released quickly in this method, but tannin and some aromatics are not. Winemakers looking to extract color in highly aromatic red hybrid wines are most likely to employ this method.

In *vinifera* red wine fermentations, many commercial winemakers like to see maximum fermentation temperatures of between 85°F and 95°F (29°C and 35°C) if high levels of tannin extraction are desired for the grape variety and style, though these temperatures are above generally recommended ranges.

You've likely heard the saying, there are a million different ways to make wine. This maxim holds true for maceration options as well. Besides punchdowns versus pumpovers and maceration frequency and temperature, some winemakers employ techniques such as cold soaking, extended maceration, and carbonic or "semi-carbonic" maceration. We'll cover each of these options in more detail next.

Cold Soak

Cold soak is a technique most commonly associated with the Burgundy region of France and Pinot Noir grapes and utilized after destemming and crushing, but before primary fermentation begins. The skins and seeds are "soaked" in contact with the juice, but the temperature of the must is kept low, 40°F to 50°F (4°C to 10°C), so alcoholic fermentation does not advance. When cold soaking, it is often recommended to add sulfur dioxide during crushing and to utilize dry ice and a cover on top of the must to prevent oxidation.

Cold soak duration is generally overnight to several days, but usually not more than a week. Even though the temperature is low enough that alcoholic fermentation is inhibited, other microbial species may be capable of metabolism in this temperature range, so it is still recommended to macerate during cold soaking, either with punchdowns or pumpovers, to ensure unwanted microbes are inhibited. Practically speaking, this can be somewhat arduous because grape must without a cap is much more difficult to punchdown!

Winemaking textbooks recommend rapid heating to standard fermentation temperatures and inoculation with a commercial yeast strain once the cold soak is complete. The danger is that a prolonged period of moderate temperatures could slow *Saccharomyces* metabolism and allow other microbes to metabolize sugar in the must. This brings to mind a couple of practical problems for the home winemaker: the ability to maintain a low temperature and the ability to rapidly heat the must to fermentation temperature. Especially in warmer climates, it can be difficult to keep a cold soak cold. Thus, what may occur in practice is a "lukewarm" soak, which could end up promoting the metabolism of non-*Saccharomyces* strains that produce unwanted aroma volatiles, like ethyl acetate (nail polish remover or solvent aroma). Similarly, even if cold temperatures can be maintained, a long warming period before fermentation also leaves the must susceptible to unwanted microbial metabolism.

There is conflicting research data on whether conducting a cold soak is beneficial in terms of color extraction, but most research seems to show little difference in color, or even a slight color loss, between cold soak and standard maceration schedules. Similar research has shown a slight decrease in tannin extraction when a cold soak is utilized, but this technique remains popular in some regions and with certain grape varieties. We mentioned Burgundy and Pinot Noir, and the idea of cold soaking appears to have initially spread to Pinot producers in Oregon and California as well. In addition, the technique has now expanded to Cabernet Sauvignon and Syrah producers in the United States and, according to the Australian Wine Research Institute, is also popular with Australian producers of many grape varieties.

Dry ice is a great way to cool a must, especially when performing a cold soak.

Besides the possible impact on color, some winemakers also like cold soaking because they believe the added time before active *Saccharomyces* fermentation may give other beneficial microbes a chance to increase the aroma complexity of the wine (similar to uninoculated, or "native" fermentations). There is some research evidence for the benefit of multi-microbe fermentation, so much so that several commercial yeast suppliers now also offer non-*Saccharomyces* strains for pre-fermentation or early fermentation use. Still for home winemakers, this technique may present more risk than reward.

Extended Maceration

Extended maceration is a technique during which the skins and seeds remain in contact with the newly fermented must well past the end of primary fermentation, often anywhere from a week to 30 days post-fermentation, and for some adventurous winemakers even longer. Extended maceration is a traditional technique used in the Burgundy, Bordeaux, and Rhône Valley regions of France, as well as in the Piedmont region of Italy. A 2009 Australian Wine Research Institute survey found it was quite common with Australian producers and most commonly used on Cabernet Sauvignon, Syrah,

Merlot, and Pinot Noir. California winemakers also sometimes employ it when making Pinot Noir and Cabernet wines.

Allowing the newly fermented wine to remain in contact with skins and seeds using extended maceration has been shown to increase the percentage of seed tannin and the overall tannin level. Anecdotally, winemakers also describe a change in tannin perception at the end of extended maceration, where the aggressive tannin of a well-extracted red wine mellows and becomes softer and smoother.

Extended maceration is a bit of a gamble if you've never tried it. It should only be performed with grapes that have ripe seeds because unripe seeds can extract too much and very harsh tannins (the fully developed seed coat is thought to slow tannin extraction). Care needs to be taken to limit oxidation and the potential for spoilage since fermentation is no longer creating carbon dioxide. Thus extended maceration should be performed in a closed tank, and preferably one that is either full or periodically purged with an inert gas, or a variable-capacity tank with a lid (for more on choosing and using inert gas, see page 90). Without this equipment, it would be difficult for home winemakers to utilize extended maceration without oxidation concerns; however, many different sizes of variable-capacity tanks are available to home winemakers. Besides limiting oxidation, extended maceration must also be monitored by tasting the wine every few days to determine the optimum time to press the wine off the skins.

Carbonic Maceration

Carbonic maceration is a relatively recent addition to the winemaking toolbox, with experiments by French researcher Michel Flanzy documenting the technique in a production capacity in 1936.

Carbonic maceration is a technique that places whole clusters of fruit in a sealed tank that has been purged with carbon dioxide. Enzymes in the grape berry will naturally break down the skin of the berry and convert some sugar into ethanol. The tank is kept quite warm, perhaps around 90°F (32°C), which helps with the enzymatic breakdown of pulp and skin tissue. After about 1 week, depending on the maximum temperature achieved, the tank is emptied to press and a traditional fermentation is continued following pressing. This technique produces very fruity wines (some call it fake fruit or "Jolly Rancher" aromas). However, the wines usually have only a moderate amount of color and low tannin.

There are not many producers practicing full-on carbonic maceration outside of Beaujolais, the French region that made this technique famous with their Beaujolais Nouveau style made from Gamay grapes. A bit more common are winemakers who utilize some percentage of whole cluster fruit in the bottom of a fermentation vat as a "semi-carbonic" process. Some winemakers also choose to destem berries, but not crush them, giving a bit of carbonic fruit lift to their fermentation.

Research has shown there are definitely organoleptic impacts on wines treated with the full carbonic maceration protocol. The effects are so dramatic that one need only compare a Beaujolais Nouveau to a common Beaujolais-Village wine to see, smell, and taste the differences. There's also some research showing differences in wines that were destemmed versus whole cluster fermentations, with whole cluster fermentations showing less color but higher total phenolics. When evaluating the impact of whole cluster fermentation versus carbonic maceration or standard maceration, it's a bit difficult to separate differences in any effects that might be coming from carbonic maceration in the berries versus the extraction of aroma and flavor coming from the included stems. Limited amounts of research regarding whole berry fermentations versus crushed fruit show subtle differences in color and phenolics (flavor differences were not categorized).

Experimenting with only destemmed whole berries is a good first step into the world of carbonic maceration. Newer commercial destemmers, and mechanical harvesters for that matter, have come a long way with gentle handling of clusters and are capable of destemming with a surprisingly large percentage of whole berries. At the top end of the

Extended maceration may be done to increase tannins.

home winemaking price range are some "gentler" destemmer-only models. Traditional small-scale destemmer/crushers will crush the fruit first, so if you, or your winemaking club, doesn't want to splurge for one of these destemmer-only models, it might be necessary to ask a larger local producer, or your local winemaking shop, to destem the fruit for you.

Another option for home producers might be to attempt carbonic maceration with whole cluster fruit in a tank that can be sealed. Poly tanks with large access lids might work, or a food-grade 55-gallon (208-L) drum with a removable lid, but getting the whole clusters back out of the tank could be difficult without a way to tip the tank. Once a suitable tank and emptying method is found, you would also need a way to purge the tank, at least daily, with carbon dioxide during the carbonic maceration period.

WineMaker Technical Editor Bob Peak offers another technique that has worked for him: "I had some success with my one experiment in a 26-gallon (100-L) variable-capacity tank. I ran a CO_2 line from the bottom of the tank before loading in whole clusters, then brought the tube out through the fermentation lock hole in the lid and over to the CO_2 tank. I burned a votive candle on the lid before charging with gas, so when the candle went out, the tank was flushed."

It's All about the Yeast

Wine yeast comprises microorganisms responsible for converting the sugar in grape juice into alcohol. However, yeast does so much more than just produce alcohol. It has a role in the resulting wine's flavor, body, structure, and color as well.

Though yeast is everywhere, including on the grapes brought in from the vineyard (known as "wild" or "native" yeast), the most common (and generally recommended, particularly for those new to winemaking) source of wine yeast, is that which has been isolated in a lab. Although the word "wild" might give the romantic impression that winemaking's native yeasts come from the grapes in the vineyard, it's just as likely that a wild fermentation is the result of yeast from winery equipment or even the floor.

Proponents of wild fermentations claim a complexity and a unique local character from the local flora makes the risk of natural fermentations worth it. That said, wild yeast fermentation is unpredictable and can be troublesome because it is more susceptible to lower levels of SO_2 and alcohol, and thus stuck fermentations. Wild yeast fermentation is also prone to microbial spoilage if not managed properly and is best left to professionals and the more adventurous amateur winemakers who are willing to dump batches that have gone astray.

Commercial yeasts, on the other hand, are isolated, bred, and characterized for behavior in laboratories and turned into powders or liquid cultures. Cultured yeast is a relatively risk-free fermentation that requires minimal monitoring because the results are highly predictable. Manufacturers of cultured wine yeasts provide a lot of data on strain characteristics and expected results.

When you want fermentation to start, simply add the yeast, either by pouring it into the must, or by adding water to rehydrate the yeast culture before pitching it—a process called "inoculation." With a wild ferment, on the other hand, it's a bit like magic: you crush the grapes and just wait until fermentation happens.

Note that concentrated and sterilized grape juices have been stripped of all yeasts during production; therefore, they always require the addition of a cultured yeast.

For home winemaking using grapes or fresh juice, it is best to inhibit wild yeasts using a small dose of SO_2; home winemakers do this by adding potassium metabisulfite to achieve a *maximum* free SO_2 level of 10 mg/L.

Saccharomyces cerevisiae is the species of yeast that is primarily responsible for wine's alcoholic fermentation, thanks to a combination of several "enological" traits: rapid and complete sugar consumption, ethanol production, and transformation of aromatic precursors as well as its tolerance to initial and final harsh conditions. There are many strains within a species, each with different physiological attributes intended for different applications and yielding different vinification results.

As mentioned, many non-*Saccharomyces* yeasts are wine spoilers. However, others have a positive effect on a wine, maintaining the desirable natural variability of wine, the so-called terroir expression, and highlighting mouthfeel, aroma, and flavor complexity. In recent years, in attempts to exploit these advantages, yeast manufacturers have isolated some of these yeasts that can be pitched a couple of days prior to a sequential *S. cerevisiae* pitch. In this way, non-*Saccharomyces* yeasts characterized by a limited sugar consumption can contribute to the chemical and sensory properties of the wine at the beginning of fermentation, before the more competitive *Saccharomyces* yeasts ensure fermentation completion. This scheme of a sequential inoculation mimics what happens in a wild ferment, bringing the best of the two techniques—the complexity of successful

wild fermentation with the safety and technical security of a controlled, alcoholic fermentation with selected strains. Isolating these non-*Saccharomyces* strains is a recent innovation and currently only a handful of species have made it to market and are starting to be widely adopted for wine production: *Torulaspora delbrueckii*, *Metschnikowia pulcherrima*, *Lachancea thermotolerans*, and, to a lesser extent, *Schizosaccharomyces pombe* and *Pichia kluyveri*.

Yeast Selection

Next to the actual fruit, yeast strain selection is the most important element that will determine the style of the wine. Yeast strain charts offer recommendations for which grape varieties are best suited for each strain, which is a great place to start in selecting a strain. However, more important is the intended outcome of the wine you plan to produce. You may choose a more neutral yeast that will complete fermentation without contributing any real character to allow the fruit to shine, or you may select a yeast that enhances or accentuates varietal or process-driven character, or contributes fermentative aromas such as esters, thiols, or terpenes. In addition, yeast can contribute to polyphenol and color extraction and some sweetness, producing different levels of glycerol. Some yeasts are more prone to autolyze and contribute better to mouthfeel than others. These are all considerations that will be dependent on the style of wine you wish to make.

Beyond the influence that the yeast strain will have on fermentation and the resulting wine, practical parameters must also be part of your decision. Consider grape characteristics that may influence yeast selection. This may include very high sugar levels that will lead to elevated alcohol levels. If you do not wish to add water and you want your wine to go dry, then you have the constraint that your chosen yeast must be able to survive those high alcohol results. Another characteristic about the grapes might include the presence of mold, which suggests a fast start and rapid fermentation to avoid further spoilage. Grapes that were over cropped or from an unusually cool growing season may contribute vegetal character, pointing toward a yeast that may reduce those attributes in the finished wine. Any risk of late sulfuring in the vineyard would suggest avoiding a yeast known to produce hydrogen sulfide during fermentation. Another factor, which may also contribute to the development of hydrogen sulfide, is a lack of nitrogen nutrition in the must. Although nutrients can and should be added to help with this problem, it may also be beneficial to select a yeast strain with relatively low nutrient demand if you expect to face this condition. Compare whatever knowledge you have about your grapes with the various comments in your yeast chart to account for as many features as you can.

In addition to limitations due to the grapes, there may be factors related to your winery that must be considered. Every yeast includes a recommended fermentation temperature. Although we usually prefer cool fermentation for white wines to preserve delicate aromas and warm fermentation for reds for color extraction and ester development, there are limits to both. Go too cool for some wine yeasts and they may just flocculate and drop out without getting the wine to dryness. Go too hot with others and they may suffer from yeast mortality or produce off aromas. Even within the recommended ranges, recognize that trying to ferment near the top or bottom of the temperature range may cause stress in your fermentation and retard a successful outcome. If you have a difficult time controlling temperature during fermentation, then you should not use a vigorous fermenting yeast that may go too fast. Also consider time. If you need to complete the fermentation early, for instance to get your fermenters empty in time to make another batch, you may want to look for yeast strains that ferment faster.

There is a plethora of yeasts available to home winemakers. The typical challenge is not that you have too few choices, but that you have too many. The better the idea you have of the resulting wine you want to make, the easier it will be to pick the yeast strain to produce it.

Alcoholic Fermentation

Bubbles from carbon dioxide are a sign of alcoholic fermentation.

By now you have collected your juice, selected the appropriate yeast, and are ready to pitch. It's time to ferment that juice into wine! Let's take a close look at what exactly is happening in your fermenter during fermentation.

Yeast go through four phases in their life cycle:

Lag phase

Log phase

Stationary phase

Death phase

The **lag phase** consists of the yeast getting used to their environment—this can last 24 to 48 hours with a commercial yeast or almost a week for a natural fermentation. During the lag phase, there is no carbon dioxide produced, but you will smell a fresh-baked bread component.

As we move into the **log phase**, we will see a small amount of carbon dioxide produced, the temperature will start to rise, and we will see a 2 to 4°Brix drop. The log phase is where we have exponential yeast growth, as the yeast is used to the environment and begins to multiply, building new yeast cells. The yeast will multiply three to four times during an alcohol fermentation, and we need those fourth-generation yeast to carry out the fermentation. Temperature becomes much harder to control during this phase because of the exponential growth. The baked-bread component is gone, and you will smell the aroma of the fruit come through.

We reach the end of the log phase and enter the **stationary phase** one-third of the way through fermentation. The growth and death of yeast are equal, and the primary function moves from growth of new cells to metabolizing the sugar into alcohol. Carbon dioxide is still present, temperature is not as hard to control, and we start to smell more of the fermentation bouquet coming through.

Fermentation finishes in the **death phase**, which begins around 5°Brix. The drop in Brix slows drastically. We can allow the temperature to rise to eliminate that as a stress and stir the sediment at the bottom. Due to the alcohol percentage increasing, we see more yeast death due to toxicity, and as they precipitate, they will take live yeast with them, trapping them in the sediment. By stirring your vessel, you can redistribute the live yeast back up to keep converting sugar to alcohol. This process will release some carbon dioxide, or you can add inert gas into the headspace as protection. Your wine is very susceptible to oxidation at this stage because of the lack of carbon dioxide being produced, so take measures not to allow oxygen to sneak into the wine. It's always better to start stirring when you see sediment collecting in the bottom or when you see the drop in Brix really slow. If you wait for it to stop and then try to get it going again, it's usually too late.

Rehydrating dried yeast in warm water helps ensure a strong yeast cell density.

The addition of must is often required after 15 minutes of yeast rehydration to bring the temperature of the yeast more in line with the must temperature.

Do not pitch the yeast slurry until the temperature is within 15°F (8°C) of the must temperature.

Next, let's look at five components that can influence the quality of the wine or can cause a sluggish or stuck fermentation—yeast cell density, high alcohol temperature, nitrogen deficiency, and nutrients.

Yeast Cell Density

Each manufacturer has different parameters that are best for the proper use of their yeast. Most of these strains are in a dried state and rehydration is necessary before inoculating. Read the manufacturer's instructions for calculating the rate and the critical temperature that should be used for rehydration. In general, the higher the starting Brix, the higher rate we will use to calculate the amount of yeast needed. Higher sugar levels cause more osmotic pressure in the yeast cell, which can be toxic to the cell and death can occur; we use a higher rate taking this into consideration. Manufacturer rates give us the recommended cell density of yeast needed for a successful fermentation. A low cell density at the beginning of fermentation or improper rehydration can affect whether you will complete fermentation. Follow directions exactly for proper rehydration, guaranteeing that you start with a strong yeast cell density. The overwhelming majority of stuck fermentations are caused by not following the directions for rehydration.

Also pay close attention to the manufactured date on your yeast. Yeast cells, even those that have been freeze-dried, have an expiration date. Using yeast that is more than six to eight months old greatly enhances your chances of encountering problems, such as stuck fermentations and off odors, down the road. So it's recommended that winemakers purchase their yeast from a reputable source before every harvest. If you use kits, make sure the yeast included hasn't been sitting on a shelf for more than six to eight months. If it has, consider buying a fresh packet to be safe. The cost of yeast is minimal compared to the expense and time committed to a batch that stalls before completing fermentation. Yeast is best stored in a cool place until ready to use, so toss your yeast in a fridge and use it before the expiration date.

High Alcohol

Saccharomyces cerevisiae is the most alcohol-tolerant of yeast species, which is why we use it for winemaking. However, alcohol is still toxic to yeast, and if your fermentation exceeds the tolerance of the yeast strain you have chosen, it will cause death to the yeast and the fermentation will not complete. If you are making a wine with a high alcohol percentage, make sure to use a yeast strain that is tolerant to your estimated alcohol level. If the Brix of your grapes is higher than the yeast you have is able to handle, it is best to make any adjustments pre-fermentation by diluting with chlorine-free water (as described on page 76).

Temperature

Each yeast strain has an optimal temperature range for use during fermentation. If your ferment goes out of that range, the result can be stressful to the yeast and hydrogen sulfide may be released from the yeast cell and into the wine. We risk the yeast going into a hibernation state if fermentation gets too cold; if it gets too warm, we risk blowing off all the fruit character, giving the wine a hot or high-alcohol sensation.

In general, the larger the fermenter the more difficult it becomes to control the temperature. Fermentation produces alcohol, carbon dioxide, and heat—the larger the mass the more heat that is produced. We're going to take a closer look at why temperature is critical and how to control it, but first we need to know how to accurately measure the temperature.

Reading Temperature

Tracking the temperature of your fermentation is important, as is knowing whether the temperature is changing and, if so, how rapidly. In a white wine fermentation of pressed juice, the natural stirring caused by the evolution of carbon dioxide will probably mix it well enough that a floating or probe thermometer anywhere in the wine will provide a reasonably accurate reading. For thin-walled tanks or carboys, a surface-mounted thermometer may suffice. Red wine fermentations are trickier. Typically hottest just below the cap, they will be cooler near the bottom. This is why getting a temperature reading right after punching down is preferable. Write down your readings at least once per day, preferably twice, and monitor the findings for trends.

Hot or Cold?

There is not just one optimum temperature for all fermentations. Rather, the style choices of the winemaker, the available grapes, and the yeast strain selected all influence the temperature. The challenge comes about because there are desirable wine characteristics to be had from cool fermentation and others from warm fermentation. In any fermentation, rapid evolution of carbon dioxide tends to sweep volatile compounds out of the must—that wonderful fermenting-wine smell is an example of desirable volatile aroma compounds leaving the wine! Because white and rosé wines rely, for much of their appeal, on the native aroma compounds that come from the grapes, keeping those compounds in the wine becomes a priority. On the other hand, higher temperatures, especially in the presence of alcohol, help extract desirable compounds from skins, as in the production of red wine.

Saccharomyces cerevisiae yeast exhibits optimum growth characteristics in the range of 77°F to 91°F (25°C to 33°C). If you are culturing yeast, use that temperature range. However, for optimum preservation of aromas in white wine, the best fermentation range is usually considered 64°F to 68°F (18°C to 20°C). For desirable extraction of color compounds and tannins in red wine, the range is usually cited as 79°F to 86°F (26°C to 30°C). During fermentation, the yeast metabolizes sugar to derive energy for its life processes and growth. There is also waste energy that is released in the form of heat, so if there is insufficient loss of heat from the fermenter, the temperature will rise. In *Concepts in Wine Chemistry*, Yair Margalit provides the theoretical outcome of this effect. As each 1°Brix that ferments releases 1.14 Kcal as heat, the complete fermentation of a 22°Brix must would result in a 40°F (25°C) rise over the initial temperature. Starting at a room temperature of 68°F (20°C), such a fermentation that was closed off to all loss of heat would rise to 113°F (45°C) by the end! Although any real-world system will necessarily lose some heat to a cooler ambient environment, this calculation makes clear that some heat management will likely be needed to keep a white wine fermentation cool and may be needed to manage the heat in red wine as well. Above 91°F (33°C), wine yeast is stressed; above 113°F (45°C), it is severely stressed; and at 122°F (50°C), 99 percent of viable cells will die within 5 minutes. For red wine fermentation, if your tank is large or ambient temperatures in your winery are high at harvest time, plan on cooling. Small tanks, because of a larger surface-to-volume ratio, lose heat to the surrounding environment faster. In a cool climate and with small fermenters, you may not need further cooling for red wine, and you may even need to warm your fermentation for optimum extraction.

In planning to ferment white wine, once you have decided to keep it cool for your style choice, you also need to pay attention to preventing it from getting too cold. The optimum range for white wine fermentation is already below the best temperature for yeast production, and there is risk of a sluggish fermentation as yeast metabolism slows at low temperatures. If allowed to drop very low, the temperature may cause the yeast to flocculate and drop out, stopping the fermentation entirely. If a white wine fermentation is allowed to stall due to cold but has only 1 or 2°Brix left, it may be very difficult to restart.

The sum of all these factors boils down to four thermal conditions that the winemaker needs to guard against:

White wine too cold

White wine too hot

Red wine too cold

Red wine too hot

White wine too cold: If cold fall weather sets in early in your climate, or if your cooling system is difficult to manage, your white wine fermentation may get too cold. The primary risk of this is a stuck or sluggish fermentation when the yeast simply cannot maintain its metabolic activity and stops working. This does not mean, however, that you cannot make wine at temperatures below the "optimum" ranges noted earlier. If your style choice or winery conditions dictate a lower temperature, make that a factor in choosing your yeast. If you do have a white fermentation that goes sluggish while residual sugar is still present, act promptly to restart it. Put the fermenter in a warmer place, or take other steps to reverse the temperature drop, but do not do it abruptly. A sudden change in temperature can shock the yeast and retard your efforts to get fermentation going again. Once you have adjusted the temperature into a range suitable for your yeast, mix it vigorously. The yeast may have settled out and "rousing" it can help get things rolling again. If fermentation does not resume within a day or two, consider re-inoculating. For that purpose, you may want to repeat with the same strain you started with, switch to one with a higher alcohol tolerance, or select one with a wider and more forgiving temperature range.

White wine too hot: If you are attempting a cool white fermentation and the heat generation gets away from you, it is unlikely that it will get so hot (above 90°F [32°C]) as to cause harm to the yeast metabolism. It may, however, cause harm to your wine quality objectives at temperatures as low as 75°F (24°C). Volatile aroma compounds are released into a wine fermentation through enzymatic actions that separate them from glucose molecules (the enzymes may be natural to the yeast and grapes or may be added by the winemaker). By their nature, as volatile compounds, their evaporation rate accelerates with higher temperatures. Particularly in white wines, where these native aromas are critical to varietal identity, as in Gewürztraminer or Viognier for example, the loss of aroma from warm fermentation may be a serious detriment to the wine. If you detect a rapid temperature rise in your fermentation, take immediate steps to cool it. Once again, however, do not shock it with a large, sudden temperature drop. Doing so could cause the yeast to immediately flocculate out and leave you with a stuck fermentation. Cool promptly, but gradually, into your desired range. You cannot replace aromas already lost, but you can minimize further losses.

Red wine too cold: Although the same sluggish fermentation problem can occur in a cold red must as in a cold white fermentation, if you are attempting a warm fermentation, it is unlikely that you will drop that low. Do note, however, that some yeast strains have a recommended minimum temperature as high as 68°F (20°C). If there is risk that your winery temperature will drop below that level, you may wish to choose a different yeast strain. More likely in a too-cool red wine scenario, it is not a failure of the fermentation but, rather, a loss in quality of the wine. The anthocyanin polyphenolic compounds that provide grape and wine color extract fairly quickly in a red must, whereas the tannin polyphenolics that provide structure and body extract more slowly. Both classes of compounds become more soluble at higher temperatures. To assure good development of color and adequate tannin balance, most red wine fermentations need to proceed under warm conditions—usually a fermentation temperature over 80°F (27°C) and allowing the must to rise to at least 90°F (32°C) at least once during the fermentation. A red wine fermented all the way to dryness at a significantly lower temperature, even if completed without stopping, may yield a wine with lighter color and a less intense tannin profile.

If you cold soak, or harvest fruit when cool, fermentation temperatures may be low for the first few days and prove difficult to start. Spoilage organisms can grow at temperatures lower than optimum red wine fermentation temperature, and you do not want those to get started before your yeast gets going. If more than a day or two passes after yeast inoculation and the temperature is still too cool, warm the must. Again, proceed gradually to avoid shocking the yeast, even if you have not seen the cap rise yet. Also consider warming if the fermentation is not generating enough heat to reach your target maximum.

Red wine too hot: Although much more likely to occur in large commercial wine tanks, overheating from fermentation heat is a condition home winemakers should keep in mind as a possibility. While 90°F (32°C) at least once may be desirable, a rise above 100°F (38°C) could cause significant loss of yeast viability, especially if it occurs quickly. If the weather is hot where you make your wine, watch the temperature closely. If you approach your desired maximum temperature and fermentation is very active, be prepared to quickly apply—gradual—cooling to the must.

Once you have determined your desired temperature of fermentations and made provisions for achieving it, ensure the manufacturer's recommended temperature range for your yeast choice will work. If you do not have good temperature control capability in your winery, avoid a yeast with a rather narrow range.

Techniques for Temperature Control

If you have the opportunity to design and build your home winery, it is most efficient to include provisions for temperature control right from the beginning. Depending on whether you make white wine or red wine, and depending on your climate, you may need heating, cooling, or both. Most home winemakers do not get to build an ideal facility and, instead, need to come up with ad hoc temperature management methods, as needed. From simplest to most elaborate setups, techniques follow for controlling temperature.

Cooling

The need for cooling is most often to maintain the temperature for white wine fermentations, for cooling red must for cold soaking, or for cellaring.

❖ **A cool cellar**: If you have a naturally cool place, such as a basement, root cellar, or even crawl space under the house, it may be worth adapting it for your white wine fermentations. Ambient cooling is not always adequate to maintain an ideal temperature for fermentation, but it can moderate temperature extremes and, once set up, requires little or no intervention.

❖ **Dry ice**: Dry ice is the solid form of carbon dioxide. It does not have a liquid state at normal atmospheric pressure, so as it warms, it turns into a gas, meaning it won't water down your fermentation when added directly into the fermenter. It is most often used at harvest when the grapes are warm or you want to initiate a cold soak. Take a hard-sided picnic cooler to your local dry ice vendor (often at welding gas supply locations) and fill it up! *Don't touch the dry ice pellets with your bare skin as they can cause burns, and be very careful of the production of large amounts of carbon dioxide gas that are released when dry ice is used. Make sure you have adequate ventilation!* Shovel the pellets directly into the fermenter. Stir periodically until the desired temperature is reached.

Placing your fermenter in a bucket of cold water is one method to cool the fermentation.

Frozen water jugs are another method of cooling a fermentation that is running hot.

❖ **Water tub**: If you are using a small fermenter, like a carboy, you can set the whole thing in a large plastic or galvanized steel tub full of water. The water will absorb some of the heat of fermentation and also serve as a ballast against wide temperature swings from day to night. If just a little more cooling is needed, put a towel over the carboy with one end of it in the water. Water will wick up and evaporate, increasing the cooling effect. Or combine this method with the next technique.

❖ **Frozen water bottles**: Buy or refill water bottles and freeze them. Sanitize the outside of the bottles and put one or two directly into a too-warm red must, or put them in a tub of water around a white wine fermenter. If more cooling is needed, put the thawed bottles back in the freezer and replace them with frozen bottles to continue the cooling.

❖ **Chillers**: Stainless or copper coils, sold at home winemaking shops, are generally used by homebrewers to cool boiled beer to fermentation temperature. You can hook up one of these to a submersible pond pump in a pail of water (iced, if needed) and put the coil into your must.

❖ **Glycol chillers**: Home glycol systems are portable and often equipped with wheels for easy moving. They operate by maintaining a tank of propylene glycol/water solution at a set temperature with pumps to circulate the chilled coolant. In home units, the reservoir tank for the glycol solution is just a few gallons (liters), and power is applied by simply plugging it into a household outlet. The chilled glycol, usually near 32°F (0°C), is pumped through flexible tubing to the tank or carboy you wish to chill. To control the fermenter temperature, a temperature sensor probe attached to an electronic controller is submerged in your wine or taped to the outside of the fermenter. To maintain sanitary conditions, you can use a stainless-steel thermowell (a tube closed at one end) to contain the probe when it is placed in the wine. The controller automatically turns the pump on and off, circulating the glycol, as needed, to maintain your wine's set point.

❖ **Chill the cellar**: A through-the-wall cellar cooling unit, like a Breezaire or CellarPro, can be sized for any well-insulated room. Purchase extra capacity if you are also going to cool tanks or carboys of white wine in the room so you can remove the heat of fermentation that is released. Air conditioners are another option. If your air-conditioned space is large enough and the mechanical equipment sized properly, you may have a suitable fermentation space. Also available are dual-purpose cooling and heating controllers like the Uni-Stat that can maintain fermentation temperatures within a repurposed refrigerator for smaller-volume fermenters. These can be rigged to cool via refrigerator or warmed via heating pad (see next section) depending on the current need for the wine.

Heating

When making wine in cooler climates, heat may be needed to keep a red wine fermentation proceeding at a favorable temperature. Heat is also used to maintain sufficient warmth when malolactic fermentation is carried out (usually above 65°F [18°C]).

❖ **Hot water bottles**: Fill plastic water or soda bottles with hot tap water, cap tightly, sanitize the outside of the bottles, and drop them right in the must.

❖ **Space blankets**: Since your fermentation is generating heat anyway, just keeping it locked in can help raise the temperature. These thin, lightweight reflective blankets are made by evaporating a very thin layer of pure aluminum onto a Mylar plastic sheet. Their highly reflective coating reflects the heat back around the fermenter. The blankets are inexpensive and readily available at camping and sporting goods stores.

❖ **Heating pad**: Electric rubber pads that are used to help with garden starts can be purchased at nurseries and home improvement stores. Placing a plastic fermenter on the pad will add some gentle heat and insulate the fermenter from a cold concrete floor, reducing heat loss.

❖ **Electric blanket**: Placed over fermenters or across barrels, an automatic electric blanket can be set with a thermostat to maintain a desired temperature. Be aware that safety concerns have led to automatic

shutoff systems in modern blankets. Most will turn off after 8 to 12 hours, and will need to be reset to keep heating.

❖ **Space heater**: If your fermentation space is small or you can partition it off with something like insulated plywood panels, a small electric space heater may be all you need. The oil-filled heaters that look like an old-fashioned radiator provide a gentle source of heat. They are not very energy efficient, but they may be suitable for short-term use during primary or secondary fermentation.

❖ **Aquarium heater**: Glass-jacketed heating elements are designed for immersion in tropical fish tanks and are equipped with thermostats. For wine, they find their best effect in barrels used for malolactic fermentation.

❖ **Heat the winery**: Just as with building in systematic cooling, a design decision to include a furnace (or ducting from the household heating system) in the winery can make operation simple. The capital cost is high, but the operating complexity is low. Make sure a thermostat is provided in the winery room, set the temperature where you want it, and go!

Nitrogen Deficiency

Nitrogen is an important nutrient that is needed by yeast to grow healthy cells and an integral part of essential pathways. Along with several factors, it can dramatically impact the complexity and organoleptic character of a wine. A minimum of 150 mg/L is often needed for successful fermentation. This number can change with the starting Brix—the higher the Brix, the more nitrogen that is required. Each yeast strain will fall into one of three categories: low, medium, or high nitrogen requirement. If your juice or must has low levels of nitrogen, it will be a stress to the yeast and result in the production of hydrogen sulfide. As a home winemaker, you may not know the level of nitrogen you have at the beginning, so you need to check your ferment daily. If you get a hint of hydrogen sulfide (rotten egg smell), feed your yeast some diammonium phosphate (DAP) or a proprietary nutrient blend, which will take the stress off the yeast and the hydrogen sulfide smell will go away, if nitrogen deficiency was the cause of the stress.

The timing of nitrogen additions is almost as critical as the addition itself. In the **log phase** of fermentation, a large portion of the nutrients are consumed in the process of yeast reproduction. Amino acids are critical to this stage of growth to build healthy, robust cells. If the only available source of nitrogen is ammonia, the yeast may become stressed and start producing reductive aromas like hydrogen sulfide.

Many manufacturers of yeast nutrients recommend breaking the addition into two or more feedings, often using a combination of organically derived nitrogen and DAP. Dividing the feeding of the fermentation into stages provides an additional level of control. More nitrogen can be added if the fermentation is too slow; less can be added if the fermentation is too fast or hot. When this action is chosen, the feeding can be divided into further parts, if needed, to make sure the entire required amount of nitrogen is added.

In the **lag phase**, it is important to wait for the addition of the fermentation yeast before any nutrient supplementation. Feeding before an active yeast strain is added may cause unwanted bacteria and spoilage yeast to grow. In a wild (uninoculated) fermentation, inoculation should be considered the point at which fermentation is observable, but with no real drop of Brix.

In the **log phase**, a large portion of the nitrogen will have been consumed by this point. At this growth stage, nitrogen is used primarily for protein synthesis and to help maintain vital cell functions.

For the **stationary phase**, when the must reaches 10 to 12°Brix, the fermentation has different needs. This is one of the most critical feedings as it will be the last opportunity for yeast to take on nitrogen vital to finishing a healthy fermentation. At this stage, a blend of DAP and amino acids is especially useful. The DAP will keep the fermentation moving and the amino acids will provide essential building blocks to help finish clean and strong. Alcohol becomes a factor at this point, and the nutrients at this stage will help fortify the yeast against toxicity. It is recommended that you not add any nitrogen past 8°Brix remaining because yeast have stored nitrogen internally and can no longer bring the nitrogen into the cell. Nitrogen left in wine after fermentation is complete can dull the perception of fruit, may become food for unwanted microbes, and has the potential to bind with ethanol to develop unwanted compounds.

Forms of Nitrogen Additions

Nutrients are commercially available as single ingredients, like autolyzed yeast, DAP, yeast extract, minerals, vitamins, and yeast hulls. These component ingredients will need to be combined with at least one or more other fundamental ingredients to create the nutrition needed for a balanced fermentation.

Base ingredients offer the advantage of fine-tuning the supplementation of a fermentation. Many suppliers have created proprietary nutrient blends. Because these complex blends differ from manufacturer to manufacturer, it is important to read the technical sheets prepared for each product. It is possible to supplement with products from different suppliers, but it is important to make sure you are not over- or underfeeding in your total additions. This is especially true with factors like thiamin, which is high in some complex blends and low or absent in others.

Often a small addition of DAP (0.06 g/L) will help stop a fermentation from creating reductive aromas by "jump-starting" the sulfur reductase pathway. In stressed conditions, yeast will stop using this process and excess hydrogen sulfide will be released into the must. This technique can only be used if the must has not dropped more than 12°Brix or the nitrogen may not be utilized.

The Australian Wine Research Institute has shown that an increase of as little as 50 ppm nitrogen can greatly increase the aromatics of a wine when compared to an unsupplemented sample of the same juice. Whether using a complex nutrient or creating a custom nutrient blend, most fermentations and wines benefit from balanced nitrogen additions.

Other Yeast Nutrients

Beyond DAP and complete nutrients used during primary fermentation, there are several specialized yeast nutrients, with the most common being a yeast rehydration nutrient. Since a high concentration of DAP can be harmful to the yeast during rehydration, these specialized nutrients contain none of that compound. They are specially selected and derived yeast-based products. Lallemand produces several variations within the Go-Ferm brand family. Although it seems counter intuitive, applying Go-Ferm early is intended mostly to help the finish of the fermentation. Research has shown that the late stages of sugar fermentation, where some wines slow, or even fail to finish, can be sharpened and made more reliable with rehydration nutrients.

Another category of yeast nutrients is even more specialized. These are the specific inactivated yeasts. They are yeast-derived, like yeast hulls or yeast extract, but are selected and prepared for specific applications. Products like Opti-Red for red wines and OptiMUM-White for white and rosé wines have been introduced by Lallemand and other fermentation suppliers. The products provide a small amount of nitrogen nutrition and are classified as

Products like Opti-Red are yeast-derived nutrients.

yeast-derived nutrients for legal compliance, but their use does not supplant your nutrient program based on the products discussed previously.

For red wines, specific inactivated yeasts are prepared to contain high levels of yeast cell wall polysaccharides. These compounds interact with newly released polyphenols from the grapes to help stabilize color and improve mouthfeel. Using the products will also reduce harshness and any "green" character that may result from less-than-ideal growing conditions. On the white side, the products have a rich glutathione concentration in addition to high polysaccharides. Added near the beginning of fermentation, they help reduce the potential for brown oxidation colors and help retain esters responsible for aromas like grapefruit and passion fruit in some grape varieties.

Is Fermentation Complete?

Specific gravity is the ratio of the density of a liquid in relation to the density of water, calibrated at a specific temperature (usually 60°F or 68°F [16°C or 20°C]). "Dry" table wine usually clocks in at about a 0.990 to 0.996 specific gravity.

Why the range? Every wine is different, and every wine does actually contain a small amount of nonfermentable sugars, and it's unusual for a wine to go so low as to achieve "no sugar" 0.00 g/L glucose + fructose. "Dry" is often defined as not enough sugar left to taste or that any yeast cell will ferment, as well as the place where the fermentation naturally stops and the yeast can't ferment anymore. Most professional winemakers chemically define this point as 2 g/L residual sugar (RS) or less (<0.2 percent RS), though some wines naturally settle at around 3 g/L RS or 0.3 percent.

Of course, specific gravity (SG) is a measure of density, and there are a lot of things other than water and sugar that can affect the density of a wine. Ethanol has a lower gravity than water, which is the reason wine often has a specific gravity below 1.000. Temperature also plays a role in gravity readings. As stated earlier, SG is usually calibrated against water at 60°F or 68°F (16°C or 20°C), measuring a specific gravity of 1.000. If your wine is warm, it'll be artificially less dense, and your reading will be off. Similarly, if your wine is colder than 60°F (16°C), it'll be artificially dense, and the hydrometer will float higher than it should. Check a hydrometer temperature correction chart to get an accurate reading. Carbon dioxide bubbles can also attach to the hydrometer, floating it artificially high. To avoid this, give it a spin in your measuring cylinder to dislodge any bubbles. Also make sure you're reading the hydrometer line at eye level. If you look down on your hydrometer from above, it can give a slightly skewed reading.

If you follow these good hydrometer-use tips and see the same measure day after day, it's likely your fermentation is finished. If you are still not confident, you can do a Clinitest (sometimes called "the sugar pill") test for residual/fermentable sugar. Drop a Clinitest tablet into a measured sample of your wine, and compare the resulting color to a calibrated chart to see if there are any residual reducing sugars in your wine. This is a great (and quick, cheap, and easy) way to see if your wine is dry or not once you start getting readings below 0.996 on the hydrometer. Be aware, however, that the tablets (copper sulfate is part of what makes them react) will also react with many of the pigments and phenolics in red wines, so red wine results tend to skew a little higher than white wines. You can work around this by diluting a sample of red wine and multiplying the result accordingly.

Note: Clinitest tablets are *not* meant for internal consumption; they are poisonous so do not drink the test sample and be sure to keep them away from pets and curious kids.

If you're still seeing bubbles on the top of your fermenter, they could just be carbon dioxide gas escaping naturally, or it could also mean you have a simultaneous malolactic fermentation going on, so bubbles in the airlock are not always the best indicator at this stage.

Stuck Fermentations

All home winemakers strive for fermentations that go smoothly and completely to the desired finish, usually dry wine. When things go wrong, a frequent problem is a stuck or sluggish fermentation, which can be defined as when there is still fermentable sugar left, but your yeast stops growing or dies. We have already gone over potential causes of sluggish and stuck fermentations; however, sometimes fermentations are unpredictable, or an addition is forgotten and fermentation does not complete.

If your fermentation seems very sluggish, but you are still seeing activity or a daily drop in Brix, aerating and agitating the wine may get it going again without a full restart protocol as described later. Use a small fan to blow the carbon dioxide off the top of a red must and vigorously splash it as you punchdown. If the cap comes up strongly again, you may have successfully invigorated the yeast. In a carboy fermentation, remove the airlock and swirl the carboy or stir with a sanitized stainless-steel spoon or rod to try for a similar effect. If those steps do not work, try to figure out the cause of your problem so you can apply the appropriate corrections.

Most stuck fermentations occur near the end of the cycle as residual sugar reaches low levels and alcohol rises. Some, however, occur in the form of failure to start (or a very weak start) or midway through the fermentation. There are many possible causes, and some have relatively simple solutions. Others are more complex, requiring significantly more labor (and supplies) to successfully restart. The following causes are grouped by the required treatments for correction.

Group 1: Temperature Correction

If your fermentation is cold and fails to start (or stops), warm it a few degrees. If it does not start again on its own, re-inoculate with a fresh pack of yeast. If it is too warm, cool it using any of the methods described earlier. Consider re-inoculation. In these cases, it is usually safe to use the same yeast strain you started with.

Group 2: Nutrient Additions

As noted earlier, if must or juice is deficient in critical nutrients, fermentation may slow or stop. If you have the opportunity to have testing done by a wine laboratory, you can find out exactly what nutrients the must needs. If not, it is best to check with your yeast supplier and determine the likely nutrient demand for the strain you are using. If you have not added nutrients and your fermentation slows, consider this a possibility. The condition is often manifested by a smell of hydrogen sulfide produced by the stressed yeast.

Adding diammonium phosphate at the rate of 1 g/gallon (3.8 L; 26 g/hL) may do the trick. For more insurance, use a complete nutrient product like Superfood, Fermaid K, or Fermaid O. Those products are generally applied at 1 or 2 g/gallon (3.8 L; 26 to 52 g/hL). Fermentation should restart within a day and, with a light aeration, off odors should disappear within a few days.

Group 3: Aeration

Two conditions merit the addition of air to your fermentation. If you oversulfited at crush, adding 50 ppm of sulfur dioxide is common, and even 75 ppm should be low enough to allow fermentation to start. If you have added a great deal more than that, aerating the must may clear it up and allow a start. In addition, yeast needs oxygen for growth and reproduction, especially early during fermentation. If activity seems to be slowing in the first few days, try adding some air and watch for improvement.

Group 4: Full Restart

This is the last resort in any sluggish or stuck fermentation (and you can try it a second time if it fails once). Several conditions can give rise to problems requiring this solution; the most common is high alcohol, particularly if you started with yeast not capable of high alcohol fermentation but you had high sugar. In this case, a restart with a stronger yeast can be very effective. Wild yeasts are particularly prone to giving up at relatively lower alcohol levels and a restart with a strong commercial yeast strain may finish the job.

Sometimes a must/wine develops a high population of yeast that carries the so-called "killer factor" that eliminates most other yeasts. If the "killer" strain cannot tolerate the final alcohol level, the fermentation will stick. Similarly various lactic acid bacteria strains can start growing in a must/wine and produce conditions that inhibit yeast. Finally, yeast growth itself may produce an excess of fatty acids that are toxic and inhibitory to yeast fermentation.

Fortunately you do not need to know exactly what is wrong for this restart protocol to work. This is also the procedure to follow if a simpler restart attempt, as described earlier, has failed to take hold.

Corrective Action:

1. Add 1 g/gallon (3.8 L; 26 g/hL) of yeast hulls to the stuck wine 24 to 48 hours before your restart attempt.

2. After 24 to 48 hours, rack the wine off the yeast hulls; they should have removed toxic fatty acids by then.

3. Add another 0.5 g/gallon (3.8 L; 13 g/hL) of yeast hulls to the racked wine.

4. Add a complete yeast nutrient, such as Fermaid K, directly to the stuck wine. If the wine is above 3°Brix, use 0.5 g/gallon (3.8 L; 13 g/hL). If the sugar is between 1 and 3°Brix, use only 0.25 g/gallon (3.8 L; 6.5 g/hL). Below 1°Brix, add none.

5. In another clean container (the restart container), mix 5 percent of your must/wine volume with an equal amount of clean, non-chlorinated water. For example, if you are restarting 20 gallons, use 20 × 0.05 = 1 gallon or 76 L × 0.05 = 3.8 L of each—water and stuck wine.

6. Measuring for the entire stuck wine volume, weigh 1.25 g/gallon (3.8 L; 32 g/hL) Go-Ferm or equivalent yeast rehydration nutrient. Dissolve that in 20 times its weight of clean, chlorine-free water at 110°F (43°C). Mix the solution and let cool to 104°F (40°C). For our 20-gallon (76 L) example, 20 gallons × 1.25 g/gallon = 25 g (0.76 hL × 32 g/hL = 25 g). Then you want 20 times that much water, so 25 g × 20 = 500 g (or, close enough, 500 ml, which is 17 oz. But trust us, go metric on this kind of calculation!)

7. Using a vigorous yeast strain that is highly alcohol tolerant, like Uvaferm 43 or EC-1118, weigh 1 g/gallon (3.8 L; 26 g/hL) for the entire restart volume, and stir it into the Go-Ferm suspension. Do this slowly, over a period of 5 minutes, stirring gently to avoid clumping. Let stand for 15 to 20 minutes.

8. Check the temperature of the stuck wine and of the yeast suspension. They should be no more than 18°F (10°C) apart. If the temperature difference is greater, mix a small amount of your wine-water mixture from your restart container into the suspension and stir again.

9. With successive additions, if needed, to adjust temperature, when the gap is small enough, stir the yeast suspension into the restart container. Wait 20 to 30 minutes.

10. Add 10 percent of your stuck wine volume into the restart container. Wait 20 to 30 minutes.

11. Add 20 percent of your stuck wine to the restart container. Wait another 20 to 30 minutes.

12. Repeat step 11 three more times.

13. Add the remaining stuck wine. Increasing the room temperature may also help.

Yeast hulls, dissolved in distilled water, are a piece of the puzzle to try to restart a stuck fermentation.

As you can see, this procedure is much more complicated and time-consuming than the simple processes described earlier. If you can avoid a full restart, you should! That means paying attention to sugar levels and adding water before fermentation, if needed, using proper yeast nutrients, and avoiding contamination or the presence of yeast toxins.

Unfortunately, despite best efforts, it is often nearly impossible to restart a stuck fermentation, particularly at a very low Brix. Sometimes the "full restart" will work as described, but even it can't get every fermentation going again. If you apply it twice without success, you probably need a different plan for your wine. If it is tolerable as a sweet wine, you may want to stabilize the wine with sulfite and sorbate and bottle it as-is. Or add more sugar (or grape concentrate) and alcohol to simulate a Port-style wine. If those ideas will not work, you may be able to blend it down to a stable residual sugar level using another dry wine.

(Intentionally) Stopping a Fermentation

We know, we know. We have spent a great part of this chapter stressing all the measures to take to ensure your fermentation completes to dryness and even drastic ways to restart your fermentation if things start to go off the rails. Of course, the caveat to all that information is that *it is for making a dry wine.* There may be times, however, that you want to cut fermentation short so you can make an off-dry wine, dessert wine, or aperitif.

The most common way to halt fermentation is with sulfite additions and cooling the wine to near freezing temperatures, which for a 13 percent ABV wine is about 22°F (–6°C) for an extended time. There is a lot of misinformation available that simply instructs to add sulfite to stop fermentation. The amount of sulfite required to stop an active fermentation depends on the active yeast population, but in almost all cases, the amount of sulfite alone required to stop an active fermentation at room temperature would have a negative effect on your wine. You must chill the wine once sulfited!

Start by sulfiting your wine to 2.0 mg/L molecular SO_2 based on your wine pH; for example, a wine with a pH of 3.2 requires 50 mg/L of free SO_2 with chilling to stop fermentation, whereas a wine with a pH of 3.6 requires 125 mg/L. Refer to the sulfite calculator at Winemakermag.com/sulfitecalculator to calculate the precise addition required for your wine. This addition will inhibit the yeast population considerably. To achieve these levels of free SO_2, you will need 4 to 10 Campden tablets per 5-gallon (19-L) batch depending on your pH. After this addition, immediately chill your wine and let it settle for at least 24 hours to ensure the treatment has been fully effective. Chilling to below freezing is ideal, if

possible, although bringing it down to 40°F (4°C) will do the trick when held for a couple of days.

Cooling the must will result in a gradual stoppage to fermentation. With that in mind, sulfite your wine and move it to a cold place when the Brix is still 1 or 2 degrees higher than desired. The time it will take fermentation to completely stop is dependent on the temperature, yeast cell count, sulfite level, and alcohol content.

Your wine should then be filtered down to a fine grade to remove as many yeast cells as possible. Once filtered, add potassium sorbate at a rate of $1/2$ teaspoon per gallon (3.8 L) of wine. Potassium sorbate does not actually kill yeast cells, but it does prevent yeast from reproducing.

An alternative way to halt fermentation is through fortification, if you are making a Port-style wine or aperitif. High alcohol levels kill yeast cells—different strains have different thresholds, but most cannot survive when alcohol levels get up around 16 to 18 percent. The addition of a spirit to bring the alcohol level above what the yeast can survive will stop fermentation fairly quickly. If your plan is to make a fortified wine, carefully plan regarding the desired residual sugar and alcohol levels in advance so your timing can be exact when adding the spirit (of course, you can also add sugar later on if you make your spirit addition too late).

No matter the technique, if you plan to stop fermentation short from the outset, you can make it easier for yourself in the process. For instance, forgo adding yeast nutrient to your must and consider underpitching your yeast. Also ferment at the low end of the recommended temperature range, which will result in a less aggressive fermentation.

Malolactic Fermentation

Malolactic fermentation (MLF) is widely used to soften the acidity of wines, increase textural aspects, and impart added flavor. A successful MLF will also increase a wine's microbial stability. However, the bacteria that cause it tend to be fastidious and often intimidate the beginning winemaker. But read on as it shouldn't.

Malolactic fermentation is the bacterial conversion of malic acid to lactic acid in wine or must. Malic acid, the primary acid in apples, is naturally occurring in grapes. It can be quite sharp, with a flavor of green apples. It can also be a substrate for lactic acid bacteria, such as *Oenococcus*, *Lactobacillus*, and *Pediococcus*.

Lactic acid, the acid found in cultured dairy products, is a softer, weaker acid than malic acid.

The conversion of malic acid to lactic acid, which is usually carried out by malolactic bacteria (*Oenococcus oeni*) during winemaking, results in a softer wine with a higher pH and lower acid. With a complete conversion, the wine becomes more microbiologically stable due to removal of the malic acid. Different strains of bacteria can have different flavor and textural effects on wine. One of the strongest flavor impacts of MLF is the creation of the buttery compound diacetyl when the bacteria consume the citric acid present in grapes.

In grapes, malic acid is the second largest contributor to the titratable acidity (or total acidity, TA) after tartaric acid. If a grape's malic acid level is found to be around 1.5 g/L, this translates to a ppm level of 1,500. That is the number we are counting on malolactic bacteria to consume down to the 30 to 100 ppm level for our end point after MLF. When *Oenococcus oeni* consume malic acid, they excrete lactic acid and CO_2 gas. Lactic acid has just one active proton instead of two. Accordingly, even though converted, molecule for molecule, from

Malolactic bacteria is available in both liquid and freeze-dried form, depending on the manufacturer.

malic acid, it will contribute only half as much TA. In consequence, MLF mellows and "rounds out" most red wines and some whites, such as Chardonnay. It also helps to know that if MLF isn't done in a controlled environment, there is a chance it will occur spontaneously after a wine has been bottled, so it's best to conduct it before bottling, if you want to avoid fizzy wine and the potential development of off flavors.

When to put a wine through MLF is up to the winemaker. The decision to either co-inoculate (during active fermentation) or sequentially inoculate (after alcoholic fermentation) can affect flavor, microbial impact, and stability.

Sequential versus Co-Inoculation

Sequential inoculation has many proponents. Sequential inoculation generally results in higher diacetyl levels. Some believe that it also results in more complexity. Adding the bacteria to a harsher environment (high alcohol) produces a longer, slower MLF. A tradeoff is that there is a risk of infection by other microbes due to increased time without SO_2. There is also a greater risk of a mixed bacterial culture that could result in biogenic amines. One recommendation by Vincent Renouf of Laffort in Bordeaux for sequential inoculation is to inoculate at 0°Brix. The wine is still warm, which helps the bacteria. With the fermentation still going, the CO_2 it generates helps keep the bacteria in suspension. Since the yeast is dying off at this point, the malolactic bacteria should quickly fill the microbial void. However if the bacteria are inoculated in an alcoholic environment, where the temperature is above 77°F (25°C), death of the population can result.

In co-inoculation, the bacteria are added 24 to 48 hours after the yeast inoculation (after the yeast lag phase). If the pH is below 3.10 or the free SO_2 is more than 50 ppm (and below 80 ppm), it is advisable to wait 48 hours. At the beginning of the alcoholic fermentation, the pH takes a temporary dip. Below 3.10, this dip could overly stress and possibly kill the bacteria in combination with active molecular SO_2. Adding at the juice stage means the bacteria will acclimate to the alcohol as it slowly rises during fermentation. Nick Smith, while doing research at the University of Minnesota, found that co-inoculated wines ended up finishing MLF at least 2 weeks before sequentially inoculated wines. This resulted in a shorter time without SO_2 and less risk of mixed bacterial strains or other microbial infections. Co-inoculated wines generally show more fruit because the live yeast will consume the diacetyl. In a German trial comparing co-inoculated Riesling with the same wine sequentially inoculated, the sequentially inoculated wine had lost all Riesling character due to diacetyl. The co-inoculated wine tasted like a traditional Riesling, just somewhat softer.

Care and Feeding of Bacteria

Malolactic bacteria have a narrow "ideal" range in which to work. Be sure to use a bacteria strain that will deal best with your winemaking conditions. In many cases, certain challenging conditions might be unavoidable. However, the more stressors you can eliminate or reduce, the better the bacteria will perform. The main stresses on bacteria are:

❖ **Alcohol**: The ideal is 13 percent ABV. This is nearly impossible with red wines from warm climates. Because the stressors are additive, as the alcohol rises, the more important it is to reduce other stress. Empirical observation is that co-inoculated wines may tolerate higher alcohol better than sequential inoculation.

❖ **pH**: The ideal range is 3.2 to 3.5. Higher than pH 3.5, *Oenococcus* is more prone to acetic acid production after degradation of malic and citric acids. Also above pH 3.5, other lactic acid bacteria species, such as *Lactobacillus* and *Pediococcus*, may take over. Lower than 3.2, the bacterial metabolism slows or stops, depending on the strain and its acid tolerance. Co-inoculated wines tend to tolerate a lower pH.

❖ **Free and total SO_2**: Free SO_2 should be <8 ppm. This is a generalization because at a higher pH the sulfur is less effective. Total SO_2 should be <50 ppm.

Much of the total SO_2 is bound to aldehydes, which the bacteria can metabolize. By consuming the aldehydes, SO_2 is released, which could potentially damage or kill the bacteria.

❖ **Temperature**: Rehydrate the bacteria at 68°F (20°C). For the actual MLF, sequentially inoculated wine should be kept at 64°F to 72°F (18°C to 22°C). Co-inoculated wines can go higher and have been successful up to 85°F (29°C).

❖ **Nutrition**: Use a complete nutrient derived from yeast. For nitrogen, bacteria cannot take up ammonia (DAP), only organic nitrogen (amino acids, peptides). Feed the bacteria, especially if the fermentation yeast had high nutrient demands or the alcoholic fermentation was a difficult one. If co-inoculating, don't feed the bacteria until after alcoholic fermentation is complete and only if it shows signs of struggling. Bâttonage treatment of the wine can also help provide nutrients to the bacteria (more on this in chapter 4).

❖ **Malic acid level**: The ideal starting level of malic acid is between 2 and 4 g/L. Less than 0.5 g/L will not sustain the bacterial population; greater than 7 g/L is highly stressful for the bacteria.

❖ **Tannin**: Recent research has shown a correlation between difficult MLFs and certain grape tannins—specifically galloylated tannins, which have a gallic acid molecule attached. Merlot is often high in these tannins and may have difficulty finishing MLF. Certain inactivated yeast preparations rich in polysaccharides seem to have a "protective" effect. When added to wine before inoculation with bacteria, they modify the effect of the tannins and make MLF easier.

Inoculating Malolactic Bacteria

Although some malolactic starter cultures can be inoculated directly to the wine, for best and fast distribution in the wine, rehydration of freeze-dried malolactic bacteria is recommended. Temperatures for rehydration and timing are very important, and the manufacturer's directions should be followed closely. Once rehydrated, follow these steps for successful MLF.

Sequential Inoculation:

1. Inoculate near the end of alcoholic fermentation (approximately 0°Brix, if fermentation is not stuck or sluggish).

2. If the yeast has high nutrient demands or the wine is nutrient-poor and/or highly tannic, supplement the wine with malolactic nutrients or rehydrate the bacteria in malolactic rehydration nutrients.

3. Once inoculated, keep the wine between 68°F and 77°F (20°C and 25°C), or 61°F and 68°F (16°C and 20°C) for high alcohol.

4. Make sure free SO_2 is less than 8 ppm, and total SO_2 is less than 50 ppm (pH dependent).

5. Do not macro-aerate after alcoholic fermentation as lactic acid bacteria are sensitive to oxygen.

Co-Inoculation:

1. Preferably, add no more than 30 ppm SO_2 to grapes or juice.

2. Add malolactic bacteria (with proper rehydration) 24 hours after yeast addition.

3. Other than yeast nutrients, other malolactic nutrients are probably not necessary. If they are, add them after the completion of the alcoholic fermentation.

4. For red wine, avoid vigorous pumpovers or vigorous punchdowns for 24 hours after inoculation, and avoid fermenting above 85°F (29°C).

5. Below a pH of 3.10, wait to inoculate until the pH has regained pH 3.10 or higher after the initial drop (approximately 48 hours).

6. Aeration during fermentation will not injure the malolactic bacteria.

Testing for Malolactic Acid

Knowing how to conduct a malolactic fermentation is only half the battle. The second half is knowing when that secondary fermentation is complete. We don't monitor the fermentation, per se, but, rather, test for the depletion of malic acid in the wine to signal that MLF is done. In looking for the disappearance of malic acid, we do not necessarily expect a result of zero. Instead, we look at some threshold value of residual malic acid that is low enough that we believe the wine is microbially stable and will not spontaneously start fermenting again in the bottle later. Commercial winemakers like to see a malic acid level below 30 mg/L (ppm) to declare the wine stable. For home use, a value as high as 100 ppm is probably safe enough. After all, even under favorable conditions, it can sometimes be difficult to get MLF to go. Once the malic acid level is low, the wine is properly sulfited, and it is stored under good cellar conditions, a spontaneous refermentation becomes very unlikely.

Although it can vary widely, MLF will generally be completed in 2 to 6 weeks. If doing a sequential inoculation, there are signs to watch for that may help you determine that MLF is underway and when it is finished. If your wine is in carboys, you may see tiny carbon dioxide bubbles rise along the walls during MLF. Another sign, when you put your ear against the carboy or barrel, is hearing a crackling sound that indicates bubble formation and active fermentation, although much less vigorous than yeast fermentation. Even if you do not see any of the telltale signs, you will need to start testing. Two or three weeks after inoculating is a good time to run your first test. If MLF is not complete, wait another week and test again.

In laboratories, there are enzymatic and instrumental tests for low levels of malic acid. At home, we use a classic wet-chemistry method: paper chromatography. Have you ever looked closely at a stain left by a coffee cup on a paper napkin? If you have, you may have noticed bands of different shades of tan and brown left behind as the spilled coffee spread through the paper. That is the principle behind paper chromatography. Different chemical components have different affinities for sticking to the paper fibers. As a liquid moves through the paper, materials that stick strongly stay where they are, whereas those that attach more weakly will move along at a faster pace. In MLF paper chromatography, a combination of paper type, solvent (called the "mobile phase"), and color indicator have been chosen to provide a semiquantitative answer.

Laboratory versions of paper chromatography use a rectangular glass tank with devices to hang a piece of chromatography paper inside the tank, with the bottom edge trailing in the solvent. For home use, we use a 1-gallon (3.8-L) pickle jar, form the paper into a cylindrical shape, and stand it in the solvent. Here's the process:

About 1 inch (2.5 cm) from the bottom edge of a piece of chromatography paper, draw a pencil line all the way from left to right. Use pencil because ink will move with the solvent and interfere with the test. Mark a small "X" for each of three acid standards plus as many samples (up to about five) as you are testing, evenly spaced along the line. Using a fresh glass capillary tube independently for each, dip the tube into standard solutions for malic, lactic, and tartaric acid. Release the contents of the capillary tube on each of the first three X marks. Label them M, L, and T to indicate which acid standard you are applying to that X. Allow the spot to dry, then put another drop of the same acid on the appropriate X. Repeat about four times, drying in between. Meanwhile, in pencil, label your other X marks with your wine sample identifications. Again using a unique capillary tube for each, spot and dry those X marks about four times.

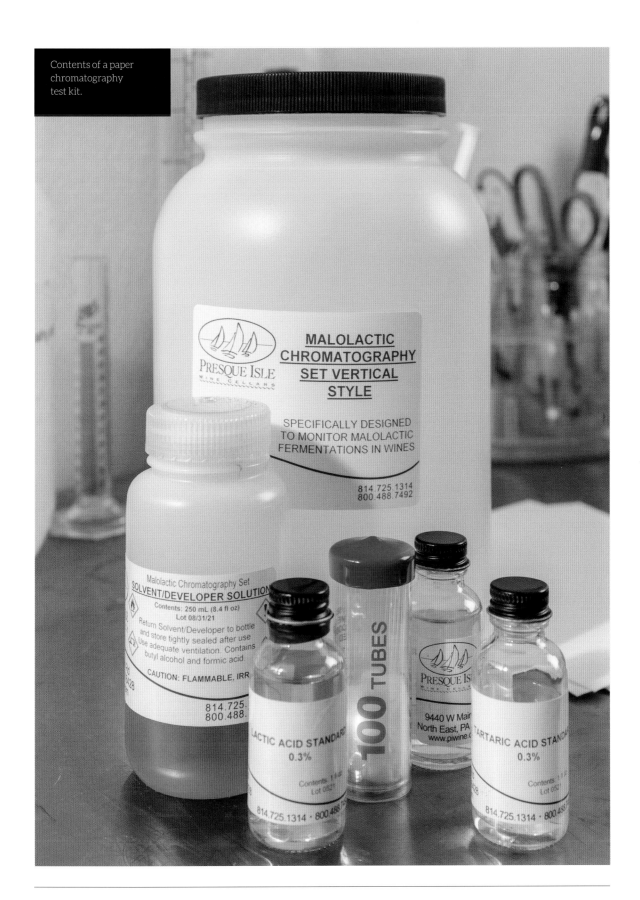

Contents of a paper chromatography test kit.

Performing a malolactic fermentation test on paper chromatography

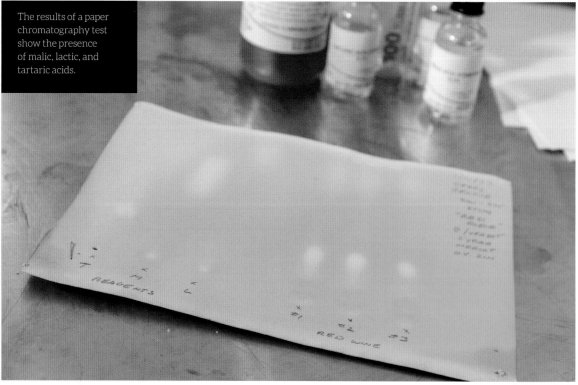

The results of a paper chromatography test show the presence of malic, lactic, and tartaric acids.

The chromatography solvent is butanol—butyl alcohol. That is the mobile phase that moves up the paper during the test. To visualize it, for this test, it contains the indicator bromocresol green, which is yellow-orange in an acid pH environment and blue-green in a basic environment. The MLF solvent also contains formic acid, which assures that it is in an acid condition and explains why the solvent is orange in the bottle. Pour your solvent into the 1-gallon (3.8-L) pickle jar, form your spotted paper into a cylinder with the line at the bottom, secure it with staples or paper clips, and stand it in the jar, resting in the solvent. Put the lid on the jar (the solvent is smelly) and go away for a few hours. During that time, the yellowish solvent will rise through the paper by surface tension. As it does, it will carry malic, lactic, and tartaric acid with it. With different affinities for the solvent and the paper, the three acids travel different distances as the solvent travels to the top of the paper. The key to the test is that a particular acid travels the same distance from all Xs. Tartaric acid remains lowest on the page, malic acid is somewhere in the middle, and lactic acid travels nearest the top.

The next key to the test is seeing where the spots ended up. Remove the paper from the jar and hang it from paper clips to dry. Formic acid is volatile and will leave the paper as it dries, while at the same time any ambient ammonia vapor in the air (which is common in buildings) will neutralize any remaining formic acid. As the formic acid clears, over a period of a few hours, the neutralized paper will turn bluish—except in those spots where target acids remain. The malic, lactic, and tartaric acid spots remain yellow and become clearly visible on a bluish background. The standard solutions are commonly either 0.1 percent (1,000 ppm) or 0.3 percent (3,000 ppm) each. The spots are clearly visible and are in the range of tartaric and malic acid in wine before MLF and lactic acid after MLF.

For any wine sample, you will always see a tartaric acid spot. If you also see a malic acid spot, MLF is not complete since malic acid is still present. If you see a lactic acid spot, it indicates conversion from malic acid to lactic acid is happening. When the malic acid spot is absent, you may conclude that MLF is complete. With careful spotting to keep the spot compact and intense, "absence" indicates a level below about 100 ppm, the approximate detection limit for this test. Over time, the entire sheet will turn blue as the acids in the spots become neutralized. If your test sheet is not turning blue after a few hours of drying, you can hurry it along by opening a bottle of household ammonia nearby. The ammonia vapors from the open bottle will neutralize the formic acid and turn the sheet blue. If you use this step, check frequently as the entire sheet may turn blue and the chromatogram will be lost if it experiences too much exposure to ammonia vapors.

To run paper chromatography tests for MLF at home, you will need to buy a kit that includes a large jar, a bottle of solvent, a package of 100 or so capillary tubes, several sheets of chromatography paper, the three acid standards, and maybe a funnel to help you put the solvent back in the bottle after the test. Detailed instructions will also be included.

Butanol is a toxic alcohol, but not strongly poisonous—it is even used in perfumes. It is flammable and has a pungent alcoholic aroma. Formic acid is an irritant and has an even more pungent aroma. The solvent stinks and you should avoid breathing the vapors. Wear safety glasses to protect your eyes against splashes. After the test, pour the solvent from the jar back into its original bottle and cap it tightly. You can keep using the same solvent again until you run low.

Chapter 4:
The Cellaring Process

Once all active fermentation is complete, wine moves into the cellaring phase of its life cycle before it gets bottled. This is a time when small but significant changes often occur to the chemical makeup of the wine as various factors influence the rate of changes. Let's start with a look at each of the factors that affects the aging process: time, temperature, oxygen, oak, yeast lees, pH, the composition of the wine, and wine stability. Then we can dig into some of these elements a little deeper.

The Main Factors

Time

The style of wine being made has a great impact on the amount of time it should be cellared before enjoyment. A Bordeaux with high acid and high tannins will take much longer to develop a balance than a softer California Cabernet. Grapes grown in cooler climates tend to need more time to age due to their higher acid and tannin structure, whereas grapes from a hotter region can usually be enjoyed earlier. But that statement is subjective. Normally we are ready to bottle whites 7 to 8 months after fermentation. Reds typically go 1 year of bulk aging before bottling, and longer is better.

Temperature

Just as all chemical reactions are influenced by temperature, so are the reactions during wine aging. Wine aging is best from 58°F to 70°F (14°C to 21°C). You don't want to overchill or overheat the wine during the aging process. You could lose a lot of positive aromas and flavors that way. If you don't have a natural "ideal" temperature in your cellar, installing an air-conditioning unit in your wine cellar could be an option to handle those warm summer days. The colder winter temperatures will not hurt the wine as much as summer heat. The biggest factor is to avoid temperature fluctuations from hot to cold. Wine likes to age at a steady temperature.

Oxygen

Excessive exposure to oxygen during aging will have a negative effect on your wine. The introduction of small amounts of oxygen during the aging process can help soften the wine and stabilize the color in red wine. This is the benefit of the barrel, as it allows micro-oxidation to occur. Too much oxygen can lead to off flavors and the browning/pinking of the color. Too much oxygen will also cause your free SO_2 levels to drop, which can then cause oxidized qualities in your wine (acetaldehyde—nuttiness, Sherry characteristic). The more phenolic material in the wine, the more oxygen the wine can safely absorb. This is why white wines are so susceptible to oxygen contact such as browning, whereas red wines carry more phenolic properties and are less likely to brown or show negative effects so quickly.

Oak

Many wine styles depend on oak aging. Oak aging highly affects the aroma and flavor profile of the wine because of the flavor that the oak itself imparts and the complexity added to the wine through micro-oxidation. Barrels can be challenging—you need to properly clean them, swell them, and consistently keep track of them by topping off your wine. If you have the funds and the time to monitor and cultivate your barrel, it will be worth the investment. If you do not, there are some great alternatives we will discuss later.

Yeast Lees

Aging on the lees is a great practice for white wines. The most popular wine to age on the lees is Chardonnay, but winemakers age Sauvignon Blanc (France), Albariño (Spain), Muscadet (France), and Champagne (France) on the lees too. Lees can provide mouthfeel to an otherwise thin wine, but there are other benefits that aging your wine on the yeast can provide, which we'll also get into later.

pH

pH is a very important factor in all stages of winemaking. If you adjust anything in your grapes before fermentation, it is the pH. When it comes to aging your wine, a high pH is dangerous as the wine is vulnerable to spoilage organisms. It is important to make sure the SO_2 is in balance with the pH. The SO_2 effectiveness is critical to color and freshness, especially in white wines, and its effectiveness is dependent upon the pH of the wine. The SO_2 and

Use a wine thief to draw a sample from a barrel.

pH balance also inhibit the growth and activity of microorganisms. So make sure to keep track of your pH and SO_2 levels. For red wines, you want it to be around a 3.5 pH; for white wines you want it to be a 3.2 to 3.4 pH.

Composition of the Wine

Starting with a good wine is key to your wine aging and finishing successfully. Starting with a faulty wine will result in an uphill battle. Always pay attention to your fermentations and the cleanliness in your home winery. If you have a wine with negative characteristics, get it tested to determine exactly what is going on. Some suppliers offer sensory tests, and there are labs that offer chemical analysis. Sometimes a little micro-oxidation is exactly what the doctor ordered. Other times you might need to introduce a chemical over time to help clean up what's going on.

Wine Stability

The wine needs to be stable before bottling—but how you get there can mean choosing among several paths. Proper SO_2 management, pH levels, cold stability (tartrate stability), heat stability (protein haze), enzyme treatments, fining and/or filtration, and tannin management, among other stabilization processes, can be utilized by winemakers. Adjusting, treating, and aging your wine properly help ensure that your wine stays safe in the bottle.

Topping Up Your Wine

Air exposure is one of the biggest enemies of wine after primary fermentation as it can cause oxidation and microbial spoilage. With that in mind, one way to prevent excessive oxygen contact is by monitoring the amount of air space in your bulk storage vessels (barrels, carboys, tanks, etc.), after primary fermentation, and limiting exposure as much as possible by topping up your wine.

When to Top Up

Air space in your fermenter during primary fermentation is not a concern the way it is after fermentation is complete, and you will actually need greater air space during fermentation to leave room for foaming that occurs during the process. You also need not worry about oxidation during active fermentation because the process of yeast consuming sugars creates carbon dioxide (CO_2), which blankets the wine with a layer of gas to protect it from oxygen contact.

This production of CO_2 ceases when fermentation is complete, however, which means that once your wine reaches dryness, it is time to make sure your fermenter is filled to the top so the wine is not exposed to oxygen and susceptible to microbial spoilage. For red wines, fresh grape winemakers will commonly press their grapes into closed containers. White wine often will be racked to a new and slightly smaller vessel.

During bulk aging, monitoring the amount of air space in your vessel is crucial as it changes over time. This is especially true when using oak barrels—even if your barrels don't have any leaks (and hopefully they don't!), wine volume can still be lost due to evaporation and the oak soaking up some of the wine. Barrels should be checked every couple of weeks, and if you see any headspace, it's time to top up! If storing in carboys, absorption isn't a concern but it is still a good idea to keep an eye on things (and if an airlock is in place, that its liquid level is properly topped up). A major time that topping up is needed for glass containers is after racking, as this process leaves sediment and some wine behind, and if racked to a similar-size vessel, air will take its place if not topped up. Carboys should be topped up so wine is above the neck, with as little space between the wine and bung as possible.

How to Top Up

One of the best ways to ensure you have wine on hand that can be used for topping up when the time comes is to make extra wine with each batch. Ferment the entire batch (this may mean fermenting the extra in a 1-gallon [3.8-L] jug if it doesn't fit in your primary fermentation vessel) and keep the extra wine separate until needed. Or, if you are making wine from fresh grapes, you could separate the pressed juice (versus the free-run juice) and use it for topping up, as needed. If you do not have extra wine from the same batch, another option is to use a previous wine from your cellar or use commercial wine of a similar style to top up (this works much better for topping off a 5-gallon [19-L] batch of wine compared to a 60-gallon [227-L] barrel, considering the added expense. Although, of course, you get back the added wine at bottling time!).

Another option that many home winemakers use is to add glass marbles to the vessel to fill the empty space. If doing this, sanitize the marbles first so as not to introduce spoilage organisms. Because of their small size, marbles work great as they can be added in small increments over time.

One last commonly used option in commercial wineries is using inert gas, such as nitrogen, argon, or CO_2. This is only recommended for short-term storage, as it will not purge all the oxygen from the container. There is no substitute for a topped-up vessel.

If you find it difficult to make enough wine for your size vessel, the best solution is either buying additional, smaller vessels so you always have one close to the size of the batch you are making, or investing in a variable-capacity tank (which will still need to be monitored).

Oak Barrels

Many factors play into the lifespan of a wine barrel. Key characteristics include the type of oak used, the degree of toasting applied, and the size of the barrel. The three main oak points of origin are the United States (*Quercus alba*), France (*Quercus robur* and *Quercus petraea*), and Hungary/ Eastern Europe (*Quercus robur* and *Quercus petraea*).

American oak products are considered to have the strongest effects on wine, cited with vanilla, coffee, coconut, and dill flavors imparted on the wines. Your big, fruit-forward wines are generally considered the best to stand up to American oak.

French oak is usually going to be from *Q. robur* trees, and barrels made with this oak are often known to have the lowest impact on wines and so are generally favored for more subtle, high- end Burgundian-style wines like Pinot Noir and Chardonnay. These barrels can lend a cinnamon, vanilla, and custard character.

Hungarian oak often will land somewhere between American and French oak, but leans more toward the French oak, often with slightly more impactful *Q. petraea* oak wood. Richer, nuttier flavors are often associated with this oak.

One thing of note is that the post-harvest conditioning period, which cures the wood, has a big impact on the flavors the wood imparts. Different regions have been shown to produce different flavors with the same wood and curing process thanks to the microflora and microfauna of the region that land and grow on the curing wood.

Oak barrels for wine will often have flames applied to the inner staves to create an aromatic boost from the char that occurs. The intensity of heat and duration of the flames will determine the toast level. Certain desired characteristic components, such as vanillin (vanilla) and furfural (caramel), will develop during the toasting process. Some compounds will continue to develop, like 4-methyl guaiacol (spice and smoke), as the toast level increases but many, like vanillin and trans-oak lactone (coconut), will begin to decline after a certain toast level. So for a more coconut and a more woody- type character, go with a less toasted oak. For a more smoke, caramel, and spice character, a heavier toast will be desired. Winemakers may come across light, medium, medium-plus, heavy, and charred toast levels in available oak products with medium through heavy being the most popular range for winemakers.

Beyond contributions from the oak itself, barrels add the unique benefit of micro-oxygenation—a slow, gradual oxygen ingress through the porous wood resulting in tannin polymerization that mellows red wine during aging and helps avoid reductive odors.

Choosing a Barrel

When you choose a new barrel for your home wine program, the choice of American or European (French, Hungarian, or others) will probably be your first big decision. Some grape varietals are most often associated with French barrels and others with American, but—as with so many decisions in winemaking—it ultimately comes down to personal taste. Try wines from producers you like for which you can get barrel information, and go from there.

The next big decision is size. Of course, there are practical considerations like the batch sizes you most often make and whether the barrel will fit through the door of your cellar, but equally important are the ways wine reacts in a given barrel size. The smaller the barrel, the greater the oak surface- to-wine volume. In *Concepts in Wine Chemistry*, Dr. Yair Margalit cites the dramatic difference in surface-to-volume ratio for different size barrels. A 5-gallon (19-L) barrel presents 214 sq. cm of wood surface for every liter/quart of wine, whereas a 53-gallon (200-L) barrel offers only 99 sq. cm per liter/quart. (The most common barrel size in North American commercial wineries is 60 gallons [227 L], but many sizes are available.) With twice the surface area for its volume, the small barrel presents more extractable material to the wine inside. As a result, it will either impart the same amount of extract in

Swell new barrels with water prior to their first use.

a shorter time, or more intense "oaky" extract if left for a standard time. About 1 year of barrel aging is common for many commercial wines, but that choice is also subject to personal preference (and economic realities).

Treating the Barrel

Regardless of size, when you are ready to place your new barrel into service, you need to prepare it by swelling it up. Although barrels are checked for water tightness at the cooperage where they are made, subsequent storage and transportation may allow them to dry out and shrink slightly. Filling the barrel with clean, odor-free water (hot water works faster) will swell it back up and restore a tight fit before you put your precious wine in it. When you determine that the barrel is watertight, transfer the water out, place the barrel in a bung-down position, and let it drain for a few hours before filling.

Reaping the Early Benefits

Once the wine is in the barrel, it begins extracting the components wine drinkers think of as "oakiness." Descriptors like vanilla, toast, and coconut are often applied to barrel-aged wines. Most of the extracted materials are in a family of chemicals known as phenolics, as their structures are based on the fundamental building block phenol. Among the phenolics are volatile (aromatic) compounds, like vanillin, and mouthfeel phenolics, like tannins. Some of the volatile compounds arise from initial breakdown of lignin in the oak wood during toasting, while the tannins come directly from the roughly 5 to 10 percent content they make up in the dry weight of oak.

Estimates vary, but Margalit cites an amount of 300 mg/L of phenolic compounds extracted from a new, 60-gallon (227-L) barrel in one year. One experiment he cites involved filling new French and American barrels with Sauvignon Blanc wine for 3 months, then emptying and filling them again with fresh Sauvignon Blanc for another 3 months. The wines were subsequently analyzed for tannin content, with the original white wine very low in native grape tannins. Extraction of

barrel tannins in French oak went from more than 140 mg/L in the first fill to less than 80 mg/L in the second. The American barrel went from about 50 mg/L in the first to only about 35 mg/L in the second. Regardless of barrel size or wood source, dramatically lower extraction comes from subsequent fills. A good general rule is to store the wine about 1 week per gallon (3.8 L) of capacity. Naturally, as seen from Margalit's figures, that time may need to be extended in repeat uses.

Because a new barrel quickly gives up lots of extractables, be sure to taste and monitor wine in a new barrel. If you think you may be getting close to as much oakiness as you want, have another trusted taster verify your conclusions. As the oak level rises in the wine, your palate may adjust to it and fail to notice when it is going too high. If you take your wine out of a new barrel before it has had sufficient bulk aging to stabilize and clarify, you will need an equal volume of neutral storage containers to complete the bulk aging process. In future vintages, or if you have another wine standing by, you will be able to leave wine in the same barrel for a longer period.

After the First Use

The best way to keep a barrel is full of wine, but if you must take the wine out before you have another batch, you need to conserve your barrel. Generally, this means either storing it wet with acidified sulfite solution, or dry after burning sulfur in it.

If used barrels are to be stored empty, rinse them several times with clean water, drain, and then burn sulfur inside. Check for the presence of SO_2 gas once a month, and replenish as required. The barrel wood will dry and shrink over time, and so will require to be swelled again before transferring wine into it.

If you prefer to store barrels full, then you need to prepare a sulfur-citric holding solution using 1 teaspoon of citric acid and $1^1/_2$ teaspoons of potassium metabisulfite for each 1 gallon (3.8 L) of barrel volume. Dissolve these in 1 gallon (3.8 L) of hot water. Fill the barrel two-thirds with water, add the holding solution, top up the barrel with cool water, and bung the barrel. Top up the barrel with a holding solution once a month to replace solution lost by evaporation and absorption into the wood. The barrel can be stored this way indefinitely without the risk of spoilage. During storage, rotate the barrel 45 degrees in either direction every time you top up to keep the bung area soaked. This will prevent the bung area from drying out and protect it from spoilage organism growth.

The real mark of continuing utility in a barrel is that it doesn't leak any more than a few dribbles. Yes, it was expensive to buy in the first place. But now that you have it, even if you have added newer barrels for more oakiness to your program, that older barrel can be a very economical wine tank. You already own it. You have gotten the expected contribution to your wines from it, and you now have a container that requires only occasional maintenance to have on hand for any wine storage needs. You can even use oak alternatives, like spirals or staves for oakiness, while the barrel provides the micro-oxygenation.

When rinsing or cleaning your barrel, avoid the use of chlorine in the rinse water by using an inline carbon water filter. The chlorine can contribute to the production of 2,4,6-trichloroanisole (TCA, or cork taint) and some molds. You can even use filtered water when mixing sulfite powder and other additives before adding it to the barrel.

If you are serious enough in your winemaking that you are getting a barrel, we also recommend the purchase of a sulfite testing kit. Testing sulfite levels as your wine ages in the barrel gives you a huge advantage and allows you to add the exact amount of sulfite needed to protect the wine from oxidation, rather than guessing and adding too much or too little. These sulfite testing kits provide clear instructions and everything you need to get started. (More on this topic can be found in the "Sulfite" section, starting on page 142.)

Oak Alternatives

If a barrel isn't in your near future (or you have a barrel that has been used so much that it is no longer contributing much in the way of oak aroma and taste), the modern home winemaker, fortunately, still has a variety of options for adding oak character to their wine, all of which are feasible, practical, and cost effective. And there is no maintenance required—these products all come ready to use, without any prepping or sterilizing needed. These oak alternatives cannot match the micro-oxygenation benefits a barrel offers; however, they are the next best thing and work tremendously well in regard to adding oak flavors to your wines.

Liquid Oak

Liquid oak is the quickest and easiest option among the alternative oak options. Flavors tend to be more stable over time yet less nuanced and, depending on the manufacturer, can have a harsh taste with less "fresh oak" taste and aroma. Liquid oak can be added at any time right up until bottling because these flavorings do not contain fermentables. Results are highly repeatable, especially when using a pipette or syringe to measure the dosage, but a little goes a long way so start with a small amount and add more to taste. Even better, remove a small, measured sample that you can dose incrementally until you are happy with the flavor, then scale up the quantity into the full batch volume.

Whenever time is a constraint, liquid flavorings are an excellent option. There are products designed for flavoring vodka or neutral spirits that are available and can instantly add specific regional flavor profiles, such as bourbons, Scotches, brandies, or liqueurs, at relatively low cost. (Manufacturers like Still Spirits and Liquor Quik provide "cloned" essences. Additionally, producers of natural fruit flavoring make liquid oak in increasing varieties.)

Occasionally winemakers are interested in adding a bourbon or spirit flavor to a big red wine or a Port-style wine, and in such a case, these products may come in handy. (Average cost for a 5-gallon [19-L] batch is between $5 and $15 USD.)

Oak Powder and Pellets

Somewhat like sawdust in texture, oak powder or pellets offers the fastest extraction of flavors over time (other than the liquid additives), requiring just 1 to 2 weeks. Wine kits often include these products, given the short contact time necessary. Country of origin may be labeled (i.e., France or the United States), but toast level is usually not, rather offering recommended flavor profiles. Oak powders and pellets are most commonly added before fermentation, even during maceration, and can sometimes be referred to as sacrificial tannins. This allows the yeast to react to the tannins and aromas of the oak, which actually modifies the oak compounds, making them smoother and less aggressive. Powders add a lot of fine particulates that can clog transfers. Once added, pellets break apart quickly, so using a bag, canister, or steeping ball may aid in fining later.

Weigh powders on a kitchen scale for consistent flavor from batch to batch. Pellets available in carboy-ready sleeves eliminate the mess associated with transferring; however, they lack the flexibility to change the quantity added to a given batch of wine. With the exception of the sleeves, oak powders or pellets are difficult to reuse in another batch later, given that they tend to offer maximum extraction on the first use. (Average cost for a 5-gallon [19-L] batch is between $4 and $8 USD for powder; $8 and $10 USD for sleeves.)

Oak Chips

Oak chips are one of the most frequently used and least expensive forms of oak available to the home winemaker. Chips are easy to toast in the oven at home to desired levels if you can't find the toast you want (or just because it's fun!). Similar quantities can have varied flavor impact on the wine due to the

Oak staves

Oak powder

inconsistent shape and size of the individual chips. Moreover, if you are used to very fine chips and find yourself using some that are considerably larger, or vice versa, the flavor profile may vary wildly. The smallest chips can clog transferring equipment, so you may consider using a bag or filter screen on your siphoning equipment. Chips can be added in primary fermentation or at post-fermentation.

Some people complain of a perceived bitterness or harshness when oak chips have been added due to the increased proportion of end cut to the long grain of the wood. Within 1 or 2 weeks of use, chips

Oak spirals

Oak chips

Oak Cubes

Roughly ¹/₂ inch (1.25 cm) to a side, cubes are typically available in either French or American oak and are often blended from various toasts; however, they can be found in individual levels. They are easy to scale up or down to accommodate desired oak character by simply counting the number of cubes, and they are highly consistent from batch to batch. It can take up to 2 months to achieve the full depth of flavor from cubes, but the resulting profile is worth the wait. However, this time constraint makes them difficult to use in the primary fermenter. They are best saved for secondary or beyond.

Much like a barrel that is toasted or charred on the inside while remaining "raw" outside, cubes offer lighter toasts the deeper the wine penetrates the wood, imparting subtleties not found in smaller-size pieces. Whether bagged or loose, there is little chance oak cubes will interfere with racking. Many will even fit into the opening of bottles and so are suitable for cellaring. Note, they may expand slightly in the bottle and become impossible to remove.

Cubes are easy to repurpose into another batch— just place them in an airtight container (mason jars and vacuum-seal bags are great for this) until the next wine is ready to be infused. In an airtight container, used wine cubes will last for months at room temperature, but consider freezing oak from a previous batch if you won't be using it right away. (Average cost for a 5-gallon [19-L] batch is between $6 and $10 USD.)

will be spent, rendering them a poor candidate for multiple reuses considering the short contact time. (Average cost for a 5-gallon [19-L] batch is between $4 and $10 USD.)

Oak Spheres

Similar to cubes, oak spheres offer a thickness that increases the depth of character in your wine. By eliminating the corners found on cubes, oak spheres are able to offer a supreme level of consistency among lots, ensuring that your favorite wine is on point time and again. They were originally designed and milled to be as large as possible for use in neutral wine barrels where other oak treatments were difficult to remove. These little balls just roll right out after you rack, making cleanup a breeze.

Since they were designed for commercial winemakers, both French and American oak is available in all toasts, but it may prove hard to find smaller quantities of any but the most popular varieties.

At 1 inch (2.5 cm) in diameter, spheres still squeeze into the narrow opening of a glass carboy and are easy to measure. They are typically added at the rate of one sphere per 1 gallon (3.8 L), but that can be changed as desired. To ensure the broadest flavor possible, allow up to 4 months of soak time post-fermentation. These are wonderful for additional uses, offering up to a year of total contact time. (Average cost for a 5-gallon [19-L] batch is between $7 and $13 USD.)

Oak Spirals

Available in a wide variety of oaks, toasts, and chars, their precise milling against the grain allows spirals to extract flavor quickly and consistently. Spirals are cut to expose more end in proportion to the long grain of the wood than other staves. The high manufacturing cost makes spirals one of the priciest oak alternative choices for the home winemaker, a cost well worth the reliability. Spirals offer infusion times as short as 3 to 6 weeks and are usually added after primary fermentation. To change the overall intensity, just measure a length and break off the desired piece.

Smaller, bottle-size spirals can be added directly to bottles and are an option if you have varying tastes in your household or among friends who you will be sharing your wines with. If you want only a portion of your bottles to be more highly oaked than others, this is an easy option rather than splitting a batch before bottling. The milling leaves the oak relatively thin so multiple reuses will yield little flavor. (Average cost for a 5-gallon [19-L] batch is between $7 and $20 USD, or single-bottle-size packages can be bought for $4 to $7 USD.)

Oak Staves

Planed smooth, oak staves have the closest relationship to a barrel in the proportion of the long grain to capillary exposure (end cut). Shy of only barrels themselves, staves take the longest time to impart their full oak character to a wine. Staves made for home winemakers are typically sized for a 5- to 6-gallon (19- to 23-L) batch. Lowering that ratio will require the use of a saw to cut down the stave to the required size. It is ill-advised to try to snap off a piece of the stave like you might do with a spiral as splitting the stave can lead to characteristics more closely resembling chips and increase the intensity (and not in a good way).

Available in every conceivable toast and char, much like spirals, manufacturers are engineering the shape and thickness of staves to decrease extraction time while providing fuller flavor. Different patterns in the wood change the overall flavor profile and are designed for wine, beer, or spirits. Follow the producers' guidelines for time, but account for at least 2 months of contact time post-fermentation. Many offer a hole drilled in one end, or both, to attach a string for easy removal or to tie several staves together in sequence. Staves are possibly the best choice for both long-term storage and reuse. (Average cost for a 5-gallon [19-L] batch is between $10 and $15 USD.)

Sur Lie Aging

In the broadest sense of the term, lees are what fall to the bottom of a fermenting or aging vat of wine. Winemakers generally will split lees into two classes, each with its own set of characteristics. *Gross lees* are, generally, the first to precipitate to the bottom of your fermenter, usually within the first 24 hours after the grapes are pressed. These include grape skins, material other than grapes (MOG), seeds, stems, dead yeast, and tartrates among other things. It is preferred that gross lees are removed after they have settled since they can contribute off flavors.

Fine lees consist mainly of dead yeast cells and take days to settle, even weeks, and, unlike gross lees, can greatly enhance the body of a wine. Although it is traditional to age some wine on the lees, not all wine is meant to be aged on them.

Making the Most of Lees

So what makes fine lees so special to winemakers? Well, we can't talk about them without understanding autolysis and mannoproteins. The term "autolysis" refers to the breakdown of the dead yeast cells that have precipitated out of the wine. Although this decomposition may seem like something winemakers would like to avoid, the dead yeast release a class of compounds from the cell wall known as mannoproteins. These compounds are a natural enhancer to the mouthfeel and body of a wine.

Mannoproteins will also interact with tannins, reducing the astringency and harshness that can be associated with excess tannins. The benefits of mannoproteins don't stop there—they can also stabilize a red wine's color, inhibit tartrate crystallization, and reduce both oxidation and protein haze.

So although winemakers want to remove the gross lees, aging wine on the fine lees can have many benefits. The only downside with aging on fine lees can be in the extreme example that they completely run out of oxygen in solution and start to produce hydrogen sulfide. This can be taken care of easily by racking wine, which will both remove the wine from the lees and reintroduce a little oxygen to the solution.

How to Age on Fine Lees

Winemakers using kits or juices are at an advantage here since most will contain very limited amounts of gross lees to start. The fine lees will be the vast

A bâttonage tool is used to stir up the lees that sink to the bottom during aging.

majority of the lees that settle to the bottom of their fermenters. Fresh grapes, on the other hand, will need an extra step to separate the two forms of lees. Since gross lees will settle within roughly 24 hours and fine lees take longer to settle, we can use the physical discrepancy to our advantage. After pressing the grapes, winemakers can allow the gross lees to settle for 24 hours and then rack the wine off the gross lees. Then most of the fine lees will settle slowly to the bottom over the course of the next several days.

Sur Lie Aging and Bâttonage

Sur lie aging simply means that the winemaker has aged their wine on the lees. An important element to sur lie aging is the bâttonage process (a French term for stirring the wine) and, in doing so, mixing the lees back into the solution. This is done for a couple of reasons. It can speed up the autolysis process and the release of the mannoproteins into your wine. And, if your wine is going through the malolactic fermentation process, the stirred lees can better provide nutrients to the bacteria as well as scavenge oxygen from solution, which the bacteria like. Finally, the bâttonage process prevents the yeast from compacting on the floor of your fermenter, which can cause problems such as creating hydrogen sulfide gas.

Just be very gentle while stirring to minimize the introduction of oxygen. Carboys and demijohns can simply be rolled around on their rim so you don't even open the fermenter. There are special tools winemakers can utilize for stirring wine in larger tanks or when aging in barrels.

So how often do you want to perform the bâttonage process on your wine when aging on the lees? Although there is no hard and fast rule, the general answer from professional winemakers is every 2 to 4 weeks. If all you're doing is rolling the carboy around, then every 2 weeks seems reasonable. If you have to open your fermenter and stir, you may want to do it every 4 weeks to minimize oxidation issues.

Fining Your Wine

Besides choosing the correct fining agent to make the right improvement in your wine, you also need to choose when to apply it. Common stages for fining include before fermentation (as juice), during the aging process (in the cellar), and just before bottling (as a final conditioning). Fining at the juice stage was already discussed in chapter 2, see page 39, so here we'll talk about post-fermentation finings.

White Wine

Every protein has a characteristic "isoelectric point"—a pH at which the oxygen atom on the carboxylic acid end of the molecule is negatively charged, and the amino hydrogen on the other end of the molecule is positively charged. If the wine pH is lower than the isoelectric point of a given protein, that protein will be positively charged. That makes it amenable to removal by negatively charged bentonite. If the remaining protein concentration is low enough, the wine will be protected against haze (more on haze in the next section). Since your wine will be kept under cellar conditions until consumed, a bentonite fining should provide the protein protection you need.

Also for general clarity, alginates may be used. Products such as Sparkolloid can be added directly to wine that is not clearing up on its own. The alginates are sometimes used as a "top dressing" over bentonite to help produce more compact lees and a more stable wine. This technique, adding a second fining agent that acts in a contrary manner from the first, is called *counter fining*. It finds application in several common pairs of fining agents.

Finally, you may want to do a fining-type addition near bottling. To maintain brilliant clarity, we need to avoid precipitation of wine components after

bottling. Gum arabic is very effective for this purpose. Adding this material, derived from the sap of acacia trees in Northern Africa, helps stabilize a wine against throwing any further deposits. It also may impart a hint of sweetness and a fuller mouthfeel.

Red Wine

It is much more common that red wines are fined in a cellar. Here tannin removal in overly astringent wines gets a great deal of attention. Tannins are polyphenolic compounds that combine with proteins and render them insoluble. The proteins lining your palate and tongue precipitate, producing the drying sensation of astringency.

Although some astringency is desirable in a well-balanced red wine, too much makes it unpalatable. Long cellaring can reduce tannic astringency, but fining can get it there sooner. A variety of water-soluble proteins, such as isinglass, gelatin, egg

whites, and casein, are available for fining astringent wine. In each case, the added protein combines with tannins in the wine, precipitates out, and can be left behind with a racking.

One additional treatment for red or white wines may be removal of sulfide aromas. This involves the addition of a copper sulfate solution to the wine to combine with hydrogen sulfide. It may be necessary to further fine the wine with inactivated yeast (yeast hulls or yeast ghosts) to adsorb excess copper and remove it. Products like Reduless from Lallemand offer the benefits of copper addition with less risk of overdoing it.

Whenever a wine has a condition that may be improved through fining, do a trial to be sure that the effort and expense will be rewarded by improving the wine. You do not need to fine every wine, but a well-chosen fining may turn a bad wine good or a good wine into a great wine.

Heat and Cold Stabilization

Both heat and cold stability issues produce aesthetic defects in wine; they affect how the wine looks in the glass but not how the wine smells or tastes (cold stability problems may slightly affect flavor by changing the acidity of the wine by a few tenths of a gram per liter—usually an imperceptible amount). As a home winemaker, are these stability issues important? The answer is literally in the eye of the beholder.

Heat (Protein) Stability

Protein haze occurs naturally when wines are subjected to warmer temperatures and can occur even if the wine has been fined and filtered if it is not protected against hazing.

Fortunately, protein haze can be prevented. During fermentation, proteins that aren't visible to the naked eye are extracted from the grapes into the juice. But when exposed to warmer temperatures, these proteins attach to each other (polymerize) and become more insoluble (depending on the pH of the wine) and remain in suspension to cause a haze. The warmer the temperature the wine is exposed to, the faster this reaction takes place. This phenomenon generally affects only white and rosé wines, as red wines contain phenolic compounds (tannins, mostly) that bind to and cause the proteins to precipitate out of the wine during winemaking. Because white and blush wines do not contain these phenolics, these wines require an additional step to remove the excess proteins.

Not all white wines have the same protein content—Sauvignon Blanc and Gewürztraminer are two varieties known to have very high protein concentrations, making them more susceptible to protein haze when exposed to warmer temperatures.

To insure against protein haze, prevention is the best defense. Once you notice a haze, it becomes harder to eliminate it completely through fining/ filtration. The best method to protect against protein haze is the addition of a suitable fining agent; bentonite is most effective. Bentonite can be added before, during, or after fermentation at a rate of 25 to 100 g/hL (1 to 4 g/gallon [3.8 L]) of juice according to the manufacturer's instructions. Store the treated wine at a temperature between 59°F and 77°F (15°C and 25°C) during the fining period and rack when the wine is completely clear.

You can test whether your wine is heat stable through a simple process. After filtering your wine, heat a sample to 176°F (80°C) in a cooking pot and maintain that temperature for 10 minutes. Remove the pot from the heat and let cool to room temperature (or put it in the refrigerator to speed the cooling process). Compare the sample to a control sample. If the tested sample is clear, then your wine is considered heat stable. If a haze forms, then it is unstable and an additional bentonite addition is necessary. Test your wine again a few days after this addition, and repeat, as needed.

If you did not add bentonite before fining, another way to determine how much bentonite to add at this point is to test multiple samples using the process described previously with different bentonite addition rates. See which sample is clear, and then treat the entire batch of wine at the same rate, but never exceed the 100 g/hL (4 g/gallon [3.8 L]) maximum as excessive bentonite can strip aromas.

Cold (Bitartrate) Stability

Done anytime between the end of fermentation to just before bottling, cold stabilization precipitates potassium bitartrate (commonly known as cream of tartar) out of wine as the compounds form crystals that settle to the bottom and sides of your fermenter.

Cold stabilization is done by allowing your wine to settle for a short time in near or below (water) freezing temperature. The colder the temperature, the less time it will take for the tartrate to fall out of suspension. Temperatures in the mid-30s°F (1°C to 3°C) may take up to 2 months, whereas a temperature in the low- to mid-20s°F (−6°C to −4°C) should only require a week or so.

So-called "wine diamonds" may form in the bottle if a wine was not cold stabilized.

If you live in a cooler climate where the temperatures fall near or below freezing, the easiest way to cold stabilize your wine is timing it right so you can put your wine in the basement, shed, or a covered area outdoors. If you live in a warmer climate, an extra chest freezer or refrigerator with the shelving removed can be used after adjusting the temperature (to the coldest setting in a fridge, or a warmer setting in a freezer).

Cold stabilization is always a good practice; however, for wines that are going to be stored in a cellar with a constant temperature at or above 59°F (15°C) and served at the same temperature, cold stabilization is not necessary as crystals will only form as the wine is chilled. Of course, it is hard to be positive a wine will never undergo an extended cooling somewhere in its lifetime, which is why cold stabilization in these cases is still a good idea as insurance.

The other times when cold stabilization may not be necessary is when a wine is already cold stable—meaning cold temperatures will no longer cause tartrates to precipitate. To test this, store a sample of the wine in a flask at 25°F (–4°C) for 3 days (or in a refrigerator set at 39°F [4°C] for a full week) and analyze the wine afterward. Hold the wine in front of a bright light and look to see whether any crystals have formed. If you don't see any, then your wine will not require cold stabilization.

If cold stabilization isn't practical in your situation, don't get discouraged. There is another option, which is adding metatartaric acid (this is not permitted in many regions for commercial wines, but home winemakers don't have to abide by these regulations). Or, you can skip cold stabilization completely. The potassium bitartrate in solution won't harm the wine or affect the taste; you just run the risk of crystals forming in the bottle if it is ever stored at a temperature lower than it was processed or stored during winemaking.

Blending

The goal of blending wine should be to add new flavors and create a wine that has more complexity and balance than the base wines from which it is made. There are as many opinions to what makes a palatable wine as there are winemakers, but most would agree a balanced wine with myriad complex flavors that go well together is going to be more enjoyable than a one-dimensional wine in which one flavor dominates.

Although blending can bring out the best in wines, it will not necessarily make a bad wine taste good. When an unpalatable wine is blended with something better, you usually just end up with a bigger volume of mediocre wine. Blending can make a good wine taste even better by compensating for any of its weaknesses, such as softening a wine that was too bitter or adding a little bit more youthful fruity aroma to a wine that has been well aged. There are many blending options to accomplish these goals. You can blend wines from different varietals, vineyards, appellations, or vintages that may have very different flavors but are complementary to each other.

Blending wines that have received different treatments is another option—such as a Cabernet Sauvignon that was aged separately in both French and American oak or combining two carboys of Marquette, each fermented with a different type of yeast. Blending a small amount of a younger wine into one that has just finished aging can be particularly useful. A full-bodied red may age for as long as 2 years, and when it is racked out of the barrel, it might have the smooth tannins and oak flavor you were looking for, but it may have lost most of its attractive fruity aromas it had in its youth. In this case, adding 5 to 15 percent of the same wine from a younger vintage will bring back a lot of that lost fruity flavor and make a blend that has the best of both wines.

Bench Blends—the Secret to Success

While experience always helps, it is not required to be successful at blending. Much more important is the process of doing bench trial blends to taste before making the blend in the cellar. To do a bench blend, you assemble sample bottles of the wines you are considering for the mix and combine a small amount of each in the same proportion that you would make in the cellar. Once the bench blend is made, taste it against the unblended wines and ask yourself, "Do I like this more or less than the original wines?" Why end there? Take it farther and try different percentages of each wine, or just some of the wines you have available to you, to dial in the best blend.

This "try it before you buy it" approach is what makes blending wine such a powerful tool. Most decisions a vintner makes are based on conjecture. You may decide to pick your grapes at a particular level of sugar, but you will never know for sure if the wine might have tasted a little better if the fruit had more hangtime on the vine. Making and tasting a trial blend before doing it in the cellar allows you to try a number of blending options without consequences to find just the right one.

But how do you go about selecting the wines to mix? First taste each wine you may use and critically examine it for its strengths and weaknesses, writing down your impressions as you go. The wine that has the highest volume, or the one with the best flavor profile that you are sure you want to use for the blend, is the *base wine*. Taste the base wine again and ask yourself, "What does this need to improve the taste?"

For example, if the base wine has most of the characteristics you are looking for but is a little too astringent, select a second wine that has soft tannins that might complement the base wine. Make up a sample blend of the two wines; a good place to start might be 80 percent base wine with 20 percent of another wine. You will need a graduated cylinder and pipet to measure 80 ml of the base wine and 20 ml of the softer wine. Gently mix the new blend and taste it against the base wine, then decide which you like best. If the new blend is now a little too soft, try again, this time adding 10 percent of the second wine to the base wine. Alternatively, if 20 percent of the second wine is still a little too rough, try upping it to 30 percent and see if it is better. Don't get discouraged if it did not make the wine taste better—just try another combination. If you have some wine-loving friends who can help make the decision, even better.

Keeping Track of the Math

If you have analysis or composition data for the wines, you can use a spreadsheet to see what the percentages for the blend would be. If you are proficient with Excel, you can make a spreadsheet of your own. Longtime professional winemaker and wine consultant Pat Henderson created his own blending template, which he has made free to download at Winemakermag.com/article/pat-hendersons-blending-spreadsheet. Using this template, enter information about each wine you have available and the amounts you want to try for a blend and it will automatically calculate the small sample amounts needed to conduct a bench trial.

The Best Time to Blend

Field blending is common with certain styles of wines such as Rhône-style wines where Syrah and Viognier (red and white grapes, respectively) are mixed at the crusher and fermented together. One downside to this method is that the different grape varieties must all ripen within a similar timeframe. A second option is blending the wines just after fermentation, which allows you to pick each variety at the optimum ripeness and gives the blended wine plenty of time to marry while it is aged. This approach also allows you to taste the blend and make further adjustments down the road if you feel they are needed.

Another option, which is the most common, is waiting until after the wines are finished aging, usually a couple of months before they are to be bottled. By this time, the wines are nearly finished and you get the most accurate estimation of what the ultimate flavor of the final blend will be when bottled.

Expanding Your Options

Your home winery may not have access to dozens of different wines to use in your blends, but if you are willing to think outside the box, there are many options open to you. If you are making a barrel of Cabernet Sauvignon from grapes, consider making a carboy of Merlot either from fruit or from a kit to complement the bigger lot in your barrel. Or if you have more than one vintage in your cellar from your home vineyard, you might benefit from mixing a little of the younger vintage into the older one to freshen it up.

You can use blending to add diversity to your wines as well. If you make a Barbera and a Zinfandel, you can bottle some of each variety by itself as well as make a red blend of the two. This is a great way to add some variety to the wines at your dinner table. You can also consider trading for a bit of wine with another home winemaker (if you are a part of a wine club, there should be a good diversity of options), or even consider buying a bottle of Syrah at the wine shop to add just a bit more body and color to your Pinot Noir.

What to Watch For

Blending is a powerful winemaking tool, but there are a few risks to be aware of. When you blend wines, you might be mixing spoilage yeast and bacteria as well. For instance, if one lot in the blend had *Brettanomyces* or *Acetobacter* growing in it, you'll spread the problem to the whole blend when you mix them. This can be avoided by tasting the wines first and not using any wine that has problems. A small volume of bad wine is one thing; it is much worse to have a big blend go bad because you did not taste each component separately before blending.

Even beneficial microbes can cause problems—when you add a wine that has finished malolactic fermentation (MLF) to one that has not gone through MLF, you will now have a blend that has the potential to go through MLF after bottling if you do not sterile filter. Usually if you mix wines that have been stabilized, the resulting blend will be stable—but this is not always the case. Sometimes the slight change in pH between the base wine and the blend will mean that wines that were once heat and cold stable now become unstable. It is best to wait until after blending before stabilizing, if you can.

Understanding the Pearson Square

If you have an understanding of a certain characteristic—such as total acidity or alcohol by volume—that you want your resultant blend to consist of, the best way to go about your blending is using the Pearson square.

The Pearson square is a tool to calculate the number of parts of two different solutions with different concentrations that are required to bring one of the solutions to a desired concentration.

To create a Pearson square, divide a square into thirds both vertically and horizontally. The upper left corner is labeled A, the lower left B, the middle C, the top right D and the bottom right E.

$$
\begin{array}{ccc}
A & & D \\
 & C & \\
B & & E
\end{array}
$$

If, for example, you want to adjust the acidity of a wine, those letters represent:

A: Acidity of the wine to be used to correct

B: Acidity of the wine to be corrected

C: Desired acidity

D: Parts of correcting wine to be used (C–B)

E: Parts of the wine to be corrected (A–C)

The equation yields your answer in "parts" (shown in D and E), which is the number of units of each component to add (whether it be ounces, milliliters, liters, or whatever unit you wish to use).

Let's plug some real numbers in here and give it a try. If you have a wine with a total acidity (TA) of 6.0 g/L that you want to bring up to 7.0 g/L, and you have a second wine with a TA of 7.5 g/L, using the Pearson square you have:

$$
\begin{array}{ccc}
7.5 & & 1.0 \\
 & 7.0 & \\
6.0 & & 0.5
\end{array}
$$

This shows that you need 1 part (7.0 – 6.0) of the correcting wine for every $1/2$ part (7.5 – 7.0) of wine you are correcting. So if you have 5 gallons (19 L) of wine at 6.0 g/L that you want to bring up to 7.0 g/L, you will need to blend it with 10 gallons (38 L) of wine at 7.5 g/L for it to result in a blended wine with a TA of 7.0 g/L.

Here is another example of how you can use the Pearson square, this time to make a fortified wine. Let's say you have a Merlot with an ABV of 12 percent and you want to make a fortified wine of 18 percent ABV using a 40 percent ABV brandy. In this case:

A: ABV of the brandy

B: ABV of the wine

C: Desired ABV

D: Parts of spirit (C–B)

E: Parts of the wine (A–C)

Using the Pearson square, it looks like:

$$
\begin{array}{ccc}
40 & & 6 \\
 & 18 & \\
12 & & 22
\end{array}
$$

So for every 22 parts (40 – 18) of Merlot, you will need to add 6 parts (18 – 12) of brandy. Adding these two, you get a total of 28 parts. This means approximately 21 percent of your fortified wine will be brandy (6 / 28) and the remaining 79 percent will be Merlot (22 / 28). If you want to make 2 gallons (7.6 L) of fortified wine, your total will be 256 fl. oz. (7.6 L) of fortified wine. So:

$256 \times 0.21 = 54$ fl. oz. (1.6 L) brandy

$256 \times 0.79 = 202$ fl. oz. (6 L) Merlot

Filtration

Filtration works, essentially, by passing wine through a filter medium, be it a cellulose pad, a pleated cartridge, or some other material of known porosity. As the wine moves through the filter, any microbes, yeast, or other particles larger than the micron rating of the filter are captured and prevented from moving through the filter media. Filtering can produce a crystal-clear product and, depending on the micron rating, a wine free of yeast and microbes—in other words: a stable wine.

Why We Filter

With anything in winemaking, there are different camps that feel strongly one way or another about various topics of the craft, and filtration is no different. We are not here to debate the pros and cons of filtration, but rather inform you of why you may choose to filter and the equipment available to home winemakers to carry out the task.

The microbes that wineries are most interested in filtering out via sterile filtration consist of a number of different yeasts and bacteria. The home winemaker is most concerned with filtering out *Saccharomyces* species (cultured wine yeast) and *Oenococcus oeni* (malolactic bacteria). This is just in case alcoholic or malolactic fermentation does not finish, and we would rather filter than use additives to stabilize the wine (which is not always an option). Yeasts are in the 5 to 10 micron (μm) range. Bacteria get smaller in size. For example, cocci can be between 0.5 and 3 μm in diameter and bacilli can range from 0.2 to 2 μm.

Filter Pore Sizes

As you can see, the filter choice makes a difference, depending on what you intend to filter. Although these sizes are simplified, it should help you choose

Filter pads come in various pore sizes, each with its own purpose.

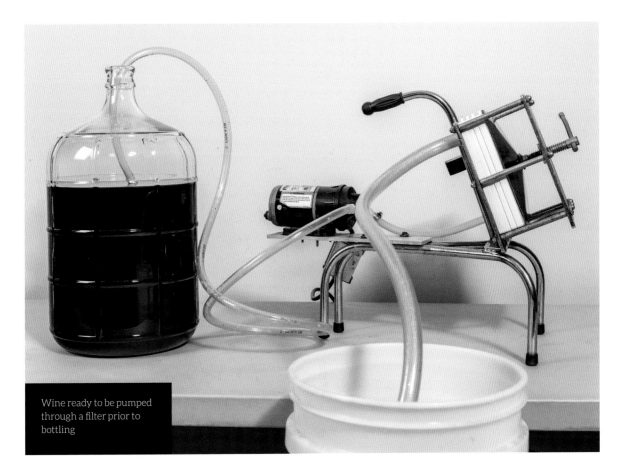

Wine ready to be pumped through a filter prior to bottling

the right filter for the job and serve as a springboard for further research.

Pore sizes are measured in microns. This means the smaller the number, the tighter the pores in the filter. The ability of the filter to remove microbes lends itself to the pore sizes, which are made to be smaller than the yeast and microbes themselves so they cannot pass through the filter media. The usual micron ratings for winemakers are 7, 5, 3, 2, 1, 0.5, and 0.45, along with other sizes for various stages in the process.

To further break down filter types, there are the "nominal" and "absolute" ratings. The *nominal* rating will filter out *most* of the microbes above the micron measurement, whereas the *absolute* filter will filter out everything above the micron rating. The industry standard for sterile filtration is 0.45 µm nominal (although sterilization by microbiological standards is usually 0.2 µm absolute, 0.45 µm is still the standard for sterile filtration in winemaking).

Plate and Frame Filters

Home winemakers have numerous filtration choices that should meet their needs based on the volume they produce and their specific requirements. To start, let's look at the plate and frame filters.

Buon Vino Mini Jet

This compact unit is made for small-scale filtration: 5 to 10 gallons (19 to 38 L) at a time and is perfect for those working with kits, juice pails, and smaller batches of wine. The Mini Jet uses a built-in self-priming Flojet pump to send the wine through the set of three cellulose filter pads. This pump can also be used to rack wine by bypassing the filter pads.

Buon Vino Super Jet

The Super Jet is made for medium-scale filtration: 13 to 26 gallons (49 to 98 L) at a time. This unit uses 20 × 20 cm cellulose filter pads to do the job, which have the same ratings as its Mini Jet counterpart.

The Super Jet also has a Flojet pump, and like the Mini, can be used for racking wine. This gives you more bang for your buck and allows you to pump large volumes of wine between tanks and other large vessels. The Super Jet is equipped with a pressure gauge so you know when the pads have become clogged with debris and need to be changed.

If you are making higher volumes of wine and have deeper pockets, the Super Jet also has a six-pad option for filtering up to 60 gallons (227 L) at a time. The three additional pads allow for a longer filtration session without the hassle of replacing pads.

The filter pads for the Mini and Super Jet come in three different grades:

1. Coarse Number 1 is approximately 7 microns and is meant for filtration of wines that are clear, but have some large, suspended particulates. Perfect for reds and preparing a wine for filtration with tighter pads.

2. Polish Number 2 is about 2 microns and is meant for filtration of white, rosé, or, if you want to further polish it, a red wine. This set of pads should be used before using the Number 3 pads.

3. Sterile Number 3 is about 0.5 microns. Although this pad set is labeled "sterile," it does not meet industry standard for sterile filtration of 0.45 nominal. This pad set may remove some yeast, but should not be used in place of potassium sorbate when there is residual sugar present, or in place of lysozyme if malolactic fermentation failed to finish. When using this pad, be sure to first filter with at least the Number 2 pad, as any particulate in the wine will quickly clog up a pad of this micron rating. This pad set would be used if the polish pads did not filter to your liking, and you desire a higher degree of brilliant clarity.

Inline Filters

The use of inline filters is becoming more popular as vacuum pumps, like the Enolmatic, the All in One Wine Pump, and homemade vacuum pump setups are being used by home winemakers for various duties around the home winery. A major benefit to using inline filters is oxygen ingress is greatly reduced thanks to the entire filter operation being enclosed. An added bonus is the filter housing is easier to clean and sanitize too. Following are the most popular inline filtration kits for home winemakers.

Enolmatic

The Enolmatic has its own filter housing and filter cartridges made specifically for the unit. Filter sizes come in 5, 1, and 0.5 microns, which can be cleaned with an alkaline agent after filtration to be used again. The filter housing is installed between the vessel of wine and the Enolmatic, and filtration takes place as the wine is bottled. This means one less step in handling the wine, which reduces exposure to oxygen and possible contaminants.

All in One Wine Pump

Among the many uses for the All in One Wine Pump, one is filtration. This unit uses an inline 10-inch (25-cm) filter housing, with cartridge filters available in many different micron ratings. It is recommended to filter and bottle in separate sessions, as a steady flow is suggested for effective filtration.

Note: The equipment list should be closely followed as the incorrect filter housing could be purchased if you are not careful. If you choose to buy the items on the list elsewhere, be sure to purchase the filter housing without the red button relief valve, as this valve may open during the vacuum operation preventing a good seal. The housing with the red button can be used with inert gas between kegs and with positive pressure wine pumps.

Filter cartridges, such as 0.45 nominal sterile cartridges by BevBright, can be purchased from numerous winemaking retailers and are said to work with any 10-inch (25-cm) housing. BevBright cartridges also come in 5-, 3-, and 1-micron ratings. When researching BevBright or other cartridges, you may see they have an efficiency rating. This simply means what percent of material will be filtered out at that particular micron rating.

As an example, following is each level of efficiency and what it means for their 3-micron filter:

❖ **High efficiency**: Removes 90 percent of the material 3 microns or larger in a single pass

❖ **Super high efficiency**: Removes 98 percent of the material 3 microns or larger in a single pass

❖ **Absolute efficiency**: Removes 99.8 percent of the material 3 microns or larger in a single pass

A few key tips: Be sure to follow the manufacturer's instructions for whichever filter you use. Before filtration, rack the clean wine off any sediment so as not to clog the filter. Be sure to sanitize everything that will touch the wine, with the exception of a new filter cartridge, which should be ready to use out of the bag. Ensure your sulfite levels are in line before filtration. Plate and frame filtration can promote oxidation, and sulfite is needed to protect the wine. If you intend to filter with a very tight pad, such as 0.5- or 0.45-micron filter media, it is necessary to step-filter down to that particular rating, for example, filtration through a 5-micron pad, then a 2-micron, and then down to 0.8 or 0.5, and then 0.45.

Filtration is one way to make a brilliantly clear wine.

Backsweetening

The technique of backsweetening means that the winemaker fermented their wine all the way to dry, then sweetened and stabilized it before bottling. Sweetening is useful for balancing acidity, as wines with different acidities require different amounts of sugar to give the same level of perceived sweetness. Trials are essential for such situations. If you decide you want a sweet or off-dry wine, or you need to balance acidity with sugar, you need to make several decisions before you get to the math of calculating your final product.

Sweeteners also require choices. Sucrose is readily available in the form of cane sugar or beet sugar. White (granulated) sugar is highly refined, very soluble, and quite pure. It tastes very sweet. Fructose tastes sweeter, but is not readily accessible for use at home. Glucose, in the form of dextrose or corn sugar, is sold at home winemaking shops. Although very useful in chaptalization because of its ready fermentability, its lower sweetness makes it less desirable for backsweetening. Honey and brown sugar offer additional flavor characteristics, but both of them may make the wine more difficult to clarify completely. Nonfermentable sweeteners, such as xylitol or stevia, may be employed without risk of refermentation, but many people perceive off flavors when they are applied to wine.

Sweetening with a natural grape product offers another option. Some sweet German wines are made by separating a portion of the original must, highly sulfiting it, and then blending it back in after the main batch has fermented to dryness. This "sweet reserve" technique could be applied at home by freezing some juice at harvest and then mixing it back in after fermentation. Sorbate and metabisulfite can be applied to a home "reserve" sweetened wine to prevent refermentation. Sweetening with grape concentrate can also be effective. Keep in mind, though, that not just the sugar is concentrated when water is evaporated from grape juice. Most of the original acids are still in there as well so an addition of concentrate may change your wine in unexpected ways. Taken together, these factors lead to sucrose, most often cane sugar, as the home winemaker's most common choice for backsweetening a finished wine.

Backsweetening Trials

You will want to run some trials to determine your sweetening level. One good way to do this is to thief out a 375-ml sample of your wine. Measure it into three separate 100-ml samples for treatment and keep the remaining 75 ml as a control. You can do any level you like, but common "off dry" sweetness is typically 1 to 3 percent, so this model lends itself to trying 1 percent, 2 percent, and 3 percent. To do your trials with sucrose, prepare a standard solution that is 50 percent weight to volume cane sugar. °Brix is percent sugar on a weight-to-weight basis, but it is so much easier to measure small volumes at home (instead of small weights), so we are preparing the standard solution on a weight to volume basis instead. That way, we can measure small amounts of solution by volume instead of trying to weigh them.

Larger amounts are easy to weigh with a small digital scale. Weigh 50 g (about 2 oz.) of sugar and place it in a small saucepan. Add 50 ml (also about 2 ounces) of distilled water and bring to a boil. Stir to dissolve. After boiling briefly, cover the pot and place it in 1 or 2 inches (2.5 to 5 cm) of cold water in the kitchen sink to cool. When the sugar syrup is completely cool, transfer it to a 100-ml volumetric flask, graduated cylinder, or graduated beaker. Dilute to exactly 100 ml with distilled water. Now you have a sugar solution that contains 50 g of sugar in 100 ml of solution, or 0.5 g in every milliliter.

You may also want to try sweetening with grape concentrate. You can do this instead of a sugar trial, or alongside a sugar trial to judge both sweetness and flavor effects. Most canned concentrate is specified at about 68°Brix. At that concentration, one producer reports that it contains about 840 grams of sugar in every liter of concentrate. To keep the math consistent, we want to prepare a standard solution of the concentrate for trials that matches our sugar solution: 0.5 grams in every milliliter. To do so, we

Always run trials with fractional amounts before sweetening an entire batch.

want to deliver 50 grams of sugar equivalent (just as with our sucrose standard) into the 100- milliliter volumetric flask, graduated cylinder, or graduated beaker. To figure out how many milliliters to use, X, we can use the ratio:

$$(X \text{ ml}/50 \text{ g}) = (1{,}000 \text{ ml}/840 \text{ g})$$

Which rearranges to

$$X \text{ ml} = 50 \times (1{,}000/840)$$

And solves to

$$X \text{ ml} = 59.2$$

Using a graduated cylinder, measure out 59 milliliters of concentrate, pour it into the volumetric flask, and dilute to exactly 100 milliliters with distilled water. Mix well and you have a solution of grape concentrate for trials that matches the sugar standard solution of 0.5 grams of sugar per milliliter, or 50 percent weight to volume. (If your grape concentrate is other than 68°Brix, check with the supplier for the appropriate sugar content value.)

Now we can proceed to trials. Since both standard solutions contain 0.5 grams of sugar in every milliliter, 2 ml contains 1 gram. For a 1 percent sweetening of a 100 milliliter wine sample, add 2 milliliters of standard solution. For a 2 percent trial, add 4 milliliters to a 100 milliliter wine sample, and for a 3 percent trial add 6 milliliters.

With 1 percent, 2 percent, and 3 percent samples prepared, do your tasting along with your untreated control sample. Have another person or two taste with you to facilitate discussion of the effects. Is the wine better sweetened? If so, what is the best level? If you are doing such a comparison, does sugar or grape concentrate taste better?

Now that you have your calculations done, you can proceed to the treatment of the batch. Some people backsweeten just before bottling: rack the wine into the bottling bucket, stir in the simple syrup (or concentrate) with a sanitized stainless-steel spoon, stir in potassium sorbate to prevent refermentation (about 1 gram per gallon [3.8 L]), and make a final sulfite addition based on your most recent free SO_2 test results. (Note that sorbate only works in conjunction with the sulfite.) This approach is convenient because it combines the last racking with bottling, and it eliminates the problem with any headspace created by thiefing out trial samples. Other winemakers prefer sweetening and stabilizing the wine with sorbate in bulk a few weeks before bottling.

Chapter 5:
Bottling

Now that fermentation is complete and the wine is stabilized, it's time to package. While kegging wine is an option, we are going to focus on the more traditional bottling of wine. If kegging wine is in your future, we recommend a search on Winemakermag.com for more in-depth coverage of that topic.

Equipment and Closure Considerations

Every bottle of wine needs some form of closure to keep oxygen out and your wine sealed inside. What you select to seal your bottles with depends on your ultimate winemaking goals. But a few generalities should be followed:

❖ Don't try to insert corks into screw-top bottles. They are not engineered for these closures.

❖ Be sure to match your tools and the wine's timeline to the cork's traits.

❖ Upgrading to a floor corker should be one of your first investments in the hobby, or you can ask about bottling at your local supply store.

With this information in mind, let's run through some of your options when looking to bottle your first or fiftieth batch of wine.

Cork Options

An important decision you need to make for bottling is what type of cork/closure you are going to use. First off, if you are using a hand corker, then opting for higher-end natural wine corks may save you a LOT of frustration. It's hard to get the leverage needed to get synthetic and composite corks fully seated in the bottle when using a hand corker. Once you have a floor corker, your cork options open up significantly.

Natural cork: Sustainably harvested from an oak tree's bark in the Mediterranean region of Europe and Africa, almost 80 percent of the world's natural wine cork is harvested from the Iberian Peninsula alone. The natural sponginess of this oak's bark allows for natural compression and expansion to occur with very little diffusion of air from one end of the cork to the other. Natural wine cork is perfectly suited as a wine closure and best used for big red wines you plan to age for more than 2 years. Natural cork is classed in various grades depending on the quality of the cork bark, with the lower-grade cork having a higher rank number. For example, grade 1 cork is considered the best and may be graded for wine storage for 20-plus years.

Some downsides of natural cork do exist. If not properly handled or of lower quality, mold can be found in the cork, which can lead to a condition known as TCA (2,4,6-trichloroanisole), or more commonly referred to as cork taint. Although occurrences are rare due to improved education of the problem in the cork-harvesting world, there are still instances of TCA in lower-grade natural corks. The price tag found on natural wine corks is also a downside, with grade 1 natural wine corks commonly running over $1 USD per cork.

Agglomerated cork: Shred natural cork into fine nuggets and then hold those cork granules together with a food-grade synthetic binding agent into the shape of a cork, and you've got yourself agglomerated corks. These are more cost-effective and provide a decent seal. These corks are often

Choosing a cork is dependent on budget and how long you plan to age a wine. Pictured from left to right: natural, agglomerated, colmated, synthetic, and two T-style cork options.

best for aging wines for 1 to 2 years. Agglomerated corks do not compress like natural corks. Therefore, it is best not to attempt corking with a hand corker, and buying a size down (#8 size as opposed to the standard #9) is sometimes recommended. Not all agglomerated corks are made alike, so be sure to assess the quality before you invest.

Colmated cork: Part natural cork, part agglomerated, colmated corks are natural corks that are not quite good enough to pass inspection on their own with their holes filled with cork powder and then bound together with a natural binding agent. These corks are very close to having all the benefits of a natural cork with a lower price tag. Just as with natural cork, though, TCA can rear its ugly head in colmated corks.

Bi-disc (1+1) cork: Less common in the hobby world but common in the professional wine world is the bi-disc cork, which takes an agglomerated cork and binds two natural cork discs onto the top and bottom of the cork. These corks are generally rated to 3 years and have a good seal, but like agglomerated corks, they can be quite difficult to get into bottles.

Synthetic cork: This class of corks comes in a wide array of compositions and qualities, but the spongy synthetic corks with a little oxygen diffusion we find to best mirror those qualities of natural cork. An

upgrade from a hand corker is highly recommended, and wines corked with these types of corks are not recommended to be aged longer than about 3 years.

Nontraditional closures: A newer product on the market is Novatwist, which provides hobby winemakers with a screw-cap option. These closures require specialty bottles and tops, though. It is worth noting commercial screw caps use an expensive machine to form the metal sleeves in place and so are not an option for home bottling.

Crown caps: These closures have been utilized for beer and cider for years and require a bottle with a lip that the cap can crimp on to (which most still wine bottles don't have). Crown caps come in handy if you make sparkling wines in the traditional Champagne method at home when used in the intermediate step of bottle re-fermentation to seal the bottle and then for simpler disgorgement later on. For this process, you will need glass bottles that are a heavier weight and designed to handle the pressures exerted by the carbonation process along with a quality capper to install the crown caps. Note there are different sizes of crown caps, so be sure to choose the correct size for your bottle type.

Champagne cork: These specialized corks are designed to stay in the bottle under the pressure that sparkling wine exerts. A specialized floor corker designed for Champagne corks is required for their insertion and a metal cage is added around the cork and held in place under the lip of the bottle as added security for keeping the cork in place. There is also a plastic option that can be inserted by hand, with a mallet, or with a tabletop bottle capper (with the added benefit of being reusable).

T-cork: These push-in style closures that typically have a plastic top with a natural or plastic cork attached are most commonly used for spirits and wines that are higher in alcohol like Port, Madeira, and Sherry where the added alcohol provides a greater level of protection from most forms of spoilage compared to typical table wines. T-corks

Corker options

important with agglomerated corks as this can remove the coating, creating a lot more friction on the surface of the cork, making them harder to install and remove from the bottle.

Cork Sizing

Choosing which size cork to purchase depends on several factors, but there are some standard sizes. Corks vary in both their length and diameter. And although length is measured in standard units such as inches/millimeters, diameter is measured by an assigned number. Generally #9-width corks are recommended for natural wine corks and colmated corks to obtain the best seal. This cork size can also be used for synthetic corks, but is not recommended for anyone using a hand corker. For the less compressible corks, such as agglomerate and bi-discs, #8-width corks can be utilized, but make sure you use a corker with good torque, and long-term aging is not recommended. Generally, #7 corks are not recommended for wine storage in normal wine bottles, but some smaller-neck bottles may require this size.

Corking Tools

Now that we've got a base understanding of the various corks that can be used, the tool that is utilized to compress and fit the cork into the bottle can make bottling day a lot easier. The elasticity (how much it will compress and re-expand) of the cork you choose should be highly dependent upon the type of corker you use.

Hand (or plunger-type) corkers are the most affordable for hobbyists, but only natural wine corks should be used with these types of corkers, and they are very labor intensive to use if you're bottling more than about 5 gallons (19 L) of wine. Natural corks with chamfered (sloped) ends make it a bit easier, but a lot of effort is still required.

Winged hand corkers provide more torque to compress the cork into the bottle and allow users to expand their field of usable corks into agglomerate, bi-discs, and compressible synthetics.

Tabletop and floor corkers are the next level up on the price scale. Both types allow for even

should never be used for long-term storage and aging of table wines, but for short-term bottles, they make for easy opening and resealing.

Special Considerations

Being a natural product, natural wine corks, generally, need the most consideration. These corks do have some moisture contained within them, allowing for the cork's inherent sponginess. If corks are stored for a long time, they can dry out and lose that elasticity. The corks can also grow mold, which can lead to TCA. So it's best to purchase natural corks fresh and use them soon after purchase. Synthetic corks have a much longer life, but upgrading to a high-torque corker is definitely recommended. Agglomerated corks often have a treated surface with a coating of wax or silicone applied by the manufacturer. No corks should be boiled (and all can be used without any treatment if used directly from the original packaging), but that is especially more torque and less effort on bottling day. Floor corkers are the largest and provide the most torque for hobby winemakers. Both types are available with either plastic or metal jaws to compress the cork evenly. Metal jaws are not recommended for use with synthetic corks as permanent crimps can develop in the cork and the wine, then, won't properly seal.

You may hear floor corkers being described as "Portuguese corkers" versus "Italian corkers." Generally speaking, the Italian models come equipped with the metal jaws whereas the Portuguese corkers come with plastic jaws. Most hobbyists view the Italian floor corker as the "Ferrari" of corkers. With metal jaws and a long handle, it can easily compress just about any cork type, though some may balk at the price tag. One other consideration is that the typical Portuguese corker has the cross leg of the T-shaped base bolted on, whereas many Italian corkers have a welded T base. No difference in use, but shipping cost and storage considerations favor the flat-packable Portuguese corker.

Bottling Time

When it comes to choosing bottles, you have a decision to make: new or recycled. Although new bottles are available at any local home winemaking store or online, they come at a price. Beyond saving your empty bottles, used bottles can often be sourced by calling a local winery, wine bar, or restaurant, and asking them to save their empties for you.

Once you have your recycled bottles home, it is time to look into each bottle, in a well-lit room, and look for any black mold or other stubborn deposits. Black mold and crusty bottle deposits can be difficult to remove and will have an unpleasant effect on your final product. Unless you are 100 percent confident in your ability to remove these growths, pitch the bottle or use it for one of those groovy color drip candles. The fun part about recycling bottles is removing the labels. (That was a joke, are you laughing?) A soak in Powdered Brewery Wash (PBW) and hot water for 30 to 60 minutes will help. Sometimes the labels will float off by themselves, sometimes not. At this point, you will be left scraping with a paint scraper (or you can buy the LabelNator, which has a curved blade and solid handle, made specifically for this purpose) and then remove any stubborn glue with a ball of steel wool.

Give reused bottles a good scrub inside with a bottle brush (the sooner you do this after the bottle is emptied, the easier they are to clean) and a quick scrub over the whole bottle with a sponge on the outside and then rinse it out with a faucet-mounted high-pressure bottle sprayer and give it a rinse on the outside. Once you think you are finished, take a final look inside. If you give it the "all clear," turn the bottle upside-down to dry (a bottle tree is a good investment to help with this). Once the bottles are sufficiently dry, put them in a box, tape it shut, and store until bottling day. The tape helps keep out bugs and dust.

Bottle Sanitizer

On bottling day, remove your clean bottles from storage and all they will need is a flush of sanitizer before being filled with wine. Depending on the volume of wine to be bottled, a spray bottle can be used to spray sanitizer into each bottle, which is then allowed to dry until it's ready to be filled.

A handful of manufacturers make a combo bottle washer/sanitizer. Models are available from All in One Wine Pump, FastBrewing, and The Vintage Shop. These units efficiently conquer the jobs of bottle washing and sanitizing by automating the tasks. The All in One High Pressure Bottle Washer/Sanitizer works with one bottle at a time. It comes with the necessary tubing, a pump, and a bottle sprayer that attaches to a 5-gallon (19-L) bucket that you provide. The FastRack FastWasher uses a pump and works in tandem with their FastRack12 in your sink to clean or sanitize a dozen wine bottles at a time. The Vintage Shop Bottle Washer also works in a sink and attaches to a faucet to clean or sanitize twelve wine bottles at a time or can be used with a pump (that you provide).

Bottle Fillers

There are a number of ways to get your wine into bottles, each allowing the flow of wine to be stopped and started at will so you can cork and organize the bottles, as needed.

A bottling wand is inexpensive, easy to use and sanitize, and perfect for the winemaker on a budget bottling 1 to 10 gallons (4 to 38 L) of wine. It connects to your siphon hose and comes with one of two tip styles. One style is spring-loaded, which means it will stop between fillings. This is convenient when you need to stop and cork a few bottles before filling more. The other style lacks the spring, which makes it a bit easier during filling (you don't need to push down to open it), but means you need to hang it up to stop the flow if you are switching to corking.

A three-spout gravity filler is a major step up from the bottling wand and allows for filling three bottles simultaneously. This filler works by gravity, which means the wine to be bottled will have to be higher than the bottle filler. A stand can be built to

Filling bottles with a bottling wand

elevate the carboys to a level that a siphon is possible, or a safer method for your back and your wine is pumping the wine up to an elevated vessel. This helps avoid lifting heavy carboys. Once a siphon is started, the filler's reservoir starts to fill with wine. The reservoir contains a floating mechanism that controls the fill level. When the reservoir gets to a certain volume, the float rises and cuts off the flow until there is room for more wine to flow into the reservoir. The spouts are then primed and the filling can begin. As the bottles are filled, the reservoir is constantly being refilled by the siphon action from the donor carboy until it is empty. These fillers also stop filling the bottle once it is full.

Buon Vino has a small family of efficient fillers. The Super Automatic Bottle Filler uses gravity to fill bottles and will stop the flow once the bottle has reached the preset fill level set by the user. The

Electric Fill Jet comes in both a tabletop version and a floor model, with self-priming pumps capable of filling a single bottle in 17 seconds. Like the Automatic Filler, the filling operation stops (the pump deactivates) when the bottle is full to prevent overfilling.

The All in One Wine Pump not only enables you to rack and degas your wine, but it is also a bottle-filler. The All in One runs on a custom-made, oil-free pump—meaning it is clean and odor-free. The kit contains everything you need for racking and bottling, with more attachments available for other tasks in the home winery. Its design ensures consistent fill levels (which are easily adjustable) with virtually any bottle style, in as little as 15 seconds. Otherwise, an inline vacuum control allows you to control the fill speed. This helps reduce foaming if there is a significant amount of residual carbon dioxide in the wine or, for first-time users, getting used to the unit.

The Enolmatic Wine Bottle Filler is also a vacuum pump operating on a continuous duty cycle with a fast and adjustable fill rate. It is capable of pulling wine from a vessel up to 13 feet (4 m) below the filler along with being able to fill a bottle in just 7 seconds. Fill levels are adjustable and, once a bottle is full, the flow stops. Along with being easy to clean, you can install an inline filter to polish your wine right before it goes into the bottle. This bottle filler can utilize more than one filler head to be able to fill more bottles simultaneously. Though it bears a higher price tag, it will stand up to years of service and would be at home in the large-scale home winery.

The Gas

Another important aspect of the home bottling line is inert gas. The use of nitrogen or argon at bottling to flush the bottle before filling it can significantly reduce oxygen uptake as wine flows into the bottle. This will lessen bottle shock, and your prebottling sulfite addition will go farther in protecting your wine. (For more on this topic, check out the "Wine Gas" section starting on page 154).

If you've chosen to use the twelve-bottle washer/sanitizer, you can use the same bottle rack and connect another base to your inert gas setup. Gas purging adapters with one end that connects directly to the sparging base and the other end that connects to your gas tank flow meter are also available. The adapter has an inline valve to be able to turn the gas on and off. Set your flow meter to your desired flow level and use the valve as you purge bottles of oxygen.

Shrink Capsules

Shrink capsules give your wine a professional look. After all the work you put into making the wine, why not dress the bottle to the nines? You have three options for getting these colorful guys onto your bottles—boiling water, a heat gun, or the heat tunnel.

❖ **Boiling water**: It's hot and steamy. Use caution and care when using this method. But it's free and you most likely have the equipment needed to do it—a pot, water, and a stove.

❖ **Heat gun**: Safer than boiling water, but this method may take more time than you want to spend applying the caps. Sometimes it is a little tricky to avoid wrinkling one side while you aim the heat gun at the other.

❖ **Heat tunnel**: Safer than boiling water, quicker than a heat gun, and the shrink cap has a professional look—but it is far more expensive than the alternatives.

Chapter 6:
Troubleshooting Wine

Now that your wine is safely stored away in bottles, it's up to you to determine how it turned out. One thing of note is the term "bottle shock," a phenomenon that occurs in part because of an uptake of oxygen that happens during the bottling process (filtration, in particular, can cause it). It is temporary and often scares winemakers into thinking their wine was somehow ruined during the bottling process. Bottle shock can sometimes take up to 6 months after bottling to disappear. So be patient if the first couple bottles that are opened show a dramatic downturn in quality since bottling day.

Wine Evaluation

The evaluation system that wine judges and home winemakers often use is based on the UC-Davis 20-Point System. Developed by some of the world's premier wine scientists, the 20-Point System is a tool that can maximize objectivity in judging wines while still retaining pertinent hedonic information about them—and to do so in a sound and reproducible manner. Though it may seem complicated, evaluating your wine (tasting) and keeping track of the results (note taking) is pretty basic if you follow the steps.

Getting Started

Before you begin randomly pouring bottles of wine, gather the following materials and find yourself a quiet space where you can sit for an hour and evaluate your homemade wines. Assume for this first time that you're only assessing one wine (though assessing more at a time is pretty easy too).

You will need:

❖ Uniform glassware—one glass per wine being tasted

❖ Shot glass for measuring pours

❖ Spit bucket (all professional tasters spit)

❖ Pencil and paper for note taking; if you type up some "official" wine-tasting sheets with the 20-point scale on it, then keeping a notebook is easier

❖ Water for rinsing your mouth between tastes

And although not necessary, an aroma definition tool, like the wine Aroma Wheel designed by Ann Noble, a professor of enology at UC-Davis, to help you come up with words to describe the aromas you're smelling is nice to have.

Using the UC-Davis 20-Point System

The basis of the 20-Point System is that certain wine characteristics are assigned a numerical value. If the wine being judged measures up to that characteristic, that wine is awarded points. If it does not, say, have a bright clarity that is desired in a

wine ready to be bottled, it is not awarded the 1 point that a brilliantly clear wine would have received. Along with awarding points, you should record your impressions of the wine and take notes along the way for future reference.

Color (1 Point)

The 1 point for color is awarded to wines that logically fall within their "color boundaries." If a new white wine is a deep gold color, bordering on brown, chances are it's been oxidized and should probably rate a 0. Similarly if your Cabernet doesn't have as much color as it should, don't award full credit. Make a note to beef up your red wine maceration program.

Clarity (1 Point)

When awarding the clarity point, feel free to be a little lenient. One way to do it is to refuse a wine the point only when the sediment or haze can't be corrected with decanting or bottle age and is a true defect, even by home-winemaking criteria. Again, record the character of the haze or sediment, if there is one, in your notebook. This can prove valuable data for future troubleshooting.

Aroma/Bouquet (5 Points)

Give your glass a big swirl to liberate the aromatic compounds in the wine and then bury your nose in it. Block out the rest of the world and concentrate on the information that your sensory organs are sending to your brain. Does the way the wine smells remind you of anything? If so, write those things down. Besides trying to define the aromas that you're smelling (use the Aroma Wheel's categories to help you here), note the overall aroma picture that the wine's giving you, including intensity.

Taste/Balance (5 Points)

Take a swig of your wine and swish, swirl, or slosh it around in your mouth. The goal is to get your entire mouth saturated with wine while allowing the volatile components of the wine to be channeled to your sensory receptors for maximum pickup. A wine can get top marks in this category for being free of unpleasant or out-of-place flavors, for being true to type and age, and for being "balanced." Even though it's a pretty subjective term, a wine is "balanced" if no one thing sticks out like a sore thumb and if all the elements seem to work together well.

Sugar (1 Point)

This one is simple: if you wanted your Muscat to have about 3 percent residual sugar, and it tastes like it does, award your wine a point. If, on the other hand, your goal was to make a dry Zinfandel and it's obviously got a little bit of sugar left, score this category a 0.

Acidity (2 Points)

There's a little bit more leeway in this category— it all depends upon the type of wine you're making. If you've got pretty high acid but a lot of tannin, alcohol, and oak to back it up, then your wine should get all 2 points. On the other hand, if your wine is too high or too low in acid for its overall composition, award it 1 point, or a 0 depending on how off mark it is.

Body (2 Points)

Body is a sensation of fullness (sometimes called "roundness" by wine critics) in the mouth that texturally differentiates wine from water. If a wine has good body, it'll feel less like the aforementioned water, and more like a wine with substance. Award 2 points if it does. If your wine lacks a little in the body department, then give it a 1 or 0. Be careful not to confuse body with sugar content. Sugar can give a wine a "fullness" that is really a taste sensation, not a textural one. Try to make a wine with higher alcohol or residual sugar next time, depending on the style. Adding glycerin as an unfermentable sugar is something that home winemakers have the freedom to do—and it adds body and some additional sweetness.

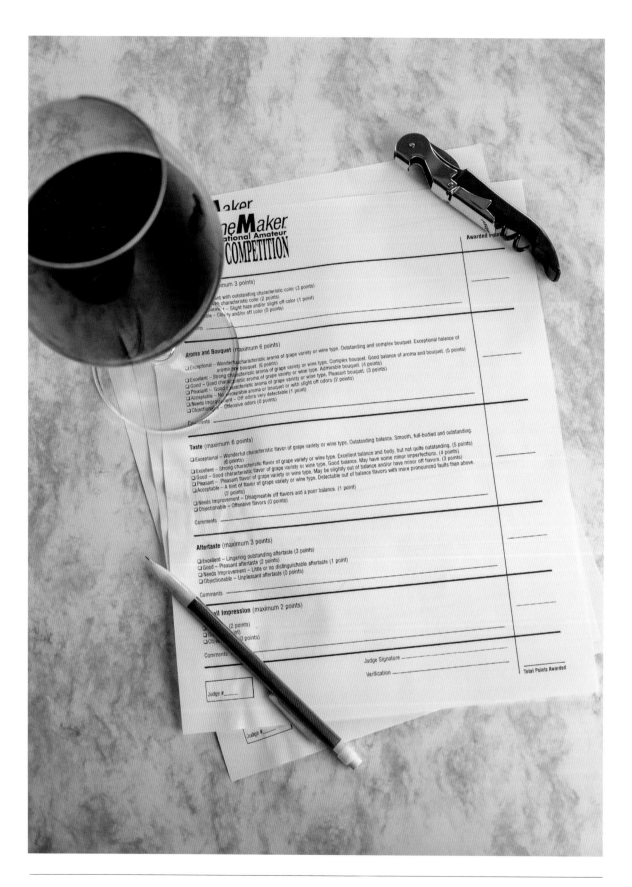

Aroma and Bouquet (maximum 6 points)

❏ Exceptional – Wonderful characteristic aroma of grape variety or wine type. Outstanding and complex bouquet. Exceptional balance of aroma and bouquet. (6 points)
❏ Excellent – Strong characteristic aroma of grape variety or wine type. Complex bouquet. Good balance of aroma and bouquet. (5 points)
❏ Good – Good characteristic aroma of grape variety or wine type. Admirable bouquet. (4 points)
❏ Pleasant – Pleasant characteristic aroma of grape variety or wine type. Pleasant bouquet. (3 points)
❏ Acceptable – No perceptible aroma or bouquet or with slight off odors (2 points)
❏ Needs improvement – Off odors very detectable (1 point)
❏ Objectionable – Offensive odors (0 points)

Comments

Taste (maximum 6 points)

❏ Exceptional – Wonderful characteristic flavor of grape variety or wine type. Outstanding balance. Smooth, full-bodied and outstanding. (6 points)
❏ Excellent – Strong characteristic flavor of grape variety or wine type. Excellent balance and body, but not quite outstanding. (5 points)
❏ Good – Good characteristic flavor of grape variety or wine type. Good balance. May have some minor imperfections. (4 points)
❏ Pleasant – Pleasant flavor of grape variety or wine type. May be slightly out of balance and/or have minor off flavors. (3 points)
❏ Acceptable – A hint of flavor of grape variety or wine type. Detectable out of balance flavors with more pronounced faults than above. (2 points)
❏ Needs improvement – Disagreeable off flavors and a poor balance. (1 point)
❏ Objectionable – Offensive flavors (0 points)

Comments

Aftertaste (maximum 3 points)

❏ Excellent – Lingering outstanding aftertaste (3 points)
❏ Good – Pleasant aftertaste (2 points)
❏ Needs improvement – Little or no distinguishable aftertaste (1 point)
❏ Objectionable – Unpleasant aftertaste (0 points)

Comments

Overall Impression (maximum 2 points)

❏ (2 points)
❏ (1 point)
❏ Objectionable (0 points)

Comments

Judge Signature

Verification

Judge #

Total Points Awarded

Tannin (1 Point)

Tannins contribute a sense or grittiness or puckering that you can feel on your tongue, cheeks, and teeth. Though tannin could possibly go under the body category because it's effect is felt as a textural quality, it really belongs in its own group because its presence (or absence) can make or break a wine, particularly red wine.

Award a wine 1 point if the level of tannin is appropriate for the wine you've made. For example, if your 6-month-old Cabernet has enough tannin to knock your socks off, it's not necessarily a defect. If you mean to age it, by all means award it the point. Similarly, if you've made a white wine but don't sense a lot of tannin—which is appropriate—also award it the point. However if your red wine is lacking a little oomph, give it a 0 and make a note to yourself to beef up your maceration strategy, to add more oak to your wine, or to add some tannic acid.

General Quality (2 Points)

Here's your chance to record your overall impressions of the wine. It's hard not to be biased, but if you like the wine so much that you wish you could make the same wine again next year, give it 2 points. If you can think of a lot of things you'd like to improve upon or if that style of wine just isn't your bag, feel free to give it a 1 or even a 0. It's nothing to be ashamed of if you make a wine that you just don't fancy; it's called a learning curve. Next time you'll make something different and probably better, and now you'll have a bunch of carefully recorded notes to go by.

Interpreting and Using the Results

Now that you've taken a wine through the 20-Point System, tally up all the points. Look at the score that it merited.

❖ An outstanding wine will usually score between 17 and 20 points, with some weaker and some stronger areas.

❖ If your wine scores lower than a 17, check out the areas where it seems to need a little help, and if improvements can be made next time, make note of them.

Be careful not to fall into the "wine magazine" trap of being too absolute in your judgments; if a wine scored an 18, it doesn't necessarily mean that it's that much "worse" than a wine that scored a 19 or 20. The 20-Point System rates many things, and the numbers are truly meaningless without your notes and comments alongside them.

Wine Faults

B efore we delve in, we must first understand the difference between a *flaw* and a *fault*. A wine exhibits any number of *flaws* when, at some point in the winemaking process, something was (or was not) done that led to the finished product developing a feature not desired for the style or varietal. Flaws can be visual (tartrate crystals, sediment, haze, minor carbonation in a nonsparkling wine); aromatic (volatile acidity, sulfur dioxide, *Brettanomyces*, lack of or nonvarietal aroma, reduced sulfur compounds at low levels, diacetyl, overoaking); or flaws of flavor (searing acidity, unintended sweetness, exceedingly high or abnormally low alcohol levels).Wine flaws are minor issues, though, and the wine may still be entirely acceptable and even enjoyable.

There is no incontrovertible point at which a flaw becomes a fault, though there are well-studied thresholds—the point at which we understand a wine's fault to be unquestionably recognizable and/or overpowering of any other characteristics in the wine. Simply put, *faulted wine* is a flawed wine that has reached very high concentrations. When a wine loses its typicity entirely, and the flaw becomes the singular defining characteristic covering up any other aroma or flavor, the wine is faulted and considered undrinkable. Many of these faults can be co-created or stem from the same underlying issues, but for the sake of understanding them best at their core, the most common faults are explained individually.

Oxidation

Though at times a purposeful and stylistic choice, such as in the production of Sherry with "oxidative characteristics," oxidation occurs when oxygen and wine interact, creating recognizable oxidative aromas by modifying the wine's chemical structure. Oxidation does not affect all wines equally nor in exactly the same way. For example, highly aromatic white wines will experience the effects of oxidation more readily and more obviously than tannic, phenolic-heavy red wines. Wine can become oxidized either before or after it is bottled.

❖ **Cause**: Excessive oxygen exposure post-fermentation, extended maceration time with inadequate inert gas usage, insufficient free sulfur dioxide (SO_2), bottling with faulty corks

❖ **Prevention**: Sufficient use of inert gas, SO_2, refrigeration, quality corks, and aging bottles on their side to prevent the cork from drying out. Using high-quality corks is important, alongside long-term storage in a cool, dark place, as heat accelerates oxidation and low humidity conditions allow the cork to dry out.

❖ **Fix**: Cannot be remedied; prevention is key.

Acetaldehyde

Acetaldehyde is the result of oxidized ethanol. It can be produced by acetic acid bacteria in low-oxygen, high-alcohol conditions. Yeasts can also convert ethanol to acetaldehyde in oxidative conditions.

❖ **Cause**: Film yeasts or *Acetobacter* in oxidative conditions, low SO_2 levels, excessive headspace, faulty corks, adding excessive amounts of SO_2 during fermentation, high pH, and allowing fermentation temperature to spike too high

❖ **Prevention**: Top up barrels to prevent excessive headspace. Be aware that increasing pH, fermentation temperature, and adding SO_2 during fermentation can increase acetaldehyde levels. Minimize a wine's exposure to oxygen after fermentation. Maintain proper free SO_2 levels.

❖ **Fix**: Add SO_2, which will bind to the acetaldehyde; however, this addition is temporary as the SO_2 will eventually diminish, allowing the acetaldehyde to be freed.

Volatile Acidity (VA)

Grape juice wants to move toward becoming vinegar, not wine. As winemakers, we interrupt this process, decelerating this natural progression as a means to our own end. VA is named for the sum of all volatile acids included in wine, the main ones being acetic acid (vinegar aroma) and ethyl acetate (nail polish remover or fresh latex paint aroma). Because yeasts produce low levels of acetic acid during alcoholic fermentation, most wines will contain low levels of VA without issue; it is when the VA exceeds a certain level that it becomes problematic.

❖ **Cause**: Its point of origin is in various spoilage yeasts and bacteria. VA is generated when bacteria convert alcohol to acetic acid in the presence of oxygen (*Acetobacter* reacting with ethanol) and creates ethyl acetate as a byproduct. *Acetobacter* creates acetic acid, which is vinegar. VA can result as a byproduct of fermentation or as post-fermentation spoilage, and will be exacerbated post-fermentation by excessive headspace. The primary cause of VA actually begins before the winemakers even have a chance to correct the problem, which is in the vineyard. Bird damage to grape skins allows bacteria and bad yeasts to gain a foothold in the grapes, which often only gets worse in the winery without necessary precautions. *Brettanomyces* is also known to manufacture VA in the presence of oxygen. Stressed yeast strains can produce acetic acid in large quantities. New oak barrels can also be the point of origin, albeit for lower levels of acetic acid, due to hydrolysis of acetyl groups in the wood.

❖ **Prevention**: Inert gas, top up barrels, maintain proper free SO_2 levels, inoculate with chosen yeast strains as opposed to allowing spontaneous fermentations of native yeasts, add SO_2 to must/juice to stop wild yeasts from producing acetic acid pre-fermentation and during fermentation, sort fruit to eliminate moldy or rotting clusters, keep winery space as free of fruit flies as possible as they are carriers of acetic acid bacteria.

❖ **Fix**: Sulfite wine as soon as VA is detected to kill the bacteria. If the wine is already bottled, chilling it before serving will help mask unpleasant aromas, as the volatile acids will vaporize less at lower temperatures.

Ethyl Acetate

Ethyl acetate is the most common ester formed in wine. This microbial fault is a result of spoilage yeasts, ethanol, and acetic acid becoming esterified. It is common in wines with higher acetic levels.

❖ **Cause**: A product of microbial spoilage yeasts within the genera *Pichia* and *Kloeckera* as well as *Acetobacter*, a genus of acetic acid bacteria; excessive headspace, lactic acid bacteria (LAB), and acetic acid bacteria (AAB) are oftentimes the culprits of high acetate production.

❖ **Prevention**: Inoculate with *Saccharomyces* yeasts, which produce a fraction of the ethyl acetate produced by other genera such as *Kloeckera*, *Pichia*, and *Candida*.

❖ **Fix**: Reverse osmosis; this is quite difficult to correct once detected.

Mercaptans (Thiols)

Mercaptans are sulfur compounds that bind with other molecules and likely formed during fermentation when amino acids containing sulfur begin to break down. They become an issue when hydrogen sulfide (H_2S) is present in wine and not removed quickly.

❖ **Cause**: Nitrogen deficiency, inadequate aeration during fermentation, prolonged contact with gross lees

❖ **Prevention**: Racking and proper aeration; don't prolong lees contact.

❖ **Fix**: Copper sulfate can alleviate this issue; however, some compounds in this class do not precipitate with copper and do not drop out with this treatment. Early detection and immediate treatment are important.

Hydrogen Sulfide (H$_2$S)

A result of alcoholic fermentation in low-nitrogen environments, caused by reduction by yeast of various sulfur compounds. Although H$_2$S is a natural product of fermentation, it can leak into the wine if more is produced than can be used.

❖ **Cause**: Yeast metabolism; elemental sulfur, stressed yeasts (nutrient deprivation), temperature stress, anaerobic conditions during fermentation

❖ **Prevention**: Be careful with elemental sulfur sprays during the growing season, as residue can remain on the grape skins even up to the time the fruit arrives in the cellar. Low yeast-assimilable nitrogen (YAN) can also cause H$_2$S to develop, and is a result of not enough sun or heat during the growing season, over cropping, low soil nutrient levels, and disease in the vineyard. If YAN levels are not high enough they cause stressful ferments, including sluggish and/or stuck fermentations. A way to prevent this is by adding an adequate amount of diammonium phosphate (DAP). Make sure the fermenting juice has enough nitrogen present so the active yeast does not excrete hydrogen sulfide. Filtering or settling out white juice before beginning fermentation can help possible sulfur-containing solids drop out, which limits the amount of H$_2$S that can be produced. Similarly, H$_2$S can be volatilized in red wines by aerating during the first racking.

❖ **Fix**: Aeration and DAP during fermentation (preventive), copper sulfate post-fermentation (remedy)

Sulfur Dioxide (SO$_2$)

This extremely important additive is used at various stages to the benefit of the wine. When added in excess, the wine takes on a "sulfitic" character.

❖ **Cause**: Adding excessive SO$_2$, wild yeast use

❖ **Prevention**: Don't oversulfite the wine; inoculate with chosen *Saccharomyces* strains.

❖ **Fix**: If bottled, decant the wine to let the SO$_2$ volatize; lowering levels prebottling runs the risk of oxidizing the wine. Blend with a wine lower in SO$_2$. You can also just leave the wine in the cellar longer; sulfite levels decline over months and years in the bottle.

Mouse Taint (Mousiness)

Mousiness is the very specific odor of caged mice and occurs due to the formation of heterocyclic ring compounds where one of the carbon atoms is replaced by nitrogen. The pyridines are among these compounds and several of them are implicated in mousiness. This is not a fault one would notice on the nose, because the compounds implicated are not volatile at the pH of wine (3.0 to 4.0). They do, however, become volatile in the pH of saliva (6.0 to 7.0), which is why this fault reveals itself once the taster has ingested the wine, giving way to a mousy aftertaste that can linger for quite some time.

❖ **Cause**: It is believed that strains of *Brettanomyces* and lactic acid bacteria are capable of producing this taint.

❖ **Prevention**: Proper levels of SO$_2$, pH, and acidity (high pH wines are more likely to experience mouse taint); limit oxygen contact.

❖ **Fix**: None known

Brettanomyces

Though it is a yeast, *Brettanomyces* is a part of a different genus than what juice or must is usually inoculated with (*Saccharomyces*). It produces volatile phenols that, at certain concentrations, can produce unpleasant aromas. Some people enjoy a certain level of *Brettanomyces* in wine, where it can add a degree of complexity. The main compounds that make up *Brettanomyces* include 4-ethylphenol, 4-ethylguaiacol, and isovaleric acid.

Natural corks are the gold standard, but as a natural product they pose a risk that can lead to cork taint.

❖ **Cause**: Contamination of surface spoilage yeast in winery, equipment, barrels, fruit, which can be exacerbated by low SO_2, high pH, high turbidity, residual sugar

❖ **Prevention**: Good winery hygiene and sanitation. *Brettanomyces* is very difficult to eliminate once it has entered the winery, so prevention is key. Keep barrels clean and cared for. Add SO_2 to maintain *Brettanomyces* population at manageable levels.

❖ **Fix**: Once the odor is in the wine, it will not come out. Prevention is integral.

❖ **Additional note**: This affects red wines most commonly because of their generally higher pH.

Cork Taint (TCA)

TCA (2,4,6-trichloroanisole) is the compound that causes this bothersome fault. You'll oftentimes hear people say that a wine is "corked," and detecting this is the reason the cork is smelled when a bottle is first opened.

❖ **Cause**: The potential for TCA begins with molds within the cork-producing tree interacting with trichlorophenol (a biocide and disinfectant that may be used during its growth and subsequent production). A wine can become corked from the cork itself or from an infection from phenols found in wood, such as pallets and oak barrels. Any time chlorine interacts with moldy material, the taint may form.

❖ **Prevention**: Invest in high-quality corks, or consider using synthetic or unconventional corks. Do not store wine near old wood or cardboard. Do not use chlorine in the wine cellar.

❖ **Fix**: If treating a single bottle, some claim putting a crumpled piece of old-style plastic wrap (made from polyvinylidene chloride or PVDC, not the now commonly used polyethylene) into a decanter and swirling it with the wine causes the plastic to absorb the TCA. This may help save a single bottle. There are no common or easily feasible large-scale equivalents of saving corked wine.

Diacetyl

A natural byproduct of malolactic bacterial conversion, diacetyl (2,3-butanedione) is a chemical compound formed when *Lactobacillus*, *Pediococcus*, *Oenococcus*, or *Leuconostoc* metabolize citric acid. Even at quite high concentrations, diacetyl may be greatly enjoyed by those who are partial to rich, buttery Chardonnays; but excessive amounts take on overwhelming odors. Diacetyl is found specifically in wines that undergo malolactic fermentation (MLF).

❖ **Cause**: Both yeast and bacteria can cause diacetyl production, though, generally, yeasts cannot produce excessive amounts of it, whereas bacteria present during malolactic fermentation can. The presence of and amount of citric acid, as well as temperature, pH, and certain bacterial strains, can all lead to the overproduction of this compound. Diacetyl is produced when citric acid is metabolized once all of the malic acid has been converted to lactic acid.

❖ **Prevention**: Halt the wine from undergoing malolactic fermentation; you can do this with SO_2 additions and by adding lysozyme. If you want the wine to go through MLF, use specified malolactic bacteria with accurate addition rates and monitor MLF closely so you can promptly add SO_2 at the completion of MLF to kill the bacteria before it goes after the citric acid. Yeast metabolize diacetyl, so leave the wine on the lees. Do not add citric acid.

❖ **Fix**: Blend with a wine that did not acquire such strong diacetyl aromas. If aging on lees, increase the time the wine spends in contact with the lees, as more time in contact will help break down diacetyl levels. Transferring a wine with very high diacetyl levels onto another batch of lees may help neutralize it as well.

Geranium Taint

This fault is particular to wines with sorbic acid added to them, as the formation of 2-ethoxyhexa-3,5-diene (crushed geranium leaf aroma) is a consequence of the metabolism of sorbic acid by lactic acid bacteria.

❖ **Cause:** Malolactic bacteria in the presence of potassium sorbate can produce 2-ethoxyhexa-3,5-diene.

❖ **Prevention:** Do not use potassium sorbate if the wine went through MLF. Sorbate is added to inhibit yeast growth in wines with residual sugar; do not allow the wine to go through MLF if you are considering keeping some sweetness to the wine. Consider dropping the temperature if you insist on having residual sugar in the wine.

❖ **Fix:** None known.

❖ **Additional note:** This taint is not found in must because its formation requires the presence of alcohol. As such, it develops in finished wine.

Light Strike (*Goût de Lumière*)

Light strike is a common yet preventable fault, where light exposure leads to the premature breakdown of the wine. It primarily affects white and rosé wines, as they are often packaged in clear bottles, allowing light damage to occur. Symptoms are akin to premature aging, such as loss of or dulled aromatics and changes in color similar to oxidation (browning of white wines, red wines taking on a lighter brick red color prematurely).

❖ **Cause:** Excessive light exposure to bottled wine.

❖ **Prevention:** Keep bottled wine in a dark, cool place; use dark-colored bottles when possible.

❖ **Fix:** None.

Chapter 7:
Advanced Winemaking Topics

Over the course of an individual's early experiences as a home winemaker, a few pitfalls may occur and some batches may not be "quite right." Wines may be perceived as out of balance or to have mild flaws. Many of these balance and flaw issues can be addressed or avoided with some simple lab analysis, both pre- and post-fermentation. Not only can laboratory testing improve the organoleptic qualities of your wines, but it will also provide the winemaker with a deeper understanding of what is actually going on inside their winemaking vessels. Hobby winemakers can test for several key metrics at home: sugar content, pH, titratable acidity, and free SO_2 counts give the winemaker some criteria to work with. Other pieces to the winemaking puzzle, like nitrogen levels, should be better understood after you have the basics down and can be determined by sending samples to a lab for testing. Other key components, like phenolics and tannins, enzymes, and using inert gas, may not be for the faint of heart, but for seasoned handlers, putting these concepts to use can separate good wines from great ones. In this chapter, we're going to dive deeper into the science and importance of some of the more complicated subjects that have been touched on earlier in this book.

pH

Having covered what to test for at home already, let's dig into what the crucial parameters signify. pH is critical to wine stability, especially in terms of the effectiveness of sulfur dioxide to prevent oxidation and spoilage. In terms of wine stability, low pH is good and high pH is bad.

There are at least four times in a wine's production cycle that you should consider measuring pH:

❖ It can support a harvest decision, along with TA and Brix. For white grapes, pH at harvest is usually between 3.1 and 3.5 and for reds, 3.3 to 3.6. For readings much lower than the bottom of these ranges, the grapes are probably not fully mature and picking should be postponed. For readings much above these ranges, the grapes are potentially overripe and should be picked right away.

❖ At crush time; in conjunction with TA readings, a pH measurement may tell you to add tartaric acid (if pH is high) or something like potassium bicarbonate (if pH is low).

❖ Measure again after fermentation is complete and you are about to begin your sulfite program. The online calculator at Winemakermag.com/sulfitecalculator will guide you to a target free SO_2 level based on your pH and wine type.

❖ Finally, you may want to measure again at bottling to verify stability for cellaring.

The original method for measuring pH is based on natural color changes of certain plant materials called "indicators." The color changes are from anthocyanin pigments in plants like cabbage, and the behavior is mirrored in red grapes—at low pH, the pigments are quite red, and at higher pH, they are purple or bluish.

We still use pH indicators like phenolphthalein for the TA titration. The indicator is colorless at low pH and turns pink at the end point near pH 8.2. pH strips use similar color changes, sometimes on more than one pad, to show the pH of a sample. Although suitable for end-point detection in a titration, they are not generally accurate enough to guide decisions like harvest or sulfite additions. Most pH sticks or papers will give you a result that is plus or minus about 0.5 pH. Without even seeing it, we can tell you

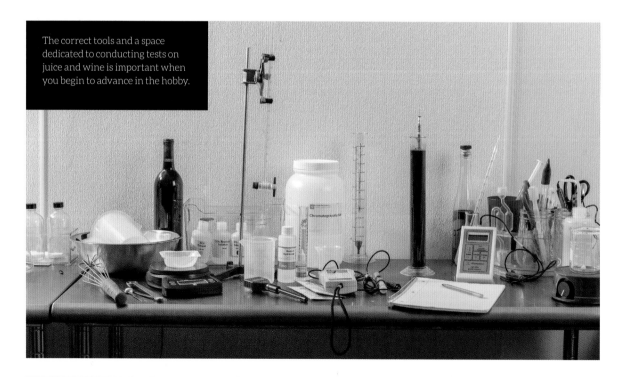

The correct tools and a space dedicated to conducting tests on juice and wine is important when you begin to advance in the hobby.

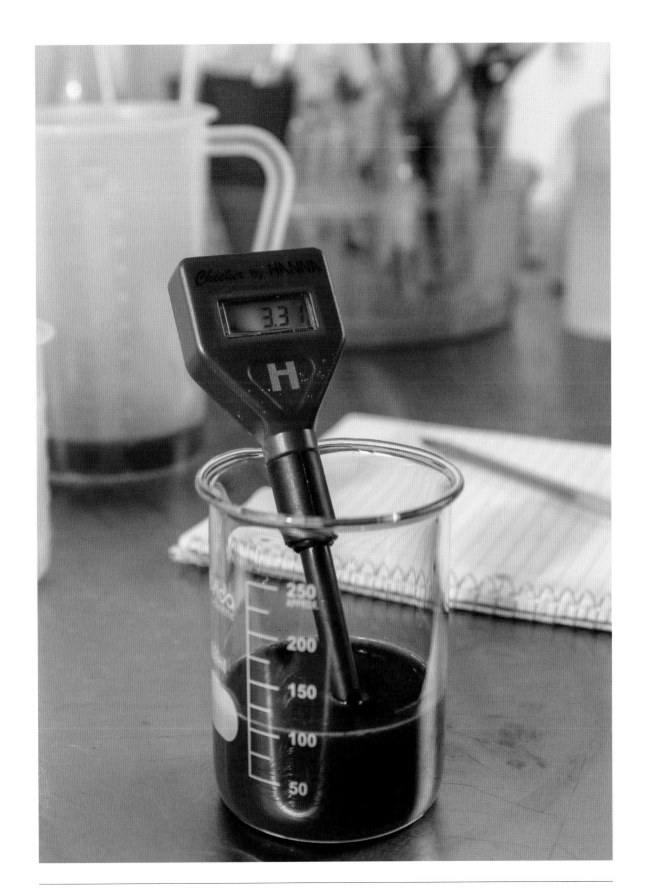

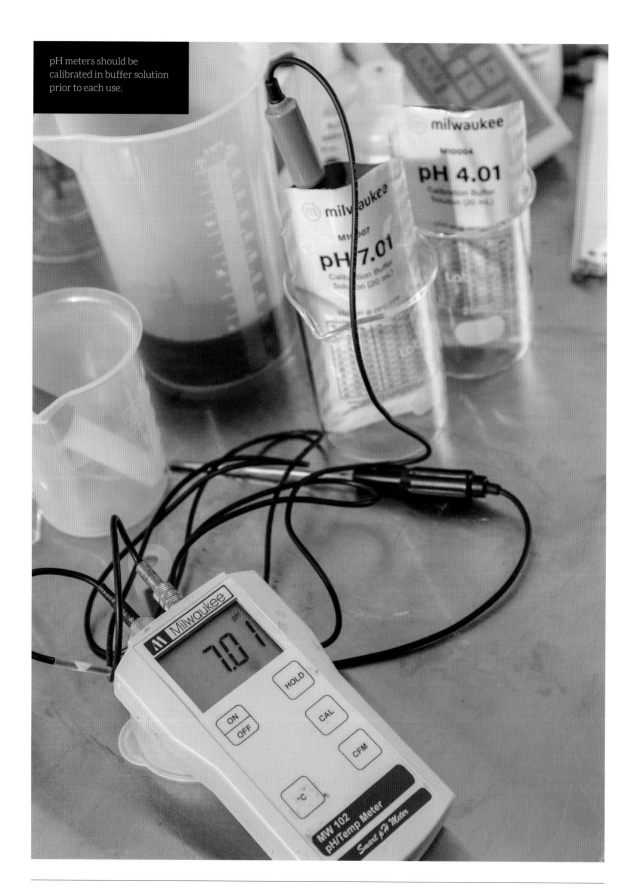

pH meters should be calibrated in buffer solution prior to each use.

that your wine is probably pH 3.5 ± 0.5, just like a pH stick might, because almost all wine is in that range.

Your other choice is the correct one all winemakers should take: purchase a pH meter. These are available in many different models at various price points, but all use the same principle: electronically measuring the voltage between a glass pH electrode and a reference electrode. A quarter century ago, there were often two separate electrodes for these functions. Now you will almost always encounter a configuration where the two are combined in a single electrode body called a combination pH electrode. The bulb of the pH electrode develops a molecular gel layer of wet glass when it is kept in aqueous solution and that layer is critical to its sensitivity—that's why pH electrodes are kept wet. When measuring, the reference electrode must be in electrical contact with the sample, so somewhere on that part of the probe you will see a fritted orifice or a small fiber that allows ions and current to pass back and forth from the reference electrode to the sample.

As the glass electrode comes to equilibrium with the solution, sodium, hydrogen, potassium, and possibly other positive ions adopt the same concentration in the gel layer as in the surrounding liquid. The ratios of those ions change the electrical potential or voltage as measured by a voltmeter between the glass electrode and the reference electrode. That voltmeter, marked as pH, is your pH meter. Although a theoretical pH response for an electrode can be calculated, the actual output of any given electrode is subject to variation. Because of this, every pH meter and electrode must first be calibrated against solutions of known pH: pH buffers. For winemaking, we usually use buffers near pH 7 and pH 4, which are commercially available. This is because the meters need to "sense" neutral pH and then "sense" pH that more resembles the wine being tested.

Testing for pH

To use a pH meter, first soak the electrode in tap water for at least 30 minutes to saturate the glass gel. Do not use distilled or deionized water for this soak as that will deplete the gel of ions and cause a slow response when you try to calibrate.

After soaking, rinse the electrode—now use distilled water—and blot dry with a tissue. Immerse the electrode tip (past any visible reference junction) in pH 7.0 (or 7.01) buffer and follow the manufacturer's instructions that came with your meter to set the first calibration point. Rinse the electrode, blot dry again, and immerse it in the pH 4.0 (or 4.01) buffer and follow the rest of the instructions to complete the calibration. For the technically minded, the first buffer calibrated the response and the second buffer calibrated the slope. Best accuracy is near the second buffer, which is why we do 7 first and 4 last when measuring wine. Users can also test their meters using the pH 7 buffer to find potential problems with the electrode. If the offset deviates significantly, the meter's readings may not be accurate and the electrode may need to be replaced. Rinse and blot the electrode again, and measure your sample the same way. Since you need to present fresh buffer or wine to the glass electrode throughout the test, swirl or stir buffers and samples.

When you are finished with your samples for the day, rinse the electrode and store it in electrode storage solution or pH 4 buffer, which will keep the glass saturated and ready to use again. The most common failure with a pH meter is a dried-out electrode. If yours has dried out, soaking in tap water as much as overnight may bring it back. Another failure is a clogged reference junction. Some ribbon-type junctions can be pulled out a small amount and clipped off, exposing a new unclogged junction. A fritted glass junction (a little white spot) may be cleaned by swirling in water with some dishwashing detergent, or by alternating between solutions of a mild acid and a base (like a solution of citric acid and another of potassium bicarbonate). Generally speaking, if your pH meter will calibrate at 4 and 7, it is working and you may proceed. If it won't, even after cleaning and soaking, you probably need a new electrode.

Effect of Temperature

Temperature has an impact on the pH of a solution, and inconsistent temperatures contribute to inaccurate readings. This can be troublesome for winemakers when calibrating with buffers that are, for example, near room temperature and then measuring the pH of a must or wine that is cold (especially in winter months where cold stabilization may be performed). To address this, ensure the sample of wine and the buffer have had time to come to the same temperature before taking any pH readings.

A quality pH meter will have a temperature compensation feature that will take into consideration the temperature of the solution before displaying a reading. Check the manufacturer's recommendations for purchasing the right probes to take advantage of this feature. They are commonly labeled "ATC" for automatic temperature compensation.

Buffer Storage and Shelf Life

❖ Buffers have a shelf life of a couple years, and this is reduced to just a few months once the buffer comes in contact with air. It is important to use buffers that are not expired and have not been open too long.

❖ To avoid contaminating the buffer, always pour a small amount of buffer from the bottle into a smaller vessel to perform a calibration and then discard the portion. Never calibrate or store the electrode in the original bottle.

❖ As an alternative to purchasing buffer in liquid form (which has a limited shelf life) consider using single-use sachets of buffer powder. They can be opened and reconstituted in distilled water on an as-needed basis.

❖ Before throwing out a costly electrode, calibrate it using brand-new buffers just to make sure that any problems in measuring pH are due to the equipment and not a buffer that is past its prime.

Titratable Acidity (TA)

Many who are new to winemaking aren't really clear about why testing for both TA and pH are needed since the two seem tied together. But it is the unknown concentration and unpredictable effect of potassium that accounts for one of the most challenging facts about pH and acid in winemaking. The pure prediction of pH from acid content or acid content from pH is confounded, leaving the winemaker needing to test both parameters to characterize must or wine. Winemakers can sometimes find themselves stuck with high TA, high pH grape juice, and wonder what they should focus on.

TA has one clearly identified method of analysis because the answer itself—titratable acidity—defines the means of determining it. It is exactly the amount of acid as determined by titration that makes it TA. Unlike, say, the tartaric acid content or the copper concentration in a wine, for TA, you apply the prescribed method and the result speaks for itself. That is, you could use any of several well-established and rugged analytical procedures to analyze for copper content, but for TA, you must do an acid-base titration of a wine sample following a specific procedure using a strong base as the titrant.

TA is mostly about tartaric acid and malic acid as those dominate in grapes. There are smaller amounts of citric and succinic acids, and lactic acid comes along later as a conversion from malic acid during MLF. All of these are referred to as fixed acids to distinguish them from the volatile acids, like acetic acid and butyric acid, which are spoilage products. All of the fixed acids, when titrated together for TA, are reported as tartaric acid equivalent.

Tartaric acid is a dicarboxylic acid, meaning it has two hydrogen atoms that can be titrated in the TA test. Malic acid is also dicarboxylic. Lactic acid, on the other hand, is a monocarboxylic acid, with each molecule featuring only one titratable hydrogen atom. That difference is what causes the drop in TA after MLF—from the dicarboxylic malic acid to the monocarboxylic lactic acid.

The combination of fixed acids produces the tart flavors of wine that contribute so much to its appeal as an adult beverage. Malic acid has a sharper taste than tartaric acid even though there is usually less of it in the grape. Indeed, Warheads Extreme Sour Hard Candy derives its sourness primarily from a coating of malic acid. Lactic acid is milder than both tartaric and malic, leading to further mellowing of flavor with MLF. If the acid level is too low in grape must, the wine is likely to taste fat or flabby, lacking sharpness and definition. Low acid content also implies high pH, which results in instability. If the TA is too high, the wine will taste excessively sharp and potentially unpleasant, although leaving some sweetness may achieve a lemonade-like balance of flavors.

At grape harvest for dry wine, we usually look for a TA of 4 to 6 g/L (0.4 to 0.6 g/100 ml) in reds and 5 to 8 g/L (0.5 to 0.8 g/100 ml) in whites. Different laboratories and test kits may report in either units, grams per liter, or grams per 100 milliliters. They differ just by the factor of 10 since 1 liter is exactly 10 times the volume of 100 milliliters. You may use either designation in your notes, but be aware that you may see either one on a wine bottle or in a wine critic's tasting notes.

A use for TA testing beyond flavor and stability is to help as a harvest indicator. That is the first time the test is applied in a particular vintage. You can collect one hundred or so grapes from throughout your vineyard, put them in a zip-top sandwich bag, and pop each grape with your fingers. Squeeze the bag a few times to release the juice and then pour out a sample for testing. If your result is much above the levels noted, it implies that your malic acid level is still too high and the grapes are not yet mature. If too low, you will either need to pick right away, add tartaric acid later, or both. When you make the picking decision (or when you receive purchased grapes) will be the next testing moment. You will crush and stir the must, then drain off or scoop out a sample of juice for testing. If crushing day has you

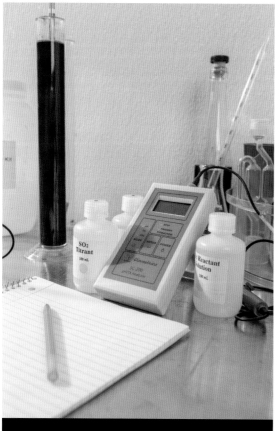
Record your measured TA each time you test for it.

conversion of malic acid to lactic acid. You cannot predict that drop from TA alone, since the original acids are titrated together and you do not know the ratio of tartaric to malic in your particular must. Once again, verify that the TA falls in the desirable range for your wine type and style.

Testing for TA

The principles of testing TA are very simple. A measured portion of juice or wine is placed in a small beaker or cup and a solution of a strong base, sodium hydroxide, is added to it in measured amounts. A syringe or burette is used for dispensing the sodium hydroxide titrant. Some test kits rely on the color-changing pH indicator phenolphthalein, which goes from colorless at acid pH to pink near pH 8.2. The indicator can be supplemented or replaced by a pH electrode and meter with a digital end point of pH 8.2. Select an electrode with a fast response time to avoid bypassing the end point as you titrate. Calculating the TA depends on the sample size you titrate and the concentration of sodium hydroxide you use. Instructions with your kit should have the details of the calculation. Following are examples of a basic kit method and a more advanced home wine lab setup.

Country Wines is one popular brand of basic TA test kit and other similar kits work the same way. A small cardboard box contains a clear plastic beaker, a 10-milliliter syringe, a bottle of 0.1 N sodium hydroxide titrant, and a dropper bottle of phenolphthalein indicator. You measure 10 milliliters of wine into the beaker and add a few drops of indicator. Rinse the syringe with distilled water, empty it, and fill to exactly the 10.0 milliliter mark with titrant. Swirling the beaker with one hand, add titrant from the syringe with the other. Watch for a flash of pink where the drops contact the wine. As you swirl, the pink will disappear as the acid neutralizes the titrant. Soon, the pink zone will last a few seconds. Stop titrating at the first persistent pink color throughout. Subtract the remaining volume in the syringe from 10.0 to determine the ml used. The TA in g/100 ml equals milliliters used × 0.075.

too busy to do the test right away, put the covered sample bottle in the refrigerator and then let it come to room temperature the next day for testing. This crush day test is probably your most critical TA analysis as it will inform you about any need to add acid or, possibly, to deacidify. When must needs acid adjustment, many winemakers prefer to do it as early in the production cycle as possible, feeling it better integrates into the final wine. If you need to add acid, you should typically begin with half of the indicated amount early and then test again later. It is much easier to add a little more acid later than it is to compensate for having added too much.

You can verify that the addition worked or that the natural acid is still in the right range by running the TA test again after fermentation. It may have changed a bit through the process, but should still be close to the desired range. If you do MLF, you can test again to see how much the TA dropped in the

The advantages of a kit like this are that it is inexpensive, quick, and easy. It is reasonably accurate for home winemaking as long as you can see the end point well. That is more difficult in red wine or dark must. To lighten a dark sample, you can dilute it 2:1 with distilled water before measuring your 10-milliliter portion, then multiply the answer by 2 to get your final result. Avoid diluting more than that. Kits cost less than $15 USD.

The best answer to titrating dark red wines is to get a pH meter setup. For the best results, use a benchtop pH meter with an electrode holder, pH buffers to calibrate it, a 10- milliliter burette for titrant, a magnetic stir plate with stir bar, a glass or plastic beaker, standardized sodium hydroxide solution (typically 0.1 N or 0.067 N), and phenolphthalein indicator. You can use the beaker, titrant, and indicator from a kit as parts of this setup.

Carbon dioxide dissolved in the wine will titrate as an acid, but is not part of TA. This could cause erroneous titration if you are testing right after fermentation before the wine has degassed. To avoid that problem, heat the wine sample to 140°F (60°C) to drive off CO_2, then let cool to room temperature. Also boil and cool distilled water that you use for the test. Add some of that water to the beaker to enough depth to submerge your pH electrode tip while remaining clear of the magnetic stir bar. Measure and add 5.0 milliliters of wine and begin stirring. Add a few drops of phenolphthalein. Fill the burette to 0.0 (at the top of the burette) with titrant and then add dropwise while watching the pH. As you approach pH 8.2, you will see the same pink zone described earlier—seeing it will help you slow your additions near the end point. When the pH reaches (or first passes) 8.2, stop adding and note the milliliters of titrant used. With this method, the calculation using 0.1 N NaOH is:

$$TA\ (g/L) = [(ml\ titrant) \times (N\ of\ titrant) \times (0.075) \times 1,000]/(ml\ of\ wine)$$

Using 0.067 N NaOH eliminates the extra math and the equation reduces to, for a 5-ml wine sample:

$$TA\ (g/L) = ml\ of\ NaOH\ used$$

Advantages of the lab method are improved accuracy and precision, independence of visual detection of the colored end point, and good correlation of results if you also send samples to a commercial laboratory. Disadvantages include higher cost, more complex execution, more cleaning, and required calibration of the pH meter. Depending on the meter and stirring options, expect to spend a couple hundred dollars. Replace titrant solution at least once a year since NaOH absorbs water and the strength of the solution changes over time. Also keep it away from heat and light.

Sodium hydroxide is the only significant safety risk with either method. The very dilute solutions we deal with during titrations are not dangerous, but clean up any spills as any dry residue is highly corrosive. As with any lab procedures, wear eye protection and rubber gloves. And when you're done, you too can start printing the TA on the back label of your wine!

Sulfite

First, let's clear up some persistent confusion about the meaning of the term "sulfite." Among the elements, sulfur is unusual in that it readily adopts several different oxidation states. Names assigned by traditional chemistry naming rules give sulfur compounds different similar names based on that oxidation state. Sulfate ion, SO_4^{2-}, is a combination of oxygen in its usual -2 oxidation state and sulfur in $+6$. This sulfate ion is common in the environment, does not provide any protection to wine, and when formed by dissolving sulfur trioxide, SO_3, in water makes sulfuric acid, H_2SO_4 (which ionizes almost completely to $2H^+$ and the SO_4^{2-}). Sulfite ion, SO_3^{2-} is similar but acts in very different ways. Here, the sulfur is in the $+4$ oxidation state and the corresponding acid would be sulfurous acid, H_2SO_3, produced by dissolving sulfur dioxide, SO_2, in water.

The –ate ending on the ion and the –ic ending on the acid represent a higher oxidation state, while the –ite ending on the ion and the –ous ending on the acid are a lower oxidation state. These names are why you variously hear winemakers refer to additions of sulfur, sulfite, or SO_2, to their wine. Regardless of which way you say it or what chemical form you add it in, the result is the presence of the sulfite ion and related compounds in your wine.

Depending on the pH of the wine, any sulfite present is distributed into three equilibrium forms. At lower pH levels, the un-ionized molecular sulfur dioxide, SO_2, is present. At higher pHs, there is a combination of the hydrogen ion, H^+, and the bisulfite ion, HSO_3^-. Moving to still higher pH yields a higher proportion of sulfite ion, SO_3^{2-}. Of all these, molecular sulfur dioxide is the most potent protection against oxidation and spoilage. It is present in very small amounts at wine pH. When combined with other bisulfite and sulfite ions and not combined with any other compound, we call the combination "free" SO_2. That is the chemical species we usually measure and then find molecular SO_2 in a chart based on the pH and the free sulfite analytical result.

The common cellar compound potassium metabisulfite is named so because it does not contain sulfite exactly but it will when dissolved. That is, the "meta" means it is about to become a sulfite compound when you dissolve it in water (or wine). In simplest terms, that can be shown as:

$$K_2S_2O_5 + H_2O \longrightarrow 2K^+ + 2\,H_2SO_3^-$$

From there, the pH determines the distribution of the sulfite forms. The way this cascades down to the molecular sulfur dioxide protecting your wine is like this:

❖ Suppose you dissolve 100 mg/L (ppm) of potassium metabisulfite in your wine. In that amount, you have added 57 ppm sulfur dioxide equivalent.

❖ Of that, if you ran a "total sulfite" test, you would find somewhat less than 57 ppm due to various losses or binding with other compounds.

❖ Depending on pH and other components in the wine, somewhat less would appear in a "free sulfite" analysis.

❖ A tiny fraction of the free would be in your wine as "molecular" sulfur dioxide, which provides the maximum protection.

Testing for Sulfites

Why do we analyze for sulfite? Sulfites have two major beneficial effects on wine. Through interactions with naturally occurring phenolic compounds, sulfite reacts with oxygen, reducing the risk of oxidizing your wine. This reaction converts the involved sulfite into sulfate, removing it from both "total" and "free" SO_2 test results. Sulfite also inhibits or kills spoilage organisms. This is so effective that native wine yeasts have evolved to be sulfite resistant and to produce sulfite in their metabolism—they inhibit competitive organisms in the rich sugar environment of juice. In both actions, molecular SO_2 is the agent and free SO_2 is the test. Winemakers generally agree that about 0.8 ppm of

molecular sulfite is needed to protect white wine and about 0.5 ppm for reds. Reds need a bit less because there are other oxidation-resistant compounds present in red wine. The table on page 37, Free SO_2 Needed at Various pH Levels, in chapter 2 shows representative "free" levels needed for these target molecular levels at different pH values.

Although we recommend a sulfite addition to the juice or must on harvest day, there is no need for testing then. That initial dose to inhibit spoilage microbes will quickly dissipate and will be long gone by the time primary fermentation is complete. Your testing program should begin then. For wines that will go through malolactic fermentation (MLF), there is no addition of sulfite before the MLF bacteria inoculation to avoid inhibiting their growth. After MLF is complete, or after primary fermentation of wines without MLF, make a first sulfite addition of about 50 ppm total SO_2. After that, make an addition every month during bulk aging. Using as a very rough guide that

sulfite is used up at a rate of about $^1/_2$ ppm per day, make a 15 ppm addition monthly. Test the wines every other month and make another addition if the free SO_2 does not conform to the target levels. You will also want to make one final test and adjustment just before bottling.

The primary winery and commercial lab method of analysis has long been a test called aeration-oxidation. A quick but somewhat less accurate method called Ripper has been used commonly in winery cellars for routine monitoring. Although both methods have had adaptations for home winery use, it was not until Dr. Richard Sportsman of Vinmetrica introduced his much-improved take on Ripper chemistry that a fast, easy, reliable home test became available.

Although TA is method-defined, sulfite, on the other hand, is a specific chemical species. A scientist can exploit any of its unique properties to render it amenable to analysis. Aeration-oxidation analysis depends on the volatility of sulfur dioxide gas and the development of an acid when reaction products are dissolved in solution. Ripper chemistry utilizes the oxidation of sulfite to sulfate by using iodine as a reactant.

Before Vinmetrica, Ripper was either a macro titration or a kit of vials. According to Zoecklein et al., in *Wine Analysis and Production*, free sulfur dioxide is measured by placing 25 milliliters of wine in a flask and adding a starch solution as an iodine indicator. The sample is acidified and then rapidly titrated with a standardized iodine solution until the blue color change of starch indicates that all free sulfite has reacted. The answer is then calculated according to a formula that includes the concentration of the iodine. The kit version of Ripper is a product called Titrets. The manufacturer, CHEMetrics, states about Titrets: "This kit is not recommended for use with red wines or white wines containing ascorbic acid or tannin. These wines often give false high test results." The same problem makes the Ripper titration method somewhat difficult to repeat with good precision. More specifically, Titrets are sealed glass vials that contain colorless iodine-iodate reagent as a stand-in for standardized iodine. The vial also contains starch indicator and is packed under vacuum. Attaching a flexible plastic hose, the user breaks the vial neck and squeezes a glass bead in the tube, allowing the vacuum to suck up the wine sample. Since the amount of iodine is fixed, this amounts to a form of back titration and you keep adding wine to it until the end point is reached. In this case, the Titret reagent turns blue on the very first bit of wine entering the vial and then wine is added until sufficient sulfite has used up all the included iodine and the blue color disappears. The more wine it takes, the lower the sulfite concentration. The vial is marked along the side with free sulfur dioxide concentration in ppm.

Using similar chemistry, the Vinmetrica meter does not depend on visual detection of a starch end point. Instead, it utilizes a platinum electrode and is an amperometric titration. When a pair of electrodes is placed in a solution and a voltage is applied, the current that results depends on the composition of the solution. Although this can be difficult to determine in an absolute sense, it is much easier to detect relative changes in the current in a changing solution. In this case, a small battery-powered meter applies a voltage between two platinum wires at the tip of the electrode. You add two Vinmetrica proprietary reagents to a wine sample, immerse the electrode, and begin titrating with an iodine-type proprietary titrant. When all of the free sulfite has reacted, the end point is reached and there is a sudden shift in the current. The meter indicates the sudden shift with a visual readout and an audible alarm. The combination of the proprietary reagents and this amperometric method produces reliable, quick, easy results.

Before Vinmetrica, the best bet at home was aeration-oxidation, or A/O. The wine sample is acidified to push the sulfite present toward the form of SO_2 molecular that can be swept out of solution by bubbling air through it. The air stream is transported through a trapping flask. In that flask, hydrogen peroxide oxidizes the sulfite to sulfate, producing sulfuric acid in place. After 10 minutes of transfer, the air is stopped and the trapping flask is titrated to a specific pH color end point with sodium hydroxide titrant. Commercial all-glass setups for A/O are quite elaborate and can cost several hundred dollars. In recent years, home winemaking suppliers have introduced systems using ordinary flasks and silicone tubing, bringing the price down to about $100 USD. Either type of system can produce accurate, reproducible analysis for free SO_2.

Yeast Assimilable Nitrogen (YAN)

Now that we've reviewed the tests that can be run at home given the right equipment, it's time to turn our attention to factors we can't test at home—key parameters like nitrogen levels in must and phenolics. You can send samples to a lab to test for these parameters, but, for some, you can use your experience and senses to guide your winemaking decisions. We'll start with one of the most important factors—the must's *yeast assimilable nitrogen* (YAN) levels.

Nitrogen is found naturally in grape juice in two forms: ammonia (NH_3) and amino nitrogen (nitrogen attached to amino acids). Yeast can metabolize all twenty naturally occurring alpha amino acids but struggles with proline due to its unique five-body pyrrolidine ring that binds the nitrogen group. As a rough average, the nitrogen in grape juice contains about one-third ammonia and two-thirds amino acids. YAN is a measure of the nitrogen available to yeast to use in fermentation. It is the combination of the available nitrogen contributed from free alpha amino acids (excluding proline), free ammonia, ammonium (ionized ammonia), and small peptides found in the grape juice.

Wine yeast has a natural preference for ammonia. "Gate proteins" in the cell wall will prevent amino acids from entering the cell in the presence of ammonia. Therefore, the natural ammonia contribution of YAN from the juice will usually be consumed during the logarithmic growth stage of the yeast. During this phase of growth, the yeast will rapidly reproduce and consume very little sugar. Once the population stabilizes, yeast will begin to break down sugars and produce alcohol. This is called the stationary phase (a reference to the stable population size).

At this point, nitrogen is consumed to help synthesize proteins and vital factors for yeast health. Winemakers can use the behavior of yeast to help influence aromatic profiles of the final wine. When yeast consume the nitrogen sourced from amino acids, the remainder of the molecule may be used to create interesting aromatic compounds, like esters and thiols, if the correct conditions exist. The active yeast need to be able to produce the correct enzymes for these types of syntheses, so the levels of thiol and ester production can be very yeast strain specific. Each unique strain has varied capabilities to produce these compounds, so yeast selection is essential.

Testing for YAN

Levels of nitrogen compounds that develop in grapes are influenced by weather, cultivation practices, vineyard sprays, irrigation, and factors from the natural environment like predation from birds and the spotted lanternfly. Testing of YAN is vital to the success of fermentation. Some fruit suppliers will provide chemical grape analysis for purchased fruit, including YAN as well as pH, TA, and other information. It is important that lab information is obtained from fruit sampled within three days of harvest. Variance of more than three days can have a big impact on this vital information.

Testing for YAN can be completed by wet chemistry, enzymatic analysis, and high-performance liquid chromatography (HPLC). There are many commercial labs that can provide a juice analysis that will include, at a minimum, YAN, pH, and TA. Testing can also be provided by any university with a wine program. These lab tests should be available for under $100 USD and are well worth the money when making larger quantities of wine. It is common to observe variations in the YAN every year with fruit sourced from the same vineyard and under similar conditions. This is something that should be tested every year and for every lot.

Note: *The wet chemistry methods for measuring YAN involve the use and subsequent disposal of formaldehyde. It is much safer and more reliable to have a wine lab or trained professional perform this analysis. Home testing is not recommended.*

Once you have the starting Brix and YAN, the state of nutrition of the must can be assessed. Under normal fermentation conditions with sugars from 22 to 24°Brix, must with a YAN under 100 ppm is considered deficient and should be supplemented to complete a healthy fermentation. Must in the range of 150 to 250 ppm YAN is at moderate risk, and supplementation should be considered to enhance the quality of the final product. Must with YAN over 250 ppm may need to be supplemented to accommodate a higher biomass from the yeast. In this case, the natural balance of resources and factors needed for growth, like magnesium, zinc, and thiamin, can become rapidly depleted due to the higher yeast cell counts.

High nitrogen fermentations tend to become stressed and produce sulfides toward the end of fermentation. Musts with sugar levels over 24°Brix generally need some nutrient additions to maintain the health of the yeast and complete fermentation. The higher level of alcohol that comes along with high sugar can often require nutrients that include yeast hulls, sterols, and vitamins, which will help support the yeast in these stressful conditions (for more on best practices when it comes to nutrient additions, see page 75).

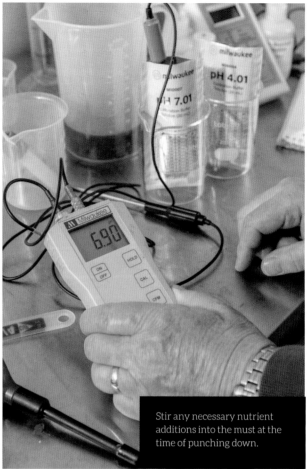

Stir any necessary nutrient additions into the must at the time of punching down.

Phenolics and Tannins

Perhaps one of the most complicated subjects in wine chemistry is phenolics, the chemistry of phenolic aroma molecules, anthocyanins, and tannin. Let's begin with a basic rundown of the chemistry of phenolic and polyphenolic molecules.

Starting with the most basic structure, a phenol is defined as a six-carbon ring with a hydroxyl (¬–OH) group attached. Phenolic molecules are plentiful in plants and have a wide range of uses. The carbon ring structure of this molecule is important because it allows the carbon molecules in the ring to "share" electrical charge from the oxygen atom attached to it, which makes it easier for the entire structure to engage in chemical reactions with other molecules. Compounds with multiple phenolic rings are collectively referred to as polyphenols.

Aromatic Phenols

Small phenolic molecules have low mass and are hydrophobic due to their carbon ring structure, thus they have a low enough vapor pressure that they are volatile and, at relatively low concentration, may be recognized in wine. Aromatic phenols in wine come from a variety of sources. They are sometimes referred to as spoilage aromas because *Brettanomyces* metabolism creates a range of volatile phenolic compounds.

Oak cooperage is another common source of volatile phenols in wine, yet these aromatic phenols are generally more well liked than the phenols of *Brettanomyces* metabolism. Oak volatile phenolic molecules may be generated by the tree itself or by the breakdown of larger polyphenolic molecules in wood lignin during seasoning and toasting. Examples of aromatic phenols in toasted oak are vanillin and eugenol, which smell like vanilla and cloves, respectively.

Another recently recognized source of aromatic phenolic molecules in wine is from smoke taint. Volatile phenols, such as guaiacol and 4-methylguaiacol, from burning vegetation may impart a charred, ashtray aroma to wines made from smoke-tainted grapes.

Finally, chlorinated phenolic molecules are the precursors to the production of TCA (cork taint). Although TCA is not considered an aromatic phenol due to its modified structure, it is produced by a range of microbes when they are exposed to chlorinated phenolic molecules often found in wood preservatives or bleached wood products.

Nonflavonoid Phenols

The nonflavonoid phenols are phenolic molecules that do not have the structure of the flavonoids. Some of the most important molecules in this category are a group of organic acids known as hydroxycinnamates. These acids are found in both red and white juices. They are easily oxidized and so can be an indication of oxygen exposure in a young must or wine. Hydroxycinnamates may also be broken into smaller molecules through the activity of spoilage microbes such as *Brettanomyces*, becoming aromatic phenols. Added enzymes may also convert hydroxycinnamates into aromatic phenols, so proper enzyme selection is important if commercial enzymes are added during crushing and pressing.

Other nonflavonoid phenols include stilbenoids, a family of molecules considered antioxidants and that have been studied for their potential health benefits. Resveratrol is the most famous molecule in the stilbenoid group. Stilbene levels increase with exposure to spoilage microbes and sunlight. Because of their correlation with sun exposure, and because sun exposure has a positive effect on many other wine quality parameters, resveratrol concentration is considered to be positively correlated with wine quality.

Flavonoids

Flavonoids are distinguished by their three-ring structure. This is where discussion of the more talked-about polyphenols, anthocyanin and tannins, begins to get interesting and complicated. There is a host of different molecules, with different properties, that originate from this base structure. The rings have a variety of different hydroxide (–OH) groups bonded in different positions, which lead to different physical properties (such as the appearance of color) and different reaction kinetics with other molecules in wine.

The base group may also be attached to one or more molecules of glucose, called "glycosylation," which, again, changes the name and reaction characteristics of the molecule. In addition, many of these molecules are often bonded together in oligomers (a few repeating units of structure) or polymers (many repeating units of the same or similar structures), which are also reactive and may add or subtract units or change structure. Finally, these molecules can react with other chemicals in the wine matrix, such as sulfur dioxide, hydrogen sulfide and other sulfur-containing molecules (thiols), and acetaldehyde, to either append these molecules onto the base flavonoid or to change the structure of the flavonoid and create other compounds. The variability of these molecules and their polymers, and the changes that occur in wines over time, make the study of wine processing impacts on flavonoid chemistry and the sensory impact of these changes quite challenging.

Next we'll dive into the flavonoid subgroups important for wine production and discuss the important chemistry of these diverse molecules.

Flavonols—Quercetin

Flavonols are a class of flavonoids that have the basic shape, but each particular molecule has added hydroxyl (–OH) units, and possibly glucose molecules, bonded onto the base ring structure. One of the most common flavonols in wine is quercetin. It acts as a sunscreen for grape berries by absorbing UV light. Thus this molecule, like the stilbenoids, shows increasing concentration in berries with increasing exposure to UV light. Flavonols are an important cofactor in the co-pigmentation of anthocyanins (discussed next), and may also contribute to color stability. There may be more to the story with flavonols and quality wine production, but research into this class of compounds and their impact on wine has been somewhat limited.

Anthocyanins

Anthocyanins, the color molecules in the flavonoid group, are colored because of the alternating single- and double-bonded carbon atoms in all three rings (in chemistry known as conjugate double bonds or conjugated pi bonds). There usually needs to be at least eight of these alternating single and double bonds for a compound to absorb color in the visible spectrum, so any disruption to the anthocyanin structure that disrupts the conjugate double bonds will cause the molecule to lose the ability to absorb visible light and appear colorless as a result.

Anthocyanins at typical wine pH levels can exist in several different forms, some colored and some colorless. The colored version of the compound is in equilibrium with several colorless forms, such that only about 25 percent of the total anthocyanin is typically in the colored form at wine pH. One of these colorless forms is caused by the addition of bisulfite ions to the middle ring, known as sulfite bleaching. This condition is temporary, and as bisulfite ions interact with other molecules in solution and become oxidized, the bisulfite will drop from the anthocyanin and the anthocyanin may revert to the colored form.

Early in the life of a wine, anthocyanins may be found as single molecules or in stacked arrangements with other anthocyanins and phenolic molecules to form "co-pigmented color." The ring structure of these compounds, and the tannin molecules discussed next, make them hydrophobic. This hydrophobicity favors these types of molecules clumping together into colloids, which is how the stacking of co-pigmentation might be imagined to occur. Co-pigmentation increases the depth of color beyond what would be expected from the individual anthocyanins alone, and also shifts the color hue to a slightly bluer color. As wine ages, anthocyanin molecules may be oxidized to colorless compounds; interact with acetaldehyde or pyruvic acid to form stable color; or polymerize with tannin molecules to become locked into what is termed "polymeric pigment." The molecules resulting from anthocyanin interaction with acetaldehyde or pyruvic acid are called pyranoanthocyanins and have several subgroups into which they may also be named (e.g., vitisins, pinotin). Pyranoanthocyanins are color shifted to a more brick red or slightly orange color, which is part of the reason older wines may take on this hue. Pyranoanthocyanins are relatively stable and are not bleached by sulfites. Anthocyanins that become locked into polymeric pigments are also stable from a color perspective, thus polymeric pigment is thought to be an important component for achieving long-term color stability.

Finally, the anthocyanins in hybrid grape cultivars are often different from the anthocyanins in *Vitis vinifera* grape cultivars. Hybrid wines may have up to 100 percent of their anthocyanins in a diglucoside form, which means there are two glucose molecules attached to the main flavonoid structure of the anthocyanin instead of the single glucose molecule in *vinifera* cultivars. This second glucose molecule appears to limit the ability of hybrid anthocyanins to form pyranoanthocyanins (one of the stable forms of color) and also greatly slows the reactions that incorporate anthocyanins into stable polymeric pigments. Couple this with the generally low level of tannin in hybrid red wines and it becomes clear that hybrid winemakers have an uphill battle in making deeply colored and color-stable wines.

Polyphenolic Monomers and Polymers—Tannin

The base structure of tannin in wine is usually described as the *catechin unit*. The catechin unit can act as a powerful, although somewhat slow, antioxidant, removing oxygen from the wine matrix and reacting with other molecules to produce a wide range of reaction products.

To make things complicated, a relatively small fraction of the total polyphenol content in grapes and wine exists in the catechin monomer form. More often, catechin is bonded to itself and other polyphenolic variants in groups from about 2 to 100 subunits in length. Catechin-based polymers have different sensory properties depending on the size of the tannin polymer. Large polymers interact with proteins in saliva, binding or precipitating the proteins and giving the feeling of roughness or dryness. Smaller polyphenols have lower astringent impact but can taste bitter. Tannin polymers are found primarily in the skins and seeds of grapes. The polymers in grape skin tend to be larger (3 to 83 subunits) than the polymers in grape seeds (2 to 16 subunits).

The sensory differences between seed tannins and skin tannins might suggest that skin tannin extraction should be encouraged and seed tannin extraction avoided. But seed tannin is important for properly structured reds, with tannin experts showing that as much as two-thirds of the total tannin in red wines is extracted from the seeds. That said, grape seeds contain an extraordinary amount of tannin, so crushing seeds to extract more tannin is definitely not a good idea.

The general ability to extract catechin and tannin from skins and seeds changes as the berry ripens and the seed coat hardens. Less ripe fruit tends to be higher in catechin monomer, not the polymeric form. There are also differences in the amount of catechin in different cultivars, including hybrid grapes. Catechin level in wine is a complicated matrix of the grape cultivar, the ripeness of the fruit, and the winemaking processes. In addition, tannin chemistry changes as the wine ages and oxidation reactions increase the size of tannin molecules and produces reaction products with other chemical components in the wine. Both catechin monomers and polymers may participate in the oxidation reactions and condensation reactions (reactions that form larger tannin polymers). These molecules are most reactive when they are first extracted, during fermentation and the early part of wine aging. The addition of oxygen in winemaking during these early stages

may actually encourage color stability and tannin polymerization into forms that are thought to be "softer" and "rounder" than the aggressive tannins in young wines.

Catechins also have a role to play in white wine production. Catechin levels have been linked to the level of yellowing and browning during aging of white wines. Catechin appears to form linkages with nonflavonoid phenol molecules, and other catechin molecules, which eventually lead to large molecules with enough conjugate double bonds to absorb visible light. Catechin levels in white wines are much lower than reds because whites are pressed immediately. However, there can still be enough catechin, especially in hybrid grapes, to cause issues with premature yellowing and browning.

Research has shown that other parameters in wine, like sweetness, acidity, and ethanol level, can affect the perception of tannin. There is much still to learn regarding these complex polyphenolic molecules and how humans perceive them in a mixture as complicated as wine.

Enzymes

It is enzymes in the yeast cells that facilitate the conversion of sugar to ethanol and carbon dioxide. Enzymes in certain bacteria strains catalyze the conversion of malic acid to lactic acid in malolactic fermentation. Even before fermentation begins, enzymes in the ripening grapes produce the color, aroma, and flavor compounds that will later define the wine. There are also some problematic enzymes natural to grapes and wine. Polyphenol oxidases, or PPOs, are the enzymes in grapes (and other fruits) that facilitate browning on exposure to air. Preventing those reactions, especially in white juice or must, depends on excluding oxygen, since the enzymes are present.

Winemaking Enzymes

Because enzymes act in different ways on different targets, there is no single "enzyme treatment" for home wine use. Purposes for adding enzymes include improved juice yield from the must, better clarification, easier filtration, better release and stabilization of red wine color, release of aroma compounds (especially in aromatic white varieties), and prevention of malolactic fermentation. Let's look more closely at some of these enzymes.

Pectinate

Pectic enzymes break down pectins in fruit. Pectins are polysaccharides (polymers of sugar molecules) that exist in the middle layer of plant cell walls. Most prominently for our purposes, they help hold together and give structure to the cell walls of grapes. As grapes ripen, natural pectic enzymes (pectinase and pectin esterase) break down some of these pectins, allowing cells to move apart and causing the fruit to soften. During maceration of red or white must after crushing, natural pectinases are further breaking down cell tissue and helping release free-run juice. Adding appropriate dosages of commercially prepared pectic enzymes will enhance that process and improve yield.

An additional benefit from pectinase additions is better clarification of juice and more reliable settling. Particularly if you crush and press white grapes, then allow the juice to settle to rack off before fermentation, your yield will gain two benefits from enzyme use: more juice at the press and more compact fruit lees when you settle. Commercial products consisting primarily of pectic enzymes include Scottzyme PEC 5L and LAFAZYM CL. Some of the pectinase enzyme preparations also contain cellulases and hemicellulases that act on other plant polysaccharides. Cellulose and hemicellulose are structural polymers in plant cell walls and woody plant material. Enzymes that break down those compounds will improve juice yield and filterability. Lallzyme EX is one of the preparations specifically noted as containing hemicellulases for action on grape cell walls.

As known by any home winemaker who has pressed red wine, a great deal of color is left in the skins following maceration, fermentation, and pressing. Some conventional winemaking techniques, such as cold soaking before fermentation or extended maceration after, are done to improve extraction and stabilization of these colors. Enzymes can also be used for similar purposes. The same Lallzyme EX, Scottzyme Color Pro, or similar pectinase products that may assist with juice yield and clarification can also help release anthocyanins for better color. They also help release other wine phenolic components and tannins, generally benefiting the wine with enhanced mouthfeel and a smoother character on the palate.

Beta Glucanase

Beta glucans form another group of polysaccharides that may inhibit juice or wine settling and may cause difficulty during filtering. In grapes with significant amounts of rot, there may be enough glucan secreted by spoilage molds such as *Botrytis* that routine wine processing becomes difficult. For these conditions, beta glucanase enzymes can break down the problematic polysaccharides and help clarify the wine or juice.

Glycosidase and Glucosidase

Aromatic white wines often contain terpenes, a large class of aromatic hydrocarbons. In grape varieties such as Gewürztraminer or Muscat one may find compounds like linalool with a floral and spicy scent and geraniol with rose-like notes. Some fraction of these aroma compounds present in the grapes will be bound to a sugar molecule, forming odorless glycosides. (When the sugar in question is glucose, the compound is a glucoside. General glycosides may involve any sugar type.) Although some of the glycosides will degrade naturally during maceration or fermentation, others may be lost with the pomace or remain bound in the wine and never manifest their aroma signature. To assist the development and release of aromas, enzyme preparations that contain glucosidases are available. If they also contain pectinases, they assist with juice yield, clarification, and filterability while helping release characteristic varietal aromas.

Note that some such products, such as Lallzyme Cuvée Blanc, are intended as macerating enzymes for use before fermentation. When formulated just as glucosidases, as with Scottzyme BG, they are, instead, used in wine after fermentation to help release remaining terpenes that are present but sugar-bound and therefore not perceptible by smell. Products like this are inhibited by high sugar levels and should not be used in the fruit must before fermentation.

Lysozyme

A completely different use of added winemaking enzymes is the use of lysozyme to inhibit, prevent, or stop malolactic fermentation (MLF). Lysozyme is a naturally occurring enzyme that has the specific antimicrobial activity of attacking the cell wall of gram-positive bacteria and killing them. (Endogenous lysozyme also occurs in human tears, protecting the eyes against gram-positive pathogens.) Winemaking lysozyme preparations, like Lallemand Lyso-Easy or Laffort Lysozym, are extracted from hen egg whites and are intended for use at several stages of winemaking. Lysozyme has no effect on gram-negative bacteria, such as *Acetobacter*, the primary source of VA spoilage. Nor is it effective against spoilage yeast such as *Brettanomyces*, so it in no way replaces the need for regular use of sulfites in clean winemaking. It is, however, highly effective against *Oenococcus oeni* (used in malolactic fermentation) and other lactic acid bacteria. In stuck or sluggish fermentations, it can be added to reduce spoilage bacteria populations that may be inhibiting yeast (exercise caution with potentially low-color reds like Pinot Noir, as a lysozyme addition may cause color to drop out). After primary fermentation, lysozyme can be added to delay or prevent the start of malolactic fermentation. It can be removed later if the winemaker wishes to proceed with MLF.

Using Enzymes

As noted earlier, enzymes are proteins so they can be fined out of wine just like any other protein. Bentonite is commonly used to remove proteins and help insure stability against protein haze formation. Because of their mutual antagonistic effects, enzymes and bentonite should not be added together. If a juice-clarification enzyme has done its work, the later addition of bentonite before fermentation may aid further clarification; it will also stop the work of the enzyme. If aroma-releasing enzymes have been employed in fermented white wine, it may be desirable to fine with bentonite to reduce the risk of a protein haze from added enzymes. This is also important in wines treated with lysozyme against bacterial spoilage or to prevent MLF. Whether the goal has been just to delay MLF or to prevent it entirely, bentonite fining after lysozyme can prevent protein haze or prepare the wine for inoculation with a selected MLF product.

You will need to further consult the manufacturer's tech sheet on your chosen product to assess the dose, method, and timing of the addition. Some of the products are dry granular materials. These are usually quite stable and need only cool, dry storage to maintain a good shelf life. Others are liquid preparations that may be subject to more

Specialized enzymes may be used to improve yield and quality in many ways.

rapid degradation. Buy fresh products at the time of each harvest to meet your specific objectives and in quantities that will be consumed in that year's production. Dose requirements vary greatly.

Wine Gas

When winemakers talk about "inert gases," they are not referring to the "noble gases" of the periodic table. Instead, winemakers consider the inert gases to include argon, nitrogen, and carbon dioxide (carbon dioxide is not really inert—more on that later). Beer gas—a blend of nitrogen and carbon dioxide—comes up in winemaking talk as well. As the name suggests, it is most commonly used by brewers (usually for dispensing beers "on nitro"), but it has a use in wineries as well. The gases used in winemaking serve mostly to prevent or minimize oxidation of wine.

For some winemaking applications, one or another of these inert gases may be clearly superior. For others, you may be able to make substitutions. After we consider the characteristics of these four gases, we will review their principal uses. In roughly the order they might come up during a winemaking cycle, we will look at cold soaking, extended maceration, container purging, wine transfer, sparging, bottling, carbonating, and dispensing.

Argon

Argon (Ar) is the lone noble gas of the periodic table used in winemaking. It is resistant to all chemical reactions and is denser than atmospheric air, giving it an advantage in filling vessels or displacing a layer of air. It has a density of about 1.78 g/L, compared with air at about 1.29 g/L. To use argon in your winery, you will need a compressed gas cylinder, a pressure regulator, and various hoses and fittings. A common size for home use is a 19-cubic-foot (538-L) cylinder, named for the volume of gas upon release at atmospheric pressure. The cylinder is about 14 inches (36 cm) tall and $5^{1}/_{4}$ inches (13.3 cm) in diameter. Argon, nitrogen, and beer gas use an

Regulators for argon, nitrogen, and beer gas are interchangeable, but a different regulator is required for carbon dioxide tanks (shown on page 155).

inert gas regulator with a connection designated CGA #580 by the Compressed Gas Association. Such a regulator can be used interchangeably on those three gases. Fermentation supply stores and welding gas outlets sell tanks and fittings.

Nitrogen

Nitrogen (N_2), the diatomic gaseous form of nitrogen, is what we are considering here. As a winemaking gas, it is unreactive and works well in many "inert" applications. For inert gas use, molecular nitrogen can be used at a lower cost for most of the same purposes as argon. The gas in contact with juice or wine does not spontaneously react with any other constituents. One drawback for nitrogen in blanketing or inerting operations is its density is slightly lower than air: 1.25 g/L for nitrogen versus the 1.29 g/L for air. It mixes easily with air and dissipates quickly.

Nitrogen is distributed in the same cylinders as argon and uses the same regulator.

Carbon Dioxide

Although it is used for many of the same oxygen-displacement purposes as argon and nitrogen, carbon dioxide (CO_2) is not inert. In contact with water or wine, some molecules combine with water according to the reaction:

$$CO_2 + H_2O \longrightarrow H_2CO_3$$

From there, a fraction of the resulting compound dissociates like this:

$$H_2CO_3 \longrightarrow HCO_3^- + H^+$$

H+ lets us know that hydrogen ions are present: an acid-forming reaction. In solution, carbon dioxide is sometimes called carbonic acid. Unreacted molecular carbon dioxide remains dissolved as well. Rising temperature or agitation causes gas to leave solution. Wines with noticeable carbon dioxide are considered spritzy, petillant, or sparkling. If you do not want spritzy wine, you must be careful in your use of carbon dioxide as your "inert gas." It has one clear advantage in its density of 1.98 g/L, making it the heaviest of the winemaking gases. CO_2 condenses to a liquid when pressurized in a cylinder. As a result, cylinders are sold by weight rather than nominal volume. Most common for home use is a 5-pounds (2.3-kg) cylinder that is about the same size as the 19–cubic-foot (538-L) cylinders argon and nitrogen come in and costs less than the other choices. Because the contents are in liquid form, a CO_2 cylinder must be kept upright in use, presenting only headspace gas to the regulator. If liquid CO_2 were to enter the regulator, its sudden evaporation would damage the equipment. CO_2 requires a specific CO_2 regulator that cannot be used with the other gases mentioned.

Beer Gas

This blend of nitrogen and carbon dioxide is most commonly found in a ratio of 75 percent nitrogen and 25 percent carbon dioxide. For winemaking, beer gas is used for the same purposes as the other inert gases. In contact with wine, some carbon dioxide will dissolve, but not usually enough to carbonate the wine or make it "sparkling." Blends with a higher carbon dioxide ratio are available, but they offer no particular advantage to the home winemaker. Because nitrogen does not condense to a liquid under pressure, the tank and regulator for beer gas are the same high-pressure equipment as for nitrogen or argon. The cost is a small price advantage over argon or nitrogen.

What Else You'll Need

Once you have purchased a full cylinder of your chosen gas and the appropriate regulator, you will need some other hardware. Most regulators have an on-off valve already fitted. Have one installed if yours does not. You will also need to buy some beverage-grade tubing that fits your regulator. Between 5 and 10 feet (1.5 and 3 m) works well for most, but consider your winery layout. If you intend to use your gas for sparging wine (more on this later), efficiency will be improved if you buy a fritted stainless-steel sparging stone. A hose-end spring-loaded squeeze valve may be convenient. You may add other fixtures, like quick disconnects, inline valves, or a flow meter.

The cylinders described here are small and portable, but keep them secure to prevent falling over, breaking off a valve, and causing a dangerous sudden release of pressure.

Before addressing specific applications, a *note of caution*: Just as these gases displace oxygen in fermentation vessels, they displace air in a room. Use only in very well ventilated spaces or outdoors to avoid a risk of asphyxiation.

Gas Uses in Winemaking
Cold Soaking and Extended Maceration

These two techniques use inert gas in the same way. In both, your juice or wine is at risk for oxidation, browning, and development of aldehydes. To minimize those risks, you can blanket the headspace with an inert gas.

Carbon dioxide is heavier than air and cheaper than the other winemaking gases, so it is a good choice for this application. All three of the other gases discussed here will work well too, but the light weight of nitrogen will cause it to dissipate more rapidly. Blended beer gas is likely to stay in the fermenter a bit better and poses no risk of carbonation as the wine is still in the very early stages of production.

For either technique, put a tank lid or heavy plastic sheet over the fermenter with the fruit or must in it. Run a hose from your gas regulator under or through the cover, set your regulator to 5 to 10 psi (35 to 70 kpa), and make sure there is an opening in the cover to let displaced air and excess gas out. Open the valve for a minute or two. If you have a flow meter fitted, calculate the volume of headspace in your fermenter and run twice that volume for the purge. This should give you reasonable protection for 24 hours. Renew the inert gas layer daily.

Purging/Flushing

Container purging, also called "flushing," is similar to must blanketing. The goal is to use inert gas to displace the atmospheric air in a carboy, tank, or barrel so oxygen contact is minimized when wine is transferred into it. Early in the fermentation cycle, carbon dioxide is a good choice for this due to its density and cost. Excess CO_2 is not a problem as the wine is already high in dissolved carbon dioxide at an early stage.

In this operation, place the end of the hose near the bottom of the vessel and open the valve. Flush a 5- or 6-gallon (19- or 23-L) carboy for 30 seconds or so. With a flow meter, three to four volumes of gas is ideal to reduce the residual oxygen level to less than 1 percent. For a larger vessel, like a 200-liter (52-gallon) variable-capacity tank, the gas used in three volume changes is substantial. At 3×200 liters, or 600 liters total, you would need more than the entire volume of a 19–cubic-foot (538-L) argon, nitrogen, or beer gas cylinder. With the larger volume of a 5-pounds (44–cubic-foot, 1,250-L) CO_2 tank, you would use about half a full cylinder. As with blanketing, make sure there is an adequate opening for displaced air and excess gas to escape while purging.

Transferring Wine

The use of inert gas in wine transfer is an extension of purging. Purge the receiving vessel, initiate your siphon or pump, and slowly bleed inert gas into the headspace of the source vessel to prevent air from entering as the wine is drawn out. You can check this by holding a lit match above the opening of the vessel being emptied and make sure the flame is extinguished by an excess of gas flowing out. That assures that air is not getting in.

Another transfer technique is to pressurize the full container. **Do not pressurize glass carboys**. PET plastic carboys can be pressurized enough to move wine. A transfer system for such carboys can be assembled easily from supplies found at most home winemaking shops. With everything arranged, start with your regulator knob backed all the way out so no pressure is being delivered. Be careful not to over pressurize the carboy! With the regulator set to zero, open the main cylinder valve, then slowly turn the regulator knob, raising the pressure until the wine begins to flow. Do not exceed 5 psi (35 kpa). When all

the wine has been moved and gas enters the racking cane, turn off the flow and disconnect. (If you are processing more than one vessel, you can transfer the water or sanitizer to the next one in line, reusing it instead of pouring it down the drain.)

Sparging

To remove unwanted dissolved gases from your wine, you may sparge with inert gas. Common nuisance gases targeted for removal are excess carbon dioxide, oxygen, and hydrogen sulfide. The technique involves placing your gas hose outlet near the bottom of the container, opening the top, and running gas bubbles through the wine. As the bubbles rise in the liquid, some of the target gas will transfer to the bubbles and exit. Finer bubbles allow better gas-to-liquid contact, so a fritted sparging stone, available at home winemaking suppliers, will make the operation more efficient.

Bottling

Some of the previously discussed operations may be combined to assist in bottling your wine with less risk of oxidation. Attach a plastic single-bottle–type filler to a hose from your regulator. Gently open the regulator to a very low pressure, like 1 or 2 psi (7 or 14 kpa). As you are ready to fill each bottle with wine, push the bottle filler against the bottom for a few seconds to purge the bottle. As the bottles are filled, slowly add inert gas to the headspace of the bulk container to minimize oxygen transfer on that end. If you use a three-spout or five-spout bottle filler, you can install a fitting with a hose barb in the lid to allow continuous flushing while bottling. For this use, argon and nitrogen are preferred as adding carbon dioxide at bottling may change the wine. Just before corking, you can shoot a puff of inert gas into the bottle's headspace.

Serving on Draft

If you serve your wine on draft instead of bottling, you have one more use for inert gas. If you use carbon dioxide, your wine will become carbonated, and you will have sparkling wine on tap. This can be a fun and easy way to create a sparkling wine, but

A simple setup for serving wine from a keg requires a keg, a tap, and a CO_2 tank.

you can also dispense still wine on tap by using argon or nitrogen. For either system, you will be dipping into the brewer's side of your local fermentation store. Originally manufactured as soda syrup tanks before the advent of bag-box packaging, 5-gallon (19-L) stainless-steel kegs are still produced and may be used for draft wine. Just be sure that if you plan to serve wine through a faucet, components need to be either stainless steel or plastic. Brass components should not be used as the low pH of wine will cause the brass to leach into the wine.

For sparkling wine, you'll need to keep the keg in a refrigerator, typically at 36°F to 40°F (2°C to 4°C) and 10 to 45 psi (70 to 310 kpa), to assure adequate dissolved gas for a pleasant sparkling wine. For

still wine, argon and nitrogen do not significantly dissolve in the wine so you can chill white or rosé wine if you want or just leave the keg at room or cellar temperature for red wines. With any of the inert gases pushing the wine, you do not need to be concerned about oxidation as the gas pressure in the keg keeps air out.

The same technique described earlier for purging a carboy can also be used for a keg to minimize air exposure during transfer. Fill the keg with clean water or sanitizer, snap an "out" fitting on the appropriate port with a hose to drain, attach your gas, and flush. If your wine is in a PET carboy, you can then push it into the keg in the same manner.

Chapter 8:
Rosé All Day,
Sparkling by Night

To this point, we have largely focused on making red and white table wines. But let's take a closer look at two additional wine styles: rosé table wines and sparkling wines made using the méthode ancestrale process. Both of these wine styles are delicious to drink and relatively easy to accomplish at the home-winemaking scale with the same equipment used to make red and white wines.

Rosé

Rosé wines are extremely popular—and for good reason. Quite simply, rosé is easy to make, quick to bottle, and delicious to drink with almost any food (or none at all). Rosé is also a fantastic way to make a drinkable wine from underripe fruit in a cold or short vintage. There are a few popular approaches to making these pink wines that we'll explain, including through direct pressing, saignée, and blending or co-fermenting white and red grapes.

Direct Press and Cold Maceration

Popular in Provence, France, the direct press or cold maceration rosé production method results in fresh, pale-pink wines primed for drinking young. In this protocol, whole red grapes are chilled before crushing, which limits extraction of texturally rough phenolic compounds during the maceration step. Once the fruit has been sufficiently chilled, it is crushed either to the press or a holding vessel. The must is then held for up to 24 hours before pressing. The amount of time the must is allowed to soak with skins is at the discretion of the winemaker and has a direct impact on the color, aroma, and texture of the resulting wine, as extended maceration time will amplify the amount of pigments, aromatic precursors, and tannins extracted.

Direct pressing (no soak time whatsoever) may be employed with color-rich grape varieties to maintain a classic, pale hue, but it may also be used to produce vin gris—an ultra-pale form of rosé that is often indistinguishable from white wine. Darker grape varieties like Marquette, Noiret, Vincent, Chambourcin, Saperavi, and Alicante Bouschet have such concentrated pigment that extended soak time often results in wines that more closely resemble reds—pressing directly following the crush limits extraction and allows for the production of rosés with the familiar pink coloration. Less pigmented varieties, like Pinot Noir or Lemberger, may be used to produce vin gris—though whole cluster pressing is advised if that's the goal.

Some cold maceration may be applied with grape varieties where color isn't as concentrated, or more textural and aromatic complexity is desired. In this case, the soak time may be adjusted to suit the stylistic aims of the finished product. For cultivars with richer phenolic profiles, like Cabernet Sauvignon or Tempranillo, a shorter maceration interval of less than 12 hours can be used to keep the resultant wine lean and fresh. For lighter varieties, like Pinot Noir, or where some herbal complexity is desired—as with the classic Provençal varieties Grenache and Mourvèdre—a longer maceration of greater than 12 hours may be desired.

When sourcing fruit for direct press or cold maceration, a few key harvest parameters must be considered. Given the fresher, more acid-driven profile of wines produced in this style, it may be advantageous to harvest the fruit a few weeks before phenological ripeness. This allows the winemaker to prioritize bright acidity and lower potential alcohol with the foreknowledge that unpleasant, underripe phenolic compounds will be largely excluded. In addition to fruit chemistry, attention must be paid to fruit cleanliness.

Saignée

French for "to bleed," saignée is a technique by which liquid is removed from a red wine fermentation to increase the ratio of skin to liquid in the fermentation vessel, allowing for more concentration in the resultant red wine. The removed fraction, however, may be fermented to produce rich, age-worthy, dry rosés. In this method, red grapes are crushed into a fermentation vessel where they'll soak for several hours, or even days, before the removal of some juice—generally 10 to 20 percent of the total volume. Unlike the cold maceration method, it may be advantageous for fermentation to start before the bleeding process, as the natural capping that occurs in red wine fermentation actually serves to streamline the separation of liquid from pulp. If you do choose to

pursue a post-inoculation saignée, be aware that it places some limits on the amount of control you'll have over the process. The wine will already be in the throes of fermentation, so techniques like cold settling your juice, adjusting its composition, or inoculating with a different yeast strain than your red ferment will become difficult, if not impossible.

The separated bleed wine produced via saignée may be fermented on its own—perfect for lighter varieties like Pinot Noir or red hybrids like Marechal Foch—or blended into white juice or wine, an excellent use of the drained fraction from richer reds like Cabernet Sauvignon or Syrah.

When working in the saignée tradition, the harvest parameters should be scaled to the goals of the desired red wine more than the rosé fraction. In this case, winemakers should prioritize phenological ripeness over acidity, as the concentration process will amplify the phenolic and aromatic content of the finished red wine. If more acid or a fresher flavor profile is desired in the rosé portion, it can always be blended with a fresher, more acid-driven wine to advance that aim.

Co-Fermentation and Blending

Maybe the simplest and most accessible way to produce dry rosé is by co-fermentation or post-fermentation blending of red and white grape varieties. This technique doesn't require intervention at any of the fruit processing steps, so it's a viable option for aspiring pink winemakers who haven't invested in crush equipment. In co-fermentation, red and white grape varieties may be processed together or blended post-pressing/draining, then allowed to ferment together, producing wine with the classic rosé color.

This co-fermentation strategy is popular in France's other rosé destination, Tavel, where saignée is often blended with less extracted rosé or even white grape juice before fermentation to produce rich, age-worthy pink wines.

Co-fermentation is an excellent way to add more complex, floral dimensions to dry rosé, by leveraging aromatic white grape varieties such as Traminette, Grüner Veltliner, or Gewürztraminer as blending bases. There are no hard and fast rules about the white-to-red juice ratio in this method, but the white portion ought to make up the bulk of the wine's volume, as a little bit of red can go a long way.

Co-fermentation is also an excellent way to use heavier press fractions of white wine juice: the rounder, more phenolic heavy-press juice that may not be ideal for a varietal Riesling or Chardonnay can be used to make compelling rosé with the addition of a little bit of Cabernet Franc or Marquette.

Blending may also be performed post-fermentation, but that can be challenging as finished red and white wines are often more difficult to harmonize. As is often the case in winemaking, early intervention tends toward more integrated, soulful wines; blending for rosé is no exception.

Fermentation Parameters

Once the juice is ready for fermentation—owing its pink color to maceration, saignée, or blending—the ideal vinification parameters closely resemble those for white wines. Fermenting rosés at cooler temperatures (55°F to 70°F [13°C to 21°C]) ensures the preservation of fresh fruit aromatic profiles. A variety of yeast strains may be chosen to flesh out the desired style of the finished product, but strains recommended for use in both red and white wine ferments are often the most effective for producing dry rosé.

Malolactic fermentation can be an effective tool for shaping acid profiles and promoting richness in rosé wines, where desired. For wines produced in the saignée method, where the concentration of phenolic compounds is higher, some acid management may be necessary to smooth out rough textural edges. If malolactic fermentation is pursued for this purpose, it may be beneficial to select a bacterial strain with limited diacetyl production, as the buttery aromatic compound can intrude on some of the more delicate elements of these wines.

Aging Considerations

Aging protocols for dry rosés are as varied as the wines themselves—the stylistic trajectories of wines produced from each of the previously enumerated

Saignée is a French term for taking juice from a red must during the early stages of fermentation to make a more concentrated red wine. The juice that is removed can then be used to make a rosé wine.

methods require different aging times, vessels, and treatments. Though much of rosé production closely resembles white winemaking, there are some unique considerations that must be weighed in order to properly respect its trademark pink hue.

For rosés where freshness is prioritized—as with those produced from direct pressing, cold maceration, and white-heavy blending—a quicker-to-bottle approach is desirable. These methods limit phenolic extraction, meaning that the resultant rosés are not only less protected against oxidation, but also not tannic enough to require long-term bulk aging. Wines produced in this style benefit from early racking to limit lees contact and bulk storage in neutral, reductive containers like well-topped glass carboys—this preserves aromatic freshness and lively acidity. It's not uncommon for dry rosé to be one of the first wines of a vintage to be bottled; the typical turnaround from harvest to bottling is generally in the range of 3 to 5 months, timing them perfectly for spring sipping.

Richer saignée or co-fermented rosés may require a bit more bulk aging than their cold macerated counterparts. The increased phenolic content of these wines often leads to wines that are awkward in their youth—clunky in both texture and aroma. In these cases, extended lees contact may be an effective method of harmonizing acid and tannin. Additionally, bulk aging in breathable vessels like Flextanks or used oak barrels may help round out some of the rougher tannic edges.

The unique chemical composition of dry rosé wine requires that care be taken to preserve its color. In red wines, red-pigmented anthocyanin molecules stabilize themselves to tannins, creating a color that persists against the myriad treatments and chemical changes that may occur over the lives of those wines. In rosés, however, the limited concentration of tannin leaves unstable anthocyanins, sensitive to fining, filtration, and sulfite additions. If you choose to employ fining or filtration in the production of rosé, be aware that color will be lost at each of these steps: limiting their use where possible is the clearest way to preserve it. Unstabilized anthocyanins also respond dramatically to the addition of sulfites—a bleaching effect that is enough to send even the most experienced winemakers into a panic. However, this bleaching is reversible and the pink coloration is likely to return in the days and weeks following the addition.

Méthode Ancestrale (Pétillant Naturel) Sparkling Wine

Hobby winemakers have a host of ways to make sparkling wine at home, including méthode Champenoise (traditional Champagne), charmat method (Italian sparkling), méthode ancestrale (pétillant naturel, or pét-nat for short), and forced carbonation. Each has its quirks, benefits, and drawbacks. Although méthode Champenoise is considered the gold standard in sparkling wine, it is also the most difficult and labor-intensive. Pét-nat is enjoying growing commercial success, but it's a style that is particularly well suited to home winemaking. With careful attention to a few key parameters, winemakers of varying experience levels can produce layered, lively, naturally sparkling wines without the extended time, effort, or equipment investments required to produce wines via méthode Champenoise or forced carbonation.

The term "pétillant naturel" (pét-nat) couldn't be a much simpler or fitting name—it's French for "naturally sparkling." Pét-nat wine is made through a very simple process, called méthode ancestrale, in which wine is bottled before the end of alcoholic fermentation and is ready to enjoy as soon as it reaches completion.

Every winemaker understands that one of the byproducts of fermentation is carbon dioxide. When crafting still wine, the racking and agitation that occur before packaging all but ensure the finished product will be bubble-free. But, if you ferment in a sealed vessel and don't allow the gas to escape, the wine gains delightful effervescence. This is the essential step in the production of naturally sparkling wines: allowing fermentation to occur without an opportunity to vent carbon dioxide, thereby forcing the gas into solution.

There are several metrics and protocols that may be used to maximize the quality of pét-nat—the most important are juice chemistry, fermentation management, and bottling protocol. But before discussing the ideal chemical parameters for pét-nat production, it makes sense to talk about some grape varieties that are particularly well suited to this unique style. Although pét-nat may be made from anything bottled before completing fermentation, varieties that showcase bright acidity, less phenolics, and lower alcohol tend to make the most compelling wines. *Vinifera* varieties such as Riesling, Albariño, and Pinot Noir are fantastic when produced in this style, but this is an avenue where hybrid and native cultivars, like Catawba, Diamond, and Marquette, really shine.

Juice Chemistry

In general, the juice characteristics that lead to a high probability of success in sparkling wine production are as follows:

High acid
Low tannin
Adequate YAN
Low sugar (17 to 19°Brix for Champagne-style wines)

In pét-nat, these ideal parameters hold true, with the exception of starting sugar, which has a lower target range unless the winemaker hopes to leave behind some sweetness. Let's look more closely at each of these parameters.

High Acid

If bubbles are the heart of any great sparkling wine, acid is the soul. Effervescence and acidity have a synergistic relationship: carbonation slightly acidifies wine and acid helps integrate carbonation in a harmonious way. In most commercial sparkling

wine production, grapes are selected for their acidity and are often harvested before reaching ripeness in an effort to retain this acid. A TA between 8 and 12 g/L tartaric acid is usually a good starting point for pét-nat.

Tannin

Although acid is a welcome and necessary component in pét-nat, the same cannot be said for tannin. Tannins interact with effervescence and acid to amplify astringency. Some tannin is unavoidable and can even lend some weight to the mouthfeel of the finished wine, but an excess of tannin will lead to a wine with less than desirable flavor and texture. Tannin extraction can be minimized by limiting the contact time between crushing and pressing, and by separating free-run juice from heavier press fractions. Not all home winemakers are equipped to process their own fruit, so these preventive steps may not be available. In that case, an assessment of the juice's tannins is necessary. The clearest way to do this in the home winery is by tasting the juice.

If the juice is judged to be overly astringent, excess tannin may be removed via protein fining with agents like egg white, skim milk, or gelatin.

YAN

The YAN of juice is the chemical parameter that most affects fermentation health. YAN requirements vary greatly across yeast strains and fermentation conditions. It's a lot to think about, but for the fermentation protocol that will be detailed later, 100 to 200 ppm is, generally, the right neighborhood.

Sugar

Although the méthode traditionnelle ideals for acid, tannin, and nitrogen hold true for pét-nat, there's definitely wiggle room on the starting sugar level—that metric can shift based on the desired effervescence, residual sugar, and alcohol of the finished product. There is a direct relationship between sugar content and the amount of alcohol and carbon dioxide produced by fermentation, both of which are critical to the character of pét-nat.

In sparkling wines, an excess of alcohol has much the same effect as an excess of tannin—producing a hot, disconnected wine that is unpleasant from both a flavor and textural standpoint. Ideally, sparkling wines will end up somewhere between 9 and 12.5 percent alcohol, with traditional pét-nats skewing toward the low end of that range. Given that one can expect between 0.5 and 0.6 percent alcohol for every degree of Brix fermented, that places the ideal starting sugar range in the 15 to 25°Brix for sparkling wines.

There is, however, one factor that may affect this range: residual sugar. If the plan is to leave some sugar to balance the acidity of the finished wine, a quick calculation can be made to adjust the starting sugar accordingly. Pressure may be leveraged to arrest fermentation. When the internal pressure of the bottle approaches 6 atmosphere of pressure (ATM), the yeast are inhibited and fermentation stops, leaving any remaining sugar unfermented.

As 1 atmosphere of CO_2 may be produced from the fermentation of 4 g/L sugar, this generally requires between 2.4 and 3°Brix more than the desired residual sugar level at bottling; packaging the wine while the sugar measures greater than 3°Brix will ensure that some residual sugar is left behind.

Fermentation Management

At first glance, the name "pétillant naturel" might lead a winemaker to believe that the only correct way to produce these wines is a hands-off approach to fermentation, but that couldn't be further from the case. Although it is true that excellent pét-nats can be made using native yeasts and limiting intervention, an embrace of commercial yeasts, nutrients, and careful monitoring increases the probability that attempts to make these wines will be successful. The most critical aspect of méthode ancestrale winemaking is timing, and engineering a little bit of predictability into the process goes a long way toward recognizing and acting upon key moments in fermentation.

In sparkling wine production, the gold standard of commercial yeast strains is Lalvin's EC-1118. A classic Prise de Mousse strain, EC-1118 is incredibly hardy; its low nitrogen requirement, competitive factor, steady fermentation speed, compact settling, and cold tolerance are all welcome attributes in méthode ancestrale winemaking.

Even when using inoculated yeast, close attention must be paid to overall fermentation health. After méthode ancestrale wines are bottled, the fermentation conditions are less than ideal for even the most robust commercial yeast strains and can lead to a variety of faults, including sulfur off aromas and volatile acidity. Assessing YAN content before inoculation and adjusting as necessary with a complex yeast nutrient, such as Fermaid K, can help keep the fermentation clean through completion. For a hardy yeast strain such as EC-1118, an initial YAN of 100 to 200 ppm should be sufficient.

As the timing of bottling is critical for achieving desired pressure and/or residual sugar, careful monitoring of fermentation speed and temperature must be observed. Daily measurements of Brix and temperature can help the winemaker determine fermentation speed and adjust if necessary. If the fermentation appears to be proceeding too quickly, it may be slowed by chilling to between 50°F and 55°F (10°C and 13°C), giving the winemaker time to track sugar depletion and prepare for bottling. As fermentation begins to approach the target for bottling, a precision hydrometer becomes an indispensable tool for accurate monitoring.

Bottling Protocol

CO_2 is generated as fermentation proceeds. Unless the fermenting wine is bottled in a timely manner, the gas will escape, leaving a less-than-pétillant final product. Appropriate timing of bottling dictates the carbonation level and residual sugar of the finished wine. The winemaker will be well served to have a target effervescence and sweetness level in mind before initiating fermentation, but on-the-fly adjustments may be made with regard to balancing sweetness and acidity. Daily Brix analysis and tasting allow for tracking of fermentation health, balance, and speed. As mentioned in the section on juice chemistry, 4 g/L sugar generates roughly one atmosphere of CO_2, and fermentations may be arrested via pressure in the range of 6 atmospheres. This information can be weighed alongside the sweetness and effervescence targets to time bottling effectively.

An additional measure that may be taken to assist in timing bottling is to arrest the fermentation by chilling. If EC-1118 is used, chilling to between 35°F and 40°F (2°C and 4°C) when the Brix reading drops to within a degree of the target should be sufficient to stop further sugar depletion without killing the yeast. A secondary benefit of chilling the wine to arrest fermentation before bottling is tartrate stabilization.

The addition of riddling adjuvants may assist in the compact settling of spent yeast. Although there is a host of commercially available additives that may be used for this, standard-issue bentonite is equally effective. Adding a properly swelled bentonite suspension of 100 to 300 ppm before bottling will have a significant effect on the clarity and stability of the finished product.

A final consideration that needs to be made for safe and effective pét-nat production is the selection of proper bottles and closures. Crown caps are the preferred closure for wines of this style, as they are cost effective, simple to use, and hold pressure well. Corks may be used, but a wire cage is required to prevent them from pushing out of the bottles as they pressurize. **For safety reasons, pét-nat wines should always be bottled in punted Champagne bottles.** As the wine may reach pressures up to 6 atmospheres (assuming it was bottled at 2.4 to 3°Brix or higher), using a heavily reinforced bottle is the surest way to prevent a fun experiment in sparkling wine production from becoming a literal time bomb.

Following bottling, cellaring the wine at 50°F to 60°F (10°C to 16°C) for 1 to 2 months should be sufficient to allow for the fermentation to finish. The winemaker is advised to open the first few bottles over a sink or outdoors; for all the planning and attention to fermentation management, there is still an element of unpredictability to pét-nat, and unpredictability in sparkling wine usually means a mess.

Chapter 9:
Country Winemaking

Country wine is a term often applied to just about any wine made from something other than wine grapes. That most often means other fruits but may also include vegetables, flowers, roots, or herbs. There are many recipes out there and lots of techniques for these very diverse wines. We'll largely focus on making country wines beginning with fresh or frozen fruit, but know that there are other great options as well, and much of the same information related to fresh fruit applies. Options like juice, concentrate, and purée are especially important if you wish to make a fruit wine during a season or in a location where fresh fruit isn't available.

All-Fruit, Part-Fruit, and Fruit-Flavored Wines

When shopping, keep in mind the quality of concentrates and juices vary. There are sources of cold-pressed concentrates that are high quality and retain the complete expression of the aromas, flavors, and colors of the source fruit. If starting from juice, avoid those containing preservatives (sorbate, benzoate, and others). If you are able to source unfiltered, unpasteurized juice locally, that's the ideal choice. UV-treated or pasteurized juice can be used, but some argue that these treatments can negatively affect the final outcome.

Commercial fruit purées are available from a variety of vendors, produced from ripened fruit that has been washed, sorted, and, where needed, pitted and peeled. One benefit of using commercial purées is that there is no need to take an additional step to sterilize the juice before fermentation as long as the purée has been pasteurized and aseptically packaged. Preparing the fruit purée for fermentation involves combining the purée with filtered or reverse-osmosis water, sugar, and other ingredients before topping with yeast. Sugar, pectic enzyme, yeast nutrient, acid blend, and grape tannin, if needed, should be stirred into the water to dissolve and then the purée can be mixed in as well.

One 49–fluid ounce (1.4-L) can of purée is recommended per 1 gallon (3.8 L) of wine you aim to make. Once the juice is fully prepared, the pH, total acidity, and Brix can be measured and adjusted, if desired. The juice can also be tasted, and bench trials conducted, to help guide any adjustments in acidity. Since the purée is sterilized as part of the packaging process, you do not need to add potassium metabisulfite at this point, rather, the yeast can be sprinkled directly on top of the juice in the primary fermenter.

For those working with fresh or frozen fruits, once you have your source of fruit, there are two critical measurements with country wines that you'll need to figure out:

❖ How much sugar is needed to get the desired alcohol level

❖ How much fruit is required to offer a pleasing profile of aroma, flavor, and appearance

Because this range of wines is so diverse, let's address it in three categories: all-fruit, part-fruit, and fruit-flavored.

All Fruit

The all-fruit category is also typical of making wine from grapes. For white (or rosé) wines, juice is expressed from the fruit and then that juice is fermented into wine. For red wine, the stems of the grapes are removed and the fruit is usually crushed, then fermentation takes place on the combination of juice, pulp, skin, and seeds (which are sometimes partially removed during fermentation). The red wine is pressed off these solids after the sugar has fermented to alcohol.

For fruits other than grapes, either of these practices may be applied, if appropriate for that fruit. It is very common to make apple wine (or hard apple cider) from the juice of apples and to make pear wine (called perry) from the juice of pears. Some softer berries, such as very ripe blackberries, may be fermented as a crushed "must" with the pulp in the manner of red wine. Cider and perry are often produced with only the native fruit sugar, yielding an alcoholic beverage with beer-like alcohol levels of 5 to 8 percent by volume (ABV). With almost all other non-grape fruits or juices, some sugar will be needed to supplement the natural fruit sugar to achieve a wine-like alcohol level of 10 to 14 percent ABV. By our definition here, the "all-fruit" category has no water added.

Before apples are pressed, they must be run through a grinder to make the juice more accessible.

Part Fruit

This category of wine covers the bulk of the country wine recipes we commonly see. Typically a recipe for 5 gallons (19 L) of fruit wine made in this manner will call for 10 to 15 pounds (4.5 to 7 kg) of fruit and 5 to 12 pounds (2.3 to 5.4 kg) of sugar. This ratio seems to produce wines that strongly represent the fruit used but require much smaller amounts than an all-fruit version.

Observing the very large amounts of fruit needed, in some cases, for an all-juice wine, it is clear why many recipes go with the part-fruit ratio. There is a contribution from the fruit, but a great deal of the wine is made from added water and sugar. Sometimes macerated fruit is mixed directly with sugar and water, whereas other recipes have you ferment the fruit in a nylon mesh bag in a bucket of sugared water.

Fruit Flavored

In the fruit-flavored category, you might find fruits that are so low in sugar or in juice yield that they're impractical to use directly. For instance, limes with only 1.7 percent sugar in the juice and yielding only 4 to 5 fluid ounces (118 to 148 ml) of juice per pound would require a whopping 142 pounds (64 kg) of fruit to make 5 gallons (19 L) of wine and it would still need more than 8 pounds (3.6 kg) of sugar to reach 20°Brix. If you want a lime wine, you will probably opt to start with much less fruit and make a lime-flavored sugar wine. The same technique applies to herbs and vegetables that yield little or no sugar or juice, such as for dandelion wine or elderflower wine.

Adding Sugar

The best approach is to provide you with the calculations for determining sugar additions. You can also juice some of your fruit and measure the sugar content with a refractometer or hydrometer and determine the yield by weighing the fruit and measuring the volume of juice produced in a measuring cup or graduated cylinder. For the calculations here, we apply some basic assumptions. Since the data from the United States Department of Agriculture (USDA) for sugar content are listed in g/100 g, it is easy for a winemaker to make the calculations. As we know, °Brix is defined as "percent of sugar by weight," which is equivalent to g/100 g.

❖ **For all-fruit country wines**: You may try just the juice or juice plus pulp. For cider or perry, the fruit must be run through a grinder or mill and then pressed to release the juice. Specialized machinery is required for that; home cidermakers will often use an InSinkErator food waste grinder for this task. Other than lining a wine press with a nylon mesh bag, home winemaking shops do not typically carry juicers for other fruits and vegetables. If you want to ferment fruit juice, a home-style juicer may be your best bet.

❖ **For citrus fruits**: A juicer may have a knurled dome on which cut fruit halves are rotated. That can be done manually or with an electrically rotated model. Also for citrus, a lever-type press can squeeze half fruits.

❖ **For most other fruits (and many vegetables)**: You may choose from two basic juicer designs. Centrifugal juicers are the least expensive. They have an upright design, looking a bit like a food processor. Fruit is pushed into a mesh basket with sharp teeth on the floor. The teeth shred the fruit and the spinning basket separates the juice, allowing it to run out of a spout. The remaining pulp is ejected separately. More expensive juicers, sometimes called masticating juice extractors, use a single- or double-auger design to crush and squeeze fruit as it passes through the machine. Juice drains out of the underside of the delivery tube and the pulp is squeezed out at the end.

Even with a juicer, it takes a tremendous amount of fruit to make all-fruit country wines, so recipes often call for the addition of water and extra sugar in a part-fruit recipe.

All-Fruit Wine

Once you determine how much fruit you will need for a 100 percent juice fermentation and have measured the Brix of that juice, you can calculate the sugar needed to supplement (chaptalize) the juice using these equations:

lb. of sugar to add = (lb. of juice) × [(desired °Brix – actual °Brix)/100]

or,

kg of sugar to add = (kg of juice) × [(desired °Brix – actual °Brix)/100]

pure water) = 54 pounds (24 kg)

You can measure the volume directly, but to get pounds or kilograms, you need to know the density. To determine the specific gravity (SG) of your target juice blend, use a formula or calculator to convert from °Brix to SG:

lb. of juice = gallons of juice × 8.33 × SG

or,

kg of juice = L of juice × SG

Note that you will be considering the target specific gravity, that is, the density the juice will have after you add your sugar. That is because Brix is percent sugar by weight of the whole solution.

To calculate the sugar addition for a crushed-fruit must, estimate your eventual juice yield and then apply the formulas just listed. For wine grapes, we may estimate 6 gallons (23 L) of juice from 100 pounds (45 kg) of fruit. At 20°Brix, the SG is 1.083, so that 6 gallons (23 L) will weigh about:

[equation] 1.083 × 6 gallons × 8.33 pounds/gallon (for pure water) = 54 pounds (24 kg)

As a fraction then, by weight, juice makes up a bit more than half of the starting weight. With an estimate of the weight of fruit you need in hand, you can source the fruit and choose a fermenter to fit.

Part-Fruit Wine

For part-fruit winemaking, you may first do a calculation as though no sugar or juice will be contributed by the fruit. For such a "sugar wine," apply the same calculation for a solution with no initial sugar. For 5 gallons (19 L) of 20°Brix sugar "juice," you need about 9 pounds (4 kg) of sugar, and for 25°Brix, about 11 pounds (5 kg).

Once you have those figures, source as much fruit as you can reasonably handle. You may grow the fruit at home, buy it from a local farmers' market, pick it up in the grocery store produce department, or even buy it from the freezer case (but check for added sugar in that case).

As noted earlier, many recipes call for 10 to 15 pounds (4.5 to 7 kg) of fruit. Whatever amount you decide to use, calculate the sugar contribution from the fruit to your wine.

pounds of sugar from fruit = lb. of fruit × (g/100 g)/100

or,

kilograms of sugar from fruit = kg of fruit × (g/100 g)/100

For example, to use 15 pounds of bananas (USDA lists bananas at 12.2 percent sugar):

Multiply 15 × 12.2/100 = 1.83 lb. of sugar from the bananas

or,

6.8 kg × 12.2/100 = 0.83 kg of sugar (from bananas)

Subtract the fruit sugar from the total sugar you calculated to get the amount of sugar to add. For the banana example at 25°B:

11 lb. – 1.83 lb. = 9.2 lb. (rounded) to add (or, 5 kg – 0.83 kg = 4.17 kg to add)

Sugar Content, Juice Yield, and 5-Gallon (19-L) Juice Example Calculations

Fruit	Sugar, g/100 g[1]	Juice Yield, oz./lb.[2]	Sugar in Juice, g/100 g[1]	For 5 Gallons (19 L) Juice, lb.	
				Fruit	Sugar to 20°Brix
Apple	9.5–11	8–10	9.5	71	4.7
Apricot	9.2	NI	13	NI	3.2
Banana	12.2	NA	NA	NA	NA
Blackberry	4.5–5	8[3]	7.7	80	5.5
Blueberry	10	NI	NI	NI	NI
Cherry, sour	8.5	6–8	NI	91	NI
Cherry, sweet	12.8	6–8	NI	91	NI
Cranberry	4	4–8	12.1	107	3.6
Date, dried	63–66	NA	NA	NA	NA
Fig	16.2	NA	NA	NA	NA
Grapefruit	7	NI	8.8	NI	5.0
Guava	9	NI	13	NI	3.2
Kiwifruit	9–11	NI	NI	NI	NI
Lemon	2.5	4–6	2.5	128	7.9
Lime	1.7	4–5	1.7	142	8.2
Mango	13.7	NI	12.5	NI	3.4
Orange	8.5–9.5	6–8	8.4	91	5.2
Papaya	7.8	3	13.9	213	2.7

Peach	8.4	1–3	12–13	320	3.4
Pear	9.7	4–8	15	106	2.2
Pineapple	10	4–6	10	128	4.5
Plum	10	10.5[3]	NI	61	NI
Pomegranate	13.7	NI	12.6	NI	3.3
Raspberry	4.4	4–5	NI	142	NI
Strawberry	4.9	4–5	NI	142	NI
Watermelon	6.2	6-1-0	NI	80	NI

KEY:

NA = not applicable (i.e., no juice from dates)

NI = not enough information from a reliable data source

1 = USDA FoodData Central

2 = juice yield from: https://juicernet.com/average-juice-yields-for-fruits-vegetables/

3 = additional data from: http://www.brsquared.org.\wine/CalcInfo/FruitDat.htm

With a fruit like bananas, dates, or figs, where there will be little or no juice contribution, you will need to add water to make the entire volume of your finished wine (5 gallons [19 L]). For juicier fruits, consult the juice yield column in the table on page 175 and above, or juice a piece of fruit and measure your yield, and subtract the anticipated juice volume from the finished wine volume to calculate the amount of water to be added. For example, with papayas that yield 3 fluid ounces per pound (198 ml per kg):

---

15 lb. of fruit × 3 oz. = 45 oz. to subtract from 5 gallons
(6.8 kg × 198 ml = 1.34 L to subtract from 19 L)

Fruit-Flavored Wine

Calculations are even easier for fruit-flavored wines. If using fruits, vegetables, herbs, or flowers that provide little or no sugar and juice, simply do the calculation described earlier for a base "sugar wine" (see page 174). For very strongly flavored herbs, like basil or cilantro, you may want to use just a few ounces. For milder flavors, you may need to use much more to achieve a pleasing result. And the amount may depend on the specific flavoring you have and to meet your taste requirements. For example, recipes for elderflower wine may call for anywhere between 1 quart (1 L) of flowers in 5 gallons (19 L), to 1 quart (1 L) per gallon (3.8 L). Some experimentation may be needed to get these wines to meet your expectations.

With the basics of making country wine calculations understood, let's look at some of the most common fruits used to make delicious wines at home.

Berry Wines

R elative to grape wine, "berry wine" is a diverse category encompassing anything from strawberries and blueberries to less common berries native to only small pockets of the world. The general idea is the same as making red wine: *crush, ferment, press or strain, rack, age, and bottle.* The maceration step is done with berry wines for some of the same reasons as with red wines—to extract tannins and color. However, there is another reason to ferment berries on the skins that is even more important—because the skin contains most of the flavor, which will also be extracted during fermentation. If possible, bagging the fruit in a mesh nylon bag that can be pulled out of the fermenter is the easiest way to separate the fruit from the juice. Pull the bag shortly before fermentation is complete and give the bag a gentle squeeze so the juice drips back into the fermenter. This "pressing" will introduce some oxygen into the wine, which is why we recommend doing this step before fermentation is complete as the yeast will consume the oxygen, reducing the risk of oxidizing the wine.

Whereas grapes often need no other ingredients beyond the fruit itself and sulfites, additions such as water, sugar, and acid are critical to the success of berry wines. Another key to making berry wines (and many other fruit wines) is getting the most from the berries by breaking down the cell walls of the fruit. Freezing the fruit before maceration is one common technique that many berry winemakers employ for this reason. The addition of pectic enzymes can also help. Let's look a little closer at some of the most popular berry wines.

Strawberry

A key component of strawberry wine is coaxing the flavor from the berries while retaining that character and color. The pigments that color strawberries are not that robust and are prone to oxidative degradation. Adding some crushed red grapes or red grape concentrate can provide a more stable rosé hue. Strawberry wines are often crafted with a sweet character, but they don't need to be, and actually can be quite delicious when dry. Look for fruit that has received a great deal of sun exposure, allowing the berries to gain that vibrant red hue from anthocyanins.

With standard greenhouse-grown strawberries, you may find sugar at 9°Brix, which should provide a great base for a strawberry wine. With the TA at 9 g/L or higher, water dilutions may require an acid addition if pH started high. Sometimes a little strawberry flavoring extract can really make the wine pop.

Blueberry

One of the great aspects of blueberries is the polyphenolic load found in their skins that are close to typical wine grapes. These compounds help provide color and structure to blueberry wine. Blueberries are fairly high in sugar with ripe, high-quality fruit coming in at 14 to 18°Brix. Some red grape concentrate can be added to enhance the fruitiness and bring the Brix up to a more common wine range.

Raspberry

Raspberries can come in both red and black, and both types can be used for winemaking. Freezing the berries before working with them is a great help to pulverize each berry. Expect them to ripen to between 8 and 13°Brix with a TA between 10 and 20 g/L. Also note that pressing raspberries can be a challenge due to their mushy character at this point. Go slow or add rice hulls to separate the juice from the pulp.

Stone Fruit Wines

Stone fruits are categorized by the pits found in their core. Think cherry, apricot, plum, peach, mango . . . even olives are considered stone fruits. In botany, they are known as drupes, and the stone contains the seed whereas the outer flesh and sugar are what the plant uses to coax a member of the animal kingdom to eat it and spread its seed afar.

Pectic enzymes help winemakers extract the sugars from the cell walls of stone fruits, with a recommended addition rate of $1/2$ teaspoon per 1 gallon (3.8 L) of must, added when the fruit is crushed. Although this isn't a requirement, it is helpful to ensure a clearer wine in the end.

Acidity may also be an issue that you'll need to address. If you have the ability to test for pH, it is recommended for microbial stability issues. Targeting pH levels of 3.2 to 3.4 is a good starting point as most of these wines will have low to no polyphenols to help stabilize the wine. Malic acid is the main acid component of stone fruits, and it's recommended that you sulfite your wine after fermentation to suppress possible malolactic bacteria activity.

Cherry

Sour cherries (sometimes called tart cherries) are the preferred cherry type for making wine. Sugar levels in this category can range from 8 up to 22°Brix depending on variety and growing season. Total acidity typically ranges from 1.3 to 2.3 g/L. These numbers are a pretty good starting place for winemaking. Add the fact that cherries provide a modest level of polyphenols, and it is easy to make the case for why cherry wine is so popular.

Sweet cherries can also be used; the main difference between the two types is that sweet cherries have less acidity and a higher pH. If using fresh fruits, discard the pits *before fermentation* as cherry pits (and some other stone fruit pits) contain low concentrations of a compound that can be converted to toxic hydrogen cyanide.

Peach/Nectarine

Although generally lower in sugar than cherries, peaches and nectarines are also great fruit choices for wine. Since their character is a little more subtle, they also make great blending partners with white grape wines. Extracts and flavorings can be utilized as well if fruit character is lacking after fermentation and aging. Fully ripened peaches and nectarines can allow sugar levels to get up toward 14°Brix in some varieties, whereas pH levels generally range from 3.3 up to 4.1. Supplemental yeast nutrients are highly recommended for peach and nectarine wines.

Plum

Like cherries, plums do contain some polyphenolic compounds, and ripe plums typically come in with similar sugar levels starting around 9°Brix and ranging up to 20°Brix, depending on variety. Their pH levels do have a high variability—from as low as 2.8 all the way up to 4.3, so getting a pH reading of your juice is important.

Chapter 10:
Recipes

This is where the rubber meets the road, as the cliché goes. This chapter includes a wide array of *vinifera*, hybrid, and country fruit recipes that are made from fresh fruit, juices, and concentrates to provide you with a path to success. Even if the grape variety or fruit you plan to make wine from isn't found here, depending on your stylistic goals, these recipes will provide some guidance that can be used for almost all wine styles in various veins. Use the introductions to each recipe to recognize the wine style it will help craft.

Standards

Yields for fresh-grape winemakers are assumed based on 6 gallons (23 L) of juice per 125 pounds (57 kg) of grapes using a crusher/ destemmer and basket press. Your actual yields will vary based on equipment used as well as the berry size.

These recipes call for specific additions of sulfur dioxide at specified intervals. Once these scripted additions are made, you must monitor and maintain to 0.8 ppm molecular SO_2. Adjust as necessary using a potassium metabisulfite (KMBS) solution. Testing can be done at a qualified laboratory or in your home cellar using various commercially available testing kits.

An equipment list should include:

❖ Food-grade plastic fermenters

❖ Several carboys of varying sizes (6-gallon [23-L], 5-gallon [19-L], 3-gallon [11-L], and 1-gallon [3.8-L])

❖ Racking cane

❖ Temperature-controlled space (such as a refrigerator)

❖ Thermometer

❖ Pipettes

❖ Some form of inert gas

❖ Bottling equipment

For fresh grape production, equipment needs include:

❖ Crusher/destemmer

❖ Wine press

❖ Various testing equipment (like pH, TA, and sulfite testing kits)

For red and rosé wines, you'll need:

❖ 15-gallon (57-L) plastic container, for the maceration period

❖ For settling wines post-press, it's best to use a 7.9-gallon (30-L) plastic bucket before racking off gross lees then transferring into a carboy for aging. Not all equipment is necessary, especially when making wines using kits, juice, and concentrates.

White Wines

Chardonnay

Yield: 5 gallons (19 L)

Chardonnay can be produced in a wide array of styles. There are three key considerations winemakers need to ponder when they decide what style they would like: oak treatment, malolactic fermentation, and sur lie aging. Are you after a big, buttery Chardonnay, a clean, crisp stainless steel–aged rendition, or something in between? This version tends toward something in the middle, with a cleaner malolactic fermentation, a touch of oak, and aged on the lees to round out the body.

Ingredients

125 pounds (57 kg) fresh Chardonnay fruit, or 6 gallons (23 L) fresh juice

15 grams potassium metabisulfite (KMBS)

Distilled water

5 grams Fermaid K or equivalent yeast nutrient

Tartaric acid (amount added based on acid testing results)

6 grams Go-Ferm or equivalent yeast starter

5 grams Premier Cuvee yeast (also known as EC-1118, Prise de Mousse)

5 grams diammonium phosphate (DAP)

Malolactic fermentation starter culture (Chr. Hansen or equivalent)

Bentonite, as needed

Step by Step

1. Clean and sanitize all your winemaking tools, supplies, and equipment.

2. Crush and press the grapes. Do not delay between crushing and pressing. Move the must directly to the press and press lightly to avoid extended contact with the skins and seeds.

3. Create a 15% potassium metabisulfite (KMBS) solution by dissolving the KMBS in about 75 ml of distilled water; when completely dissolved, add distilled water up to 100 ml.

4. Transfer the juice to a 7.9-gallon (30-L) bucket. During the transfer, add 7 ml of the KMBS solution (equivalent to 50 ppm SO_2).

5. Move the juice to a refrigerator.

6. Test the juice for acidity and pH.

7. Let the juice settle at least overnight. Layer the headspace with inert gas and keep covered.

8. When sufficiently settled, rack the juice off the solids into a 5-gallon (19-L) carboy.

9. Suspend the Fermaid K in about 20 ml of distilled water, mix well, and add it to the juice.

10. If you need to adjust for acid, mix in tartaric acid, as needed.

11. Prepare the yeast. Heat about 50 ml of non-chlorinated water to 110°F (43°C). Mix in the Go-Ferm. Measure the temperature. When the temperature drops to 104°F (40°C)—do not exceed this temperature as it will kill the

yeast—sprinkle the yeast on the water's surface and gently mix so no clumps remain. Let sit for 15 minutes, undisturbed. Measure the temperature of the yeast suspension, then measure the temperature of the juice. You do not want to add the yeast to cool juice if the temperature difference exceeds 15°F (8°C). Acclimate your yeast by adding about 10 ml of cold juice to the yeast suspension. Wait 15 minutes, then measure the temperature again. Do this until you are within the specified temperature range. When the yeast is ready, add it to the carboy and move the carboy to an area where the ambient temperature is 55°F to 60°F (13°C to 16°C).

12. You should see signs of fermentation within 2 to 3 days, appearing as some foaming on the surface, and the airlock will have bubbles moving through it. If the fermentation has not started by day 4, try warming the juice to between 60°F and 65°F (16°C and 18°C) temporarily to stimulate the yeast. Once fermentation starts, move back to the lower temperature. If that does not work, consider repitching the yeast as described in step 10.

13. Dissolve the DAP in as little distilled water as needed to go completely into solution (usually about 20 ml) and add it to the carboy. This addition is typically done at one-third sugar depletion. However, since we are going on visual cues to avoid entering the carboy, then add 36 to 48 hours after noticeable fermentation

(assuming a 22 to 25°Brix initially, 36 hours for the low end and 48 hours for the high end).

14. Normally you would monitor the progress of the fermentation by measuring Brix. One of the biggest problems with making white wine at home is maintaining a clean fermentation. Entering the carboy to measure the sugar is a prime way to infect the fermentation with undesirable microbes. So at this point, the presence of noticeable fermentation is good enough. If your airlock becomes dirty by foaming over, remove, clean, and sanitize it, and replace it as quickly and cleanly as possible. Sanitize anything that will come in contact with the juice.

15. Assuming the fermentation has progressed, after about 2 weeks it is time to start measuring the sugar. Sanitize your wine thief; remove just enough liquid for your hydrometer. Record your results. If the Brix is greater than 7, wait another week before remeasuring. If the Brix is less than 7, begin measuring every other day. Continue to measure the Brix every other day until you have two readings in a row that are negative and about the same.

16. Inoculate the wine with malolactic bacteria according to the manufacturer's instructions. MLF should be conducted at a temperature above 64°F (18°C). If the wine smells good, let the lees settle for about 2 weeks, then stir them up. Repeat this step every 2 weeks for 8 weeks total. This will be a total of five stirs.

17. Monitor MLF using a paper chromatography assay according to the kit instructions.

18. When MLF is complete, add 8 ml of 15% KMBS solution (40 ppm SO_2) and lower the temperature to about 40°F (4°C). The refrigerator works best for this.

19. After 8 weeks, let the lees settle. At this point, the wine may be crystal clear or a little cloudy. If the wine is crystal clear, great! If the wine is cloudy, then, presumably, if you have kept up with the SO_2 additions and adjustments, temperature control, kept a sanitary environment, and there are no visible signs of a re-fermentation, this is most likely a protein haze, and you have two options: do nothing— it is just aesthetics, or clarify with bentonite.

20. While aging, test for SO_2 and keep it maintained at between 30 and 35 ppm free.

21. Once the wine is cleared, it is time to move it to the bottle. This would be about 6 months after the onset of fermentation. If all has gone well to this point, given the quantity made, it can probably be bottled without filtration. Your losses during filtration could be significant. Maintain sanitary conditions while bottling, and you should have a fine example of a Chardonnay that pairs well with a wide array of culinary dishes.

Pinot Gris

Yield: 5 gallons (19 L)

This is a simple way to make a clean white wine from juice concentrate. For this recipe, we'll use Pinot Gris concentrate, but juice concentrates, generally, are adjusted for pH and acidity so no further adjustments are necessary. Consult the manufacturer's specifications included with the juice.

Ingredients

Distilled water

5 (46-ounce , or 1.3-L) cans Pinot Gris juice concentrate (68 to 70°Brix)

10 grams Fermaid K or equivalent yeast nutrient

6 grams Go-Ferm or equivalent yeast starter

5 grams Lallemand QA23 yeast or Premier Cuvée (if using Premier Cuvée, reduce yeast nutrients by half—5 g Fermaid K and 2.5 g DAP)

5 grams diammonium phosphate (DAP)

10 grams potassium metabisulfite (KMBS)

Step by Step

1. Clean and sanitize all your winemaking tools, supplies, and equipment.

2. Warm 3½ gallons (13 L) of distilled water to about 65°F (18°C).

3. Add the juice concentrate to the warm water, using the water to dissolve any remaining concentrate in the can. Mix well. This can be done in the bucket or a pot on the stove. In the end, you will have about 5½ gallons (21 L) of juice in the bucket at about 22.5°Brix.

4. Suspend the Fermaid K in about 20 ml of distilled water, mix well, and add it to the juice.

5. Prepare the yeast. Heat about 50 ml of non-chlorinated water to 110°F (43°C). Mix in the Go-Ferm. Measure the temperature. When the temperature drops to 104°F (40°C)—do not exceed this temperature as it will kill the yeast—sprinkle the yeast on the water's surface and gently mix so no clumps remain. Let sit for 15 minutes, undisturbed. Measure the temperature of the yeast suspension, then measure the temperature of the juice. You do not want to add the yeast to cool juice if the temperature difference exceeds 15°F (8°C). Acclimate your yeast by adding about 10 ml of cold juice to the yeast suspension. Wait 15 minutes, then measure the temperature again. Do this until you are within the specified temperature range. When the yeast is ready, add it to the fermenter and mix.

6. Initiate the fermentation at room temperature (65°F to 68°F [18°C to 20°C]). Once you notice fermentation (within 1 to 2 days), move to a location where the temperature can be maintained at 55°F to 58°F (13°C to 15°C).

7. Two days after fermentation starts, dissolve the DAP in as little distilled water as needed to go completely into solution (usually about 20 ml), and add it to the juice.

8. Normally you would monitor the progress of the fermentation by measuring Brix. One of the biggest problems with making white wine at home is maintaining a clean fermentation. Entering the carboy to measure the sugar is a prime way to infect the fermentation with undesirable microbes. So at this point, the presence of noticeable fermentation is good enough. If your airlock becomes dirty by foaming over, remove, clean, and sanitize it, and replace it as quickly and cleanly as possible. Sanitize anything that will come in contact with the juice.

9. Leave the mixture alone until the airlock shows about one bubble per minute. This usually takes 2 to 3 weeks. Begin measuring the Brix every 2 to 3 days.

10. Make a 10% potassium metabisulfite solution by dissolving the KMBS into about 75 ml of distilled water; when dissolved, add up to 100 ml total distilled water. The wine is considered dry, or nearly dry, when the Brix reaches –1.5 or less. Add 3 ml of the KMBS solution per 1 gallon (3.8 L) of wine (equivalent to about 40 ppm addition).

11. Use inert gas to purge a 5-gallon (19-L) carboy to minimize oxygen exposure, then transfer the wine to the carboy. Lower the temperature to between 38°F and 40°F (3°C and 4°C).

12. After 2 weeks, test for pH and SO_2 and adjust as necessary to attain 0.8 ppm molecular SO_2.

13. In another 2 weeks, check the SO_2 again and adjust while racking to another sanitized carboy or bucket. In the case of the latter, clean the original carboy and transfer the wine back to it. This is done at 4 to 6 weeks after the first SO_2 addition. Once the free SO_2 is adjusted, maintain it at this target level, checking every 3 to 4 weeks.

14. Fine and/or filter, if desired.

15. At about 3 months you are ready to bottle. Maintain sanitary conditions while bottling.

Sauvignon Blanc

Yield: 5 gallons (19 L)

Keep the wine cool during active fermentation, and especially post-fermentation, to retain the esters and thiols that Sauvignon Blanc varietal wines are highly regarded for. Aging the wine on the lees and with a little lightly toasted oak is an option for the winemaker and would not be out of character for some renditions of Sauvignon Blanc.

Ingredients

125 pounds (57 kg) fresh Sauvignon Blanc fruit, or 6 gallons (23 L) fresh juice, racked off the grape solids

10 grams potassium metabisulfite (KMBS)

Distilled water

10 grams Fermaid K or equivalent yeast nutrient

6 grams Go-Ferm

5 grams Lallemand QA23 yeast

5 grams diammonium phosphate (DAP)

Bentonite, as needed

Step by Step

1. Clean and sanitize all your winemaking, tools, supplies, equipment.

2. If you are using fresh fruit, crush and press the grapes. Do not delay between crushing and pressing. Move the must directly to the press and press lightly to avoid extended contact with the skins and seeds.

3. Make a 10% potassium metabisulfite solution by dissolving the KMBS into about 75 ml of distilled water; when dissolved, add up to 100 ml total of distilled water.

4. Transfer the juice to a 7.9-gallon (30-L) bucket. If you are using fresh-crushed grape juice, add 16 ml of the solution to the juice (equivalent to 40 ppm SO_2 addition). If you are starting with 5 gallons (19 L) of juice, add 13 ml of the solution. Move the juice to the refrigerator.

5. Let the juice settle at least overnight. Layer the headspace with inert gas and keep covered.

6. When sufficiently settled, rack the juice off the solids into a 6-gallon (23-L) carboy.

7. Suspend the Fermaid K in about 20 ml of little distilled water, mix well, and add it to the juice.

8. Prepare the yeast. Heat about 50 ml of non-chlorinated water to 110°F (43°C). Mix in the Go-Ferm. Measure the temperature. When the temperature drops to 104°F (40°C)—do not exceed this temperature as it will kill the yeast—sprinkle the yeast on the water's surface and gently mix so no clumps remain. Let sit for 15 minutes, undisturbed. Measure the temperature of the yeast suspension, then measure the temperature of the juice. You do not want to add the yeast to cool juice if the temperature difference exceeds 15°F (8°C). Acclimate your yeast by adding about 10 ml of cold juice to the yeast suspension. Wait 15 minutes, then measure the temperature again. Do this until you are within the specified temperature range. When the yeast is ready, add it to the carboy.

9. Initiate the fermentation at room temperature (65°F to 68°F [18°C to 20°C]). Once fermentation starts, (about 24 hours), move the mixture to a location where the temperature can be kept at 55°F (13°C).

10. Two days after fermentation starts, dissolve the DAP in as little distilled water as needed to go completely into solution (usually about 20 ml), and add it to the carboy.

11. Normally you would monitor the progress of the fermentation by measuring Brix. Entering the carboy to measure the sugar is a prime way to infect the fermentation with undesirable microbes. So at this point, the presence of noticeable fermentation is good enough. If your airlock becomes dirty by foaming over, remove, clean, and sanitize it, and replace it as quickly and cleanly as possible. Sanitize anything that will come in contact with the juice.

12. Leave the mixture alone until bubbles in the airlock are about one per minute, usually 2 to 3 weeks.

13. At this point, start measuring the sugar. Test and record your results. If the Brix is greater than 7°Brix, wait another week before measuring again. If the Brix is less than 7°Brix, begin measuring every other day.

14. Continue to measure the Brix every other day until you have two readings in a row that are negative and about the same. This should be –1.5°Brix or lower for a dry wine.

15. Measure the residual sugar using a Clinitest kit, following the kit instructions.

16. If the wine is dry, less than 0.2%, rack to a 5-gallon (19-L) carboy and control for headspace. Add 16 ml of the 10% KMBS solution to inhibit the MLF, and lower the temperature to about 45°F (7°C).

17. Let the lees settle for about 2 weeks, then stir them up. Repeat this every 2 weeks for 8 weeks.

18. After the second stir (after the fourth week), check the SO_2 and adjust to between 30 and 35 ppm free.

19. Let the lees settle for another 2 weeks. At this point, the wine may be crystal clear or a little cloudy. If the wine is cloudy, then, presumably, if you have kept up with the SO_2 additions and adjustments, temperature control, kept a sanitary environment, and there are no visible signs of a

refermentation, this is most likely a protein haze. Fine with bentonite to clarify, if desired.

20. While aging, test for SO_2 and keep it maintained at between 30 and 35 ppm. Test for titratable acidity. The target is about 6.5 g/L. The pH target is 3.1 to 3.5, but rely more on the TA as that contributes to mouthfeel.

21. Once the wine is cleared, it is time to bottle. This is about 6 months after the onset of fermentation. Maintain sanitary conditions while bottling.

Riesling

Yield: 5 gallons (19 L)

This recipe covers a dry and sweet style of Riesling wine. Making a sweeter version requires advanced skills, specifically with mathematical calculations. We have done some for you. You can use this recipe to make a sweeter version of Riesling by adjusting your initial dilution and yeast hydration procedures as outlined.

Ingredients

Distilled water

5 (46-ounce., or 1.3-liter) cans Riesling juice concentrate (68 to 70°Brix)

10 grams Fermaid K or equivalent yeast nutrient

6 grams Go-Ferm or equivalent yeast starter

5 grams Lalvin QA23 yeast (10 g if making a sweet version)

5 grams diammonium phosphate (DAP)

10 grams potassium metabisulfite (KMBS)

Step by Step

1. Clean and sanitize all your winemaking tools, supplies, and equipment.

2. Warm 3¹/₂ gallons (13 L) of distilled water to about 65°F (18°C).

3. Add the juice concentrate, using the warmed water to completely dissolve any remaining concentrate in the can. Mix well. You should have about 5¹/₂ gallons (21 L) of juice in the bucket at about 22.5°Brix.

4. Suspend the Fermaid K in about 20 ml of distilled water, mix well, and add it to the juice.

5. Prepare the yeast. Heat about 50 ml of non-chlorinated water to 110°F (43°C). Mix in the Go-Ferm. Measure the temperature. When the temperature drops to 104°F (40°C)—do not exceed this temperature as it will kill the yeast—sprinkle the yeast on the water's surface and gently mix so no clumps remain. Let sit for 15 minutes, undisturbed. Measure the temperature of the yeast suspension, then measure the temperature of the juice. You do not want to add the yeast to cool juice if the temperature difference exceeds 15°F (8°C). Acclimate the yeast by adding about 10 ml of cold juice to the yeast suspension. Wait 15 minutes, then measure the temperature again. Do this until you are within the specified temperature range. When the yeast is ready, add it to the fermenter and mix.

6. Initiate the fermentation at room temperature (65°F to 68°F [18°C to 20°C]). Once fermentation is noticed (24 to 48 hours), appearing as some foaming on the juice, move the mixture to a location where the temperature can be maintained at 55°F to 58°F (13°C to 15°C). If using a refrigerator, be sure to monitor the temperature as some older models can be too cold even at their warmest temperature. If your fridge is colder than 55°F (13°C), consider placing the carboy in an ice bath and add ice to the water, as needed, while monitoring the temperature.

7. Two days after fermentation starts, dissolve the DAP in as little distilled water as needed to go completely into solution (usually about 20 ml), and add it to the juice.

8. Normally you would monitor the progress of the fermentation by measuring Brix. One of the biggest problems with making white wine at home is maintaining a clean fermentation. Entering the carboy to measure the sugar is a prime way to infect the fermentation with undesirable microbes. So at this point, the presence of noticeable fermentation is good enough.

9. Leave the mixture alone until bubbles in the airlock are about one bubble per minute, usually 2 to 3 weeks, then measure the Brix every 2 to 3 days.

10. The wine is considered dry, or nearly dry, when the Brix reaches –1.5 or less. *For the sweet version,*

the absence of fermentation is the key that the "end is near." Make a 10% potassium metabisulfite solution by dissolving the KMBS into about 75 ml of distilled water; when dissolved, add up to 100 ml total of distilled water. Add 3 ml of the solution per gallon (3.8 L) of wine (equivalent to about 40 ppm addition). Transfer the wine to a 5-gallon (19-L) carboy, and lower the temperature to between 38°F and 40°F (3°C and 4°C).

11. After 2 weeks, test for pH and SO_2 and adjust as necessary to attain 0.8 ppm molecular SO_2.

12. In another 2 weeks, check the SO_2 again before next racking, and adjust while racking. This is done at 4 to 6 weeks after the first SO_2 addition. Once the free SO_2 is adjusted, maintain it at this target level, checking every 3 to 4 weeks.

13. At about 3 months, you are ready to bottle. Maintain sanitary conditions while bottling.

Modifications for Sweeter (Ice) Version

1. Adjust your initial dilution: use 7 (46-ounce, or 1.3-liter) cans of concentrate to 3 gallons (11 L) of distilled water.

2. Measure the dehydrated yeast by pouring it into a disposable weigh boat on a scale. Weigh 2 to $2^1/_2$ times the amount stated on the package (50 to 65 g/hL).

3. Measure the Go-Ferm by pouring it into a disposable weigh boat on a scale. Weigh 50 g/hL.

Pour carefully; the dust is fine and can be irritating.

4. Heat 10 times the weight of the yeast in non-chlorinated water to 110°F (43°C). Mix in the Go-Ferm. Measure the temperature. When the temperature drops to 104°F (40°C)—do not exceed this temperature as it will kill the yeast—sprinkle the yeast on the water's surface and gently mix so no clumps remain. Let sit for 15 minutes, undisturbed. While waiting, dilute a small amount of wine must to about 20°Brix and warm it to 77°F (25°C). Once rehydration is complete, add an equal volume of the diluted room-temperature must to the yeast hydration container. Maintain this mixture at 86°F (30°C) for 1 hour, stirring every 30 minutes with a whisk. A water bath may be helpful to maintain a constant temperature.

5. After 1 hour, add another equal volume of 77°F (25°C) high-Brix must. Maintain the mixture for 2 hours at 77°F (25°C), mixing every 30 minutes with a whisk. The yeast starter culture is now at about 20°Brix. The must should be preheated to 68°F (20°C), then add the yeast starter culture to the main ice wine must tank. Maintain this temperature for 24 hours to allow the yeast to further acclimate, then drop the temperature to 59°F (15°C) for the remainder of the fermentation.

Seyval Blanc

Yield: 5 gallons (19 L)

The quality and style of Seyval Blanc wine is very similar to Chenin Blanc or Chablis styles, which are lighter, with notes of grapefruit, green apple, hay, and melon. It can be thin in the mouth and, in some cases, benefits greatly from barrel fermentation and malolactic fermentation, especially if the acid is high. Some winemakers offset the thinness by making a semisweet version.

Ingredients

125 pounds (57 kg) fresh Seyval Blanc fruit, or 6 gallons (23 L) commercial clarified juice

20 grams potassium metabisulfite (KMBS), divided

Distilled water

Cane sugar, as needed

Potassium carbonate, as needed

6 grams Go-Ferm or equivalent yeast starter

5 grams Lallemand QA23 yeast or Premier Cuvee yeast

5 grams Fermaid K or equivalent yeast nutrient

5 grams diammonium phosphate (DAP)

Bentonite, as needed

Step by Step

1. Clean and sanitize all your winemaking tools, supplies, and equipment.

2. If you are using fresh juice, skip to step 6. If starting with grapes, crush and press the grapes. Do not delay between crushing and pressing. Move the must directly to the press and press lightly to avoid extended contact with the skins and seeds.

3. Make a 10% potassium metabisulfite solution by dissolving 10 g of KMBS into about 75 ml of distilled water; when dissolved, add up to 100 ml total of distilled water.

4. Transfer the juice to a 7.9-gallon (30-L) bucket. During the transfer, add 16 ml of the solution (equivalent to 40 ppm SO_2 addition). Move the juice to the refrigerator.

5. Let the juice settle at least overnight. Layer the headspace with inert gas and keep the juice covered.

6. Measure the Brix. Ideal styles of this wine are around 11% alcohol, which is produced when the sugar is at 18 to 19°Brix. A higher Brix will produce a higher-alcohol wine. You do not want anything greater than 13% alcohol. If the Brix is low, add cane sugar (sucrose).

7. Adjust the acidity to 6 to 7 g/L. Given the high acidity of this grape, you will probably have to de-acidify using potassium carbonate.

8. When sufficiently settled, rack the juice off the solids into a 6-gallon (23-L) carboy.

9. Prepare the yeast. Heat about 50 ml of non-chlorinated water to 110°F (43°C). Mix in the Go-Ferm. Measure the temperature. When the temperature drops to 104°F (40°C)—do not exceed this temperature as it will kill the yeast—sprinkle the yeast on the water's surface and gently mix so no clumps remain. Let sit for 15 minutes, undisturbed. Measure the temperature of the yeast suspension, then measure the temperature of the juice. You do not want to add the yeast to cool juice if the temperature difference exceeds 15°F (8°C). Acclimate your yeast by adding about 10 ml of cold juice to the yeast suspension. Wait 15 minutes, then measure the temperature again. Do this until you are within the specified temperature range. When the yeast is ready, add it to the fermenter and mix.

10. Suspend the Fermaid K in about 20 ml of distilled water, mix well, and add it to the carboy.

11. Initiate the fermentation at room temperature (65°F to 68°F [18°C to 20°C]). Once fermentation is noticed (about 24 hours), move the mixture to a location where the temperature can be maintained at 55°F (13°C).

12. Two days after fermentation starts, dissolve the DAP in as little distilled water as needed to go completely into solution (usually about 20 ml), and add it to the carboy.

13. Normally you would monitor the progress of the fermentation by measuring Brix. One of the biggest problems with making white wine at home is maintaining a clean fermentation. Entering the carboy to measure the sugar is a prime way to infect the fermentation with undesirable microbes. So at this point, the presence of noticeable fermentation is good enough. If your airlock becomes dirty by foaming over, remove, clean, and sanitize it, and replace it as quickly and cleanly as possible. Sanitize anything that will come in contact with the juice.

14. Leave the mixture alone until bubbles in the airlock are about one bubble per minute, usually 2 to 3 weeks, then measure the Brix every 2 to 3 days.

15. The wine is considered dry, or nearly dry, when the Brix reaches –1.5 or less. Measure the residual sugar using a Clinitest kit, following the kit instructions. When the result is less than 0.5%, make a fresh batch of 10% potassium metabisulfite solution using the remaining 10 g of KMBS (see step 3) and add 15 ml of fresh solution per 1 gallon (3.8 L) of wine (equivalent to about a 40 ppm addition). Transfer the wine to a 5-gallon (19-L) carboy and lower the temperature to between 38°F and 40°F (3°C and 4°C).

16. After 2 weeks, test for pH and SO_2 and adjust as necessary to attain 0.8 ppm molecular SO_2.

17. In another 2 weeks, check the SO_2 again before the next racking, and adjust while racking. This is done at 4 to 6 weeks after the first SO_2 addition. Once the free SO_2 is adjusted, maintain it at this target level, checking every 3 to 4 weeks.

18. It is possible you may experience a protein haze, so bentonite fining is recommended.

19. At about 3 months, you are ready to bottle. Maintain sanitary conditions while bottling.

Red and Rosé Wines

Cabernet Sauvignon

Yield: 5 gallons (19 L)

The tannins in Cabernet Sauvignon can be quite harsh, including powerful sensations of bitterness and astringency. Commercial winemakers are not afraid to barrel down these wines for up to 2 years to add small doses of oxygen to help polymerize and soften the tannins. Both French and American barrels are often used from a number of different coopers.

Ingredients

125 pounds (57 kg) fresh Cabernet Sauvignon fruit

20 grams potassium metabisulfite (KMBS), divided

Distilled water

5 grams Fermaid K or equivalent yeast nutrient

Tartaric acid (addition rate based on acid testing results)

6 grams Go-Ferm or equivalent yeast starter

5 grams Lallemand D254 yeast

5 grams diammonium phosphate (DAP)

Malolactic fermentation starter culture (Chr. Hansen or equivalent)

Egg whites, as needed

Step by Step

1. Clean and sanitize all your winemaking tools, supplies, and equipment.

2. Crush and destem the grapes.

3. Make a 10% potassium metabisulfite solution by dissolving 10 g of KMBS into about 75 ml of distilled water; when dissolved, add up to 100 ml total of distilled water.

4. Transfer the must to your fermenter. During the transfer, add 15 ml of the solution (equivalent to about 50 ppm SO_2).

5. Take a sample to test for Brix, acidity, and pH. Record the results and keep them handy.

6. Layer the headspace with inert gas and keep covered and in a cool place overnight.

7. Suspend the Fermaid K in about 20 ml of distilled water, mix well, and add it to the must.

8. Go back to those results you took yesterday. Typical Brix for this wine style is 24 to 25°Brix. Typical acid levels will be 0.58 to 0.62%. Adjust as necessary using tartaric acid. If the acid is higher than 0.70%, don't panic, this recipe calls for a minimum final acidity of 0.55%.

9. Prepare the yeast. Heat about 50 ml of non-chlorinated water to 110°F (43°C). Mix in the Go-Ferm. Measure the temperature. When the temperature drops to 104°F (40°C)—do not exceed this temperature as it will kill the yeast—sprinkle the yeast on the water's surface and gently mix so no clumps remain. Let sit for 15 minutes, undisturbed. Measure the temperature of the yeast suspension, then measure the temperature of the juice. You do not want to add the yeast to cool juice if the temperature difference exceeds 15°F (8°C). Acclimate your yeast by adding about 10 ml of cold juice to the yeast suspension. Wait 15 minutes, then measure the temperature again. Do this until you are within the specified temperature range. When the yeast is ready, add it to the fermenter and mix.

10. You should see signs of fermentation within 1 to 2 days, appearing as some foaming on the must surface, and it will seem as though the berries are rising out of the medium. This is called the cap rise.

11. Push the grapes back into the juice to promote color and tannin extraction. This is called punching down and should be done at least once a day, but twice is preferred. Use a sanitized utensil.

12. Monitor the Brix and temperature twice daily during peak fermentation (10 to 21°Brix). Maintain a fermentation temperature of between 81°F and 86°F (27°C to 30°C).

13. At about 19°Brix, sprinkle in the DAP and punchdown.

14. When the must reaches 4°Brix, transfer it to your press and press the cake dry, collecting the free-run juice in a 7.9-gallon (30-L) bucket. Keep the free-run wine

separate from the press portion for now, and label the vessels. Your press fraction may be only a gallon or two (up to 8 L).

15. After settling for a day, transfer the wine to a carboy. Make sure you do not have any headspace. Place an airlock on the vessel(s).

16. Inoculate the wine with malolactic bacteria according to the manufacturer's instructions. Cover the tops with an airlock to allow CO_2 to escape.

17. Monitor MLF using a paper chromatography assay according to the kit instructions.

18. When MLF is complete, measure the residual sugar. You are shooting for 0.5% or lower. If the sugar is higher, give it more time to finish fermentation.

19. Make a fresh 10% potassium metabisulfite solution using the remaining 10 g of KMBS (see step 3) and add 2 ml of fresh solution per 1 gallon (3.8 L) of wine (0.5 ml per L of wine, equivalent to about 40 ppm addition).

20. Measure the pH and titratable acidity. Most important, you want a finished TA of 0.55 to 0.60%. The pH is secondary but should be around 3.6. Add tartaric acid to adjust the TA before settling. Place the wine in a cool place to settle.

21. After 2 weeks, test for SO_2 and adjust as necessary to attain 0.8 ppm molecular SO_2.

22. In another 2 weeks, check the SO_2 again and adjust. Once the free SO_2 is adjusted, maintain it at this

target level, checking every 2 months, and before racking.

23. Rack the wine clean twice over the next 6 to 8 months to clarify.

24. Blend the wine to integrate the press fraction back into the free run. You may not need it all; use your judgment. Fining with egg whites may be necessary to tame the tannins.

25. Filter as desired.

26. Once the wine is cleared, it is time to bottle. Maintain sanitary conditions while bottling.

Pinot Noir

Yield: 5 gallons (19 L)

Pinot Noir has much less color (anthocyanins) and so the grapes must be processed differently than, say, a Syrah to extract as much color as possible. Regimens of cold soaking before fermentation, elevated temperature during fermentation, seed removal, and harvesting on lunar cycles are used, but there is no sound research on the best means to translate the color from the grape to the wine other than sound viticultural practices.

Ingredients

125 pounds (57 kg) fresh Pinot Noir fruit, or 6 gallons (23 L) fresh juice

20 grams potassium metabisulfite (KMBS), divided

Distilled water

10 grams Fermaid K or equivalent yeast nutrient

Tartaric acid (addition rate based on acid testing results)

6 grams Go-Ferm or equivalent yeast starter

5 grams Lallemand BGY (UCD-51) yeast or Premier Cuvée

10 grams diammonium phosphate (DAP)

Malolactic fermentation starter culture (Chr. Hansen or equivalent)

Step by Step

1. Clean and sanitize all your winemaking tools, supplies, and equipment.

2. Crush and destem the grapes.

3. Make a 10% potassium metabisulfite solution by dissolving 10 g of KMBS into about 75 ml of distilled water; when dissolved, add up to 100 ml total of distilled water.

4. Transfer the must or juice to your fermenter. During the transfer, add 15 ml of the solution (addition equivalent to about 50 ppm SO_2). Mix well.

5. Take a sample to test for Brix, acidity, and pH. Record the results and keep them handy.

6. Layer the headspace with inert gas and keep covered. Keep the mixture in a cool place overnight.

7. The next day, suspend the Fermaid K in about 20 ml of distilled water and add it to the must or juice. Mix well.

8. Go back to those results you took yesterday. Typical Brix for this wine style is 24 to 25°Brix. Typical acid levels will be between 0.65 and 0.70%. Adjust as necessary using tartaric acid. If the acid is higher than 0.70%, don't panic, this recipe calls for a minimum final acidity of 0.50%.

9. Prepare the yeast. Heat about 50 ml of non-chlorinated water to 110°F (43°C). Mix in the Go-Ferm. Measure the temperature. When the temperature drops to 104°F (40°C)—do not exceed this temperature as it will kill the

yeast—sprinkle the yeast on the water's surface and gently mix so no clumps remain. Let sit for 15 minutes, undisturbed. Measure the temperature of the yeast suspension, then measure the temperature of the juice. You do not want to add the yeast to cool juice if the temperature difference exceeds 15°F (8°C). Acclimate your yeast by adding about 10 ml of cold juice to the yeast suspension. Wait 15 minutes, then measure the temperature again. Do this until you are within the specified temperature range. When the yeast is ready, add it to the fermenter and mix.

10. You should see signs of fermentation within 1 to 2 days, appearing as some foaming on the must surface, and it will seem as though the berries are rising out of the medium. This is called the cap rise.

11. Push the grapes back into the juice to promote color and tannin extraction. This is called punching down and should be done at least once each day. Use a sanitized utensil.

12. Monitor the Brix and temperature twice daily during peak fermentation (10 to 21°Brix). Morning and evening are best and more often if the temperature shows any indication of exceeding 85°F (29°C). Keep the temperature between 80°F and 85°F (27°C and 29°C). Do not cool to less than 80°F (27°C).

13. At about 19°Brix, dissolve the DAP in about 20 ml of distilled water and mix it into the must.

14. When the Brix reaches 0 (5 to 7 days), transfer to your press and press the cake dry, collecting the free-run juice in a 7.9-gallon (30-L) bucket. Keep the free-run wine separate from the press portion for now and label the vessels. Your press fraction may be only a gallon or two (up to 8 L).

15. After settling for a day, transfer the wine to a carboy. Make sure you do not have any headspace. Place an airlock on the vessel(s).

16. Inoculate the wine with malolactic bacteria according to the manufacturer's instructions. Cover the tops with an airlock to allow CO_2 to escape.

17. Monitor MLF using a paper chromatography assay according to the kit instructions.

18. When MLF is complete, measure the residual sugar using a Clinitest kit, following the kit instructions. You are looking for the results to be 0.5% or lower.

19. Make a fresh 10% potassium metabisulfite solution using the remaining 10 g of KMBS (see step 3) and add 2 ml of fresh solution per 1 gallon (3.8 L) of wine (0.5 ml per L of wine, equivalent to about 40 ppm addition).

20. Let the wine settle in a cool place.

21. Add oak chips to your press fractions. Do not treat the entire lot of wine.

22. After 2 weeks, test for pH and SO_2 and adjust the SO_2 as necessary to attain 0.8 ppm molecular SO_2.

23. In another 2 weeks, check the SO_2 again and adjust. Maintain this level, checking every 2 months or so and before racking.

24. Rack the wine clean twice over the next 6 to 8 months to clarify. Fine and/or filter, as needed.

25. Once the wine is cleared, it is time to bottle (about 12 months after fermentation is complete).

26. Blend to integrate the oak fraction back into the free run. You may not need it all.

27. If all has gone well, you can filter, if desired, and bottle. Maintain sanitary conditions while bottling.

Zinfandel

Yield: 5 gallons (19 L)

Also known as Primitivo in Italy and Tribidrag in its native Croatia, Zinfandel is an early ripening variety. It is best to showcase the fruit up front but subtly balance in some wood character. If you are using oak alternatives, work with a small lot of wine, and blend it back into the original to taste.

Ingredients

125 pounds (57 kg) fresh Zinfandel fruit, or 6 gallons (23 L) fresh juice

30 grams potassium metabisulfite (KMBS), divided

Distilled water

5 grams diammonium phosphate (DAP)

Tartaric acid (addition rate based on acid testing results)

Sugar, as needed

6 grams Go-Ferm or equivalent yeast starter

5 grams Lallemand Syrah yeast

5 grams Fermaid K or equivalent yeast nutrient

Malolactic fermentation starter culture (Chr. Hansen or equivalent)

Step by Step

1. Clean and sanitize all your winemaking tools, supplies, and equipment.

2. If you are using fresh fruit, crush and destem the grapes.

3. Make a 15% potassium metabisulfite solution by dissolving 15 g KMBS into about 75 ml of distilled water; when dissolved, add up to 100 ml total of distilled water.

4. Transfer the must or juice to your fermenter. During the transfer, add 8 ml of the solution (equivalent to about 25 ppm SO_2). Mix well. **Please note** that if you are purchasing fresh juice, check the SO_2 level before adding any more as you want it to be around 25 ppm.

5. Layer the headspace with inert gas and keep covered. Keep the mixture in a cool place overnight.

6. Take a sample to test for Brix, acidity, and pH.

7. Dissolve the DAP in as little distilled water as needed to go completely into solution (usually about 20 ml), and add it to the must or juice and mix well.

8. If you need to adjust for acid or Brix, this is the time to mix in tartaric acid or sugar. If you are adjusting Brix levels, heat just enough distilled water to dissolve your sugar.

9. Prepare the yeast. Heat about 50 ml of non-chlorinated water to 110°F (43°C). Mix in the Go-Ferm. Measure the temperature. When the temperature drops to 104°F (40°C)—do not exceed this temperature as it will kill the yeast—sprinkle the yeast on the water's surface and gently mix so no clumps remain. Let sit for 15 minutes, undisturbed. Measure the temperature of the yeast suspension, then measure the temperature of the juice. You do not want to add the yeast to cool juice if the temperature difference exceeds 15°F (8°C). Acclimate your yeast by adding about 10 ml of cold juice to the yeast suspension. Wait 15 minutes, then measure the temperature again. Do this until you are within the specified temperature range. When the yeast is ready, add it to the fermenter and mix.

10. You should see signs of fermentation within 1 to 2 days, appearing as some foaming on the must surface, and it will seem as though the berries are rising out of the medium. This is called the cap rise.

11. Push the grapes back into the juice to promote color and tannin extraction. This is called punching down and should be done at least once a day, but twice is preferred. Use a sanitized utensil.

12. Rehydrate the Fermaid K according to the manufacturer's instructions. At about 19°Brix, mix in the Fermaid K. If you are using grapes, put it directly on the cap and mix it in as part of your punchdown.

13. Monitor the Brix and temperature twice daily during peak fermentation (10 to 21°Brix). You want to keep the temperature between 85°F and 90°F (29°C and 32°C).

14. When the Brix reaches 0 (5 to 7 days), it is time to press. If you are using just fresh juice, rack the wine to the secondary fermenter (carboy) and skip steps 15 and 16.

15. If you are using grapes, transfer to your press and press the cake dry, collecting the free-run juice in a 7.9-gallon (30-L) bucket. Keep the free-run wine separate from the press portion for now and label the vessels. Your press fraction may be only a gallon or two (up to 8 L).

16. After settling for a day, transfer the wine to a carboy. Make sure you do not have any headspace. Place an airlock on the vessel(s).

17. Inoculate the wine with malolactic bacteria according to the manufacturer's instructions. MLF should be conducted at a temperature above 64°F (18°C).

18. Monitor MLF using a paper chromatography assay according to the kit instructions.

19. When MLF is complete, measure the residual sugar using a Clinitest kit, following the kit instructions.

20. Make a fresh 15% potassium metabisulfite solution using the remaining 15 g KMBS (see step 3). Add 2 ml of the fresh solution per 1 gallon (3.8 L) of wine (0.5 ml per L of wine, equivalent to about 40 ppm addition).

21. Place the wine in a cool place to settle.

22. Consider adding oak chips to your press fractions. Do not treat the entire lot of wine. Make the project fun by having a blending party to integrate the oak fraction back into the free run.

23. While aging, test for SO_2 and keep it maintained at 30 to 35 ppm.

24. Rack the wine once or twice over the next 8 to 12 months to clarify. If your wine is still cloudy after that time, you may choose to fine and/or filter.

25. Once the wine is cleared, it is time to bottle (about 12 months after fermentation is complete). Check the SO_2 level and adjust to 35 ppm. Maintain sanitary conditions while bottling.

Sangiovese

Yield: 5 gallons (19 L)

Sangiovese should be picked at optimal ripeness when flavors of strawberry and cherry are evident. In a well-balanced vineyard, this is typically at 24 to 25°Brix. Due to its tendency to over crop and extended time to maturity, fruit may come in before fully ripening. Consider making a Blanc de Noir rosé-style wine if that is the case.

Ingredients

125 pounds (57 kg) fresh Sangiovese fruit

20 grams potassium metabisulfite (KMBS), divided

Distilled water

5 grams Fermaid K or equivalent yeast nutrient

Tartaric acid (addition rate based on acid testing results)

6 grams Go-Ferm or equivalent yeast starter

5 grams Lallemand D254 yeast

5 grams diammonium phosphate (DAP)

Malolactic fermentation starter culture (Chr. Hansen or equivalent)

Step by Step

1. Clean and sanitize all your winemaking tools, supplies, and equipment.

2. Crush and destem the grapes.

3. Make a 10% potassium metabisulfite solution by dissolving 10 g of KMBS into about 75 ml of distilled water; when dissolved, add up to 100 ml total of distilled water.

4. Transfer the must to your fermenter. During the transfer, add 15 ml of the solution (equivalent to about 50 ppm SO_2 addition). Mix well.

5. Take a sample to test for Brix, acidity, and pH. Record the results and keep them handy.

6. Layer the headspace with inert gas and keep covered. Keep the mixture in a cool place overnight.

7. The next day, suspend the Fermaid K in about 20 ml of distilled water, mix well, and add it to the must.

8. Go back to those results you took yesterday. Typical Brix for this wine style is 24 to 25°Brix. Typical acid levels are between 0.58 and 0.62%. Adjust as necessary using tartaric acid. If the acid is higher than 0.70%, don't panic, this recipe calls for a minimum final acidity of 0.55%. Higher acid won't hurt here.

9. Prepare the yeast. Heat about 50 ml of non-chlorinated water to 110°F (43°C). Mix in the Go-Ferm. Measure the temperature. When the temperature drops to 104°F (40°C)—do not exceed this temperature as it will kill the

yeast—sprinkle the yeast on the water's surface and gently mix so no clumps remain. Let sit for 15 minutes, undisturbed. Measure the temperature of the yeast suspension, then measure the temperature of the juice. You do not want to add the yeast to cool juice if the temperature difference exceeds 15°F (8°C). Acclimate your yeast by adding about 10 ml of cold juice to the yeast suspension. Wait 15 minutes, then measure the temperature again. Do this until you are within the specified temperature range. When the yeast is ready, add it to the fermenter and mix.

10. You should see signs of fermentation within 1 to 2 days, appearing as some foaming on the must surface, and it will seem as though the berries are rising out of the medium. This is called the cap rise.

11. Push the grapes back into the juice to promote color and tannin extraction. This is called punching down and should be done at least once a day, but twice is preferred. Use a sanitized utensil.

12. At about 19°Brix, sprinkle in the DAP and punchdown.

13. Monitor the Brix and temperature twice daily during peak fermentation (10 to 21°Brix). Mix the must. Wait 15 minutes, mix and check the temperature again. Keep the temperature between 81°F and 86°F (27°C and 30°C).

14. When it reaches 0°Brix (5 to 7 days), transfer to your press and press the cake dry, collecting the free-run juice in a 7.9-gallon (30-L) bucket. Keep the free-run wine separate from the press portion for now and label the vessels. Your press fraction may be only a gallon or two (up to 8 L).

15. After settling for a day, transfer the wine to a carboy. Make sure you do not have any headspace. Place an airlock on the vessel(s).

16. Inoculate the wine with malolactic bacteria according to the manufacturer's instructions. Cover the tops with an airlock to allow CO_2 to escape.

17. Monitor MLF using a paper chromatography assay according to the kit instructions.

18. When MLF is complete, taste the wine for dryness. A dry wine is the stylistic goal here.

19. Make a fresh 10% potassium metabisulfite solution using the remaining 10 g of KMBS (see step 3) and add 2 ml of fresh solution per 1 gallon (3.8 L) of wine (0.5 ml per L of wine, equivalent to about 40 ppm addition).

20. Measure the pH and titratable acidity. Most important, you want a finished TA of between 0.55 and 0.60%. The pH is secondary but should be around 3.7. Add acid to adjust the TA before settling.

21. Place the wine in a cool place to settle.

22. After 2 weeks, test for SO_2 and adjust as necessary to attain 0.8 ppm molecular SO_2.

23. In another 2 weeks, check the SO_2 again and adjust. Once the free SO_2 is adjusted, maintain it at this target level, checking every 2 months or so and before racking.

24. Rack the wine clean twice over the next 6 to 8 months to clarify.

25. Once the wine is cleared, it is time to bottle (about 8 months after fermentation is complete).

26. Integrate the press fraction back into the free run. You may not need all of it.

27. Fining and/or filtrations are generally not needed if SO_2 levels are maintained and there are no surface films or indications of subsequent fermentations. Maintain sanitary conditions while bottling.

Tempranillo

Yield: 5 gallons (19 L)

With so many versions and sources of inspiration of Tempranillo-made wines (like Rioja), it's a good time for home winemakers to tackle this grape. However, because of its sometimes harsh tannins and acidity issues, the grape requires skillful handling.

Ingredients

125 pounds (57 kg) fresh Tempranillo fruit

20 grams potassium metabisulfite (KMBS), divided

Distilled water

5 grams diammonium phosphate (DAP)

Sugar, as needed

Tartaric acid (addition rate based on acid testing results)

6 grams Go-Ferm or equivalent yeast starter

5 grams Premier Cuvée yeast

5 grams Fermaid K or equivalent yeast nutrient

5 grams diammonium phosphate (DAP)

Malolactic fermentation starter culture (Chr. Hansen or equivalent)

Step by Step

1. Clean and sanitize all your winemaking tools, supplies, and equipment.

2. Crush and destem the grapes.

3. Make a 10% potassium metabisulfite solution by dissolving 10 g of KMBS into about 75 ml of distilled water. When dissolved, add up to 100 ml total of distilled water.

4. Transfer the must or juice to your fermenter. During the transfer, add 15 ml of 10% KMBS the solution. (This addition is equivalent to about 50 ppm SO_2.) Mix the solution well.

5. Take a sample to test for Brix, acidity, and pH. Record the results and keep them handy. We'll take this up later.

6. Layer the headspace with inert gas and keep covered. Keep the mixture in a cool place overnight.

7. The next day, dissolve the DAP in as little distilled water as required needed to go completely into solution (usually about 20 ml). Add the solution to the must or juice and mix well.

8. Go back to those lab results you took yesterday. Typical sugar for this style is 24 to 25 °Brix. Typical acid levels will be between 0.65 and 0.70%. Adjust the levels as necessary using sugar (if the Brix is low) and tartaric acid (if the acid is low).

9. Prepare the yeast. Heat about 50 ml distilled water to 104°F (40°C). Do not exceed this temperature as you will kill the yeast. If you overshoot the temperature, start over, or add some cooler water to get the temperature just right. Sprinkle the yeast on the surface and gently mix so that no clumps exist. Let sit for 15 minutes, undisturbed. Measure the temperature of the yeast suspension, then measure the temperature of the juice. You do not want to add the yeast to your cool juice if the temperature difference exceeds 15°F (8°C). Acclimate your yeast by taking about 10 ml of the cold juice and adding it to the yeast suspension. Wait 15 minutes, then measure the temperature again. Do this until you are within the specified temperature range. When the yeast is ready, add it to the fermenter and mix.

10. You should see signs of fermentation within 1 to 2 days. This will appear as some foaming on the must surface, and it will seem as though the berries are rising out of the medium. This is called the "cap rise."

11. Push the grapes back into the juice to promote color and tannin extraction. This is called punching down and should be done at least once a day, but twice per day is preferred. Use a sanitized utensil.

12. Monitor the Brix and temperature twice daily during peak fermentation (10 to 21°Brix). You want to keep the temperature between 85°F and 90°F (29°C and 32°C).

13. At about 19°Brix, suspend the Fermaid K in about 20 ml of distilled water, mix well, and add it to the must before punching down.

14. When the Brix reaches 0°Brix (about 5 to 7 days), transfer to your press, and press the cake dry, collecting the free-run juice in a 7.9-gallon (30-L) bucket. Keep the free-run wine separate from the press portion for now and label the vessels. Your press fraction may be only a gallon or two (up to 8 L).

15. After settling for a day, transfer the wine to a carboy. Make sure you do not have any headspace. Place an airlock on the vessel(s).

16. Inoculate the wine with your malolactic bacteria. Check according to the manufacturer's instructions on how to prepare and inoculate. Cover the tops with an airlock to allow CO_2 to escape.

17. Monitor the MLF using a thin paper chromatography assay according to the kit instructions.

18. When the MLF is complete, measure the residual sugar using a kit, following the kit instructions. Adjust, if necessary.

19. Make a fresh 10% potassium metabisulfite solution using the remaining 10 g of KMBS (see step 3) and add 2 ml of fresh KMBS 10% solution per 1 gallon (3.8 L) of wine (0.5 ml per L of wine). This is the equivalent to about 40 ppm addition).

20. Place the wine in a cool place to settle.

21. Consider adding some French or American oak chips (use American oak if you are looking for more of a Rioja-style Tempranillo wine) to your press fractions. Do not treat the entire lot of wine.

22. After 2 weeks, test for pH and SO_2 and adjust the SO_2 as necessary to attain 0.8 ppm molecular SO_2.

23. In another 2 weeks, check the SO_2 again and adjust. Once the free SO_2 is adjusted, maintain it at this target level, checking every 2 months or so.

24. Rack the wine clean twice over the next 8 to 12 months to clarify. Fining and/or filtration are generally not needed if SO_2 is maintained and there are no surface films or indications of subsequent fermentations.

25. Once the wine is cleared (after about 12 months), it is almost time to bottle. Make the project fun by having a blending party to integrate the press fraction back into the free run.

26. Now it is time to bottle. Maintain sanitary conditions while bottling.

Syrah/Shiraz

Yield: 5 gallons (19 L)

Australia recognizes Syrah as Shiraz, whereas in the United States the variety is made into wine under both names depending on the market and wine style. Maintaining a solid acid balance is key to producing a good varietal wine, most notably from grapes grown in hotter climates. Oak is recommended most often for tannin management.

Ingredients

125 pounds (57 kg) fresh Syrah fruit

20 grams potassium metabisulfite (KMBS), divided

Distilled water

5 grams Fermaid K or equivalent yeast nutrient

Tartaric acid (addition rate based on acid testing results)

6 grams Go-Ferm or equivalent yeast starter

5 grams Lallemand Syrah yeast

5 grams diammonium phosphate (DAP)

Malolactic fermentation starter culture (Chr. Hansen or equivalent)

Step by Step

1. Clean and sanitize all your winemaking tools, supplies, and equipment.

2. Crush and destem the grapes.

3. Make a 10% potassium metabisulfite solution by dissolving 10 g of KMBS into about 75 ml of distilled water; when dissolved, add up to 100 ml total of distilled water.

4. Transfer the must to your fermenter. During the transfer, add 15 ml of the solution to the must (equivalent to about 50 ppm SO_2 addition). Mix well.

5. Take a sample to test for Brix, acidity, and pH. Record the results and keep them handy.

6. Layer the headspace with inert gas and keep covered. Keep the mixture in a cool place overnight.

7. The next day, suspend the Fermaid K in about 20 ml of distilled water, mix well, and add it to the must.

8. Go back to those results you took yesterday. Typical Brix for this wine style is 24 to 25°Brix. Typical pre-fermentation acid levels will be between 5.0 and 7.0 g/L. Adjust using tartaric acid to the pre-fermentation level of 7.5 to 8.0 g/L. Malolactic conversion will drop the acid levels so slightly high acid is okay.

9. Prepare the yeast. Heat about 50 ml of non-chlorinated water to 110°F (43°C). Mix in the Go-Ferm. Measure the temperature. When the temperature drops to 104°F (40°C)—do not exceed this temperature as it will kill the yeast—sprinkle the yeast on the water's surface and gently mix so no clumps remain. Let sit for 15 minutes, undisturbed. Measure the temperature of the yeast suspension, then measure the temperature of the juice. You do not want to add the yeast to cool juice if the temperature difference exceeds 15°F (8°C). Acclimate your yeast by adding about 10 ml of cold juice to the yeast suspension. Wait 15 minutes, then measure the temperature again. Do this until you are within the specified temperature range. When the yeast is ready, add it to the fermenter and mix.

10. You should see signs of fermentation within 1 to 2 days, appearing as some foaming on the must surface, and it will seem as though the berries are rising out of the medium. This is called the cap rise.

11. Push the grapes back into the juice to promote color and tannin extraction. This is called punching down and should be done at least once a day, but twice is preferred. Use a sanitized utensil.

12. Monitor the Brix and temperature twice daily during peak fermentation (10 to 21°Brix). If the temperature exceeds 86°F (30°C), cool it down. Do not cool to less than 81°F (27°C).

13. At about 19°Brix, sprinkle in the DAP and punchdown.

14. When the Brix reaches 0 (5 to 7 days), transfer to your press and

press the cake dry, collecting the free-run juice in a 7.9-gallon (30-L) bucket. Keep the free-run wine separate from the press portion for now and label the vessels. Your press fraction may be only a gallon or two (up to 8 L).

15. After settling for a day, transfer the wine to a carboy. Make sure you do not have any headspace. Place an airlock on the vessel(s).

16. Inoculate the wine with malolactic bacteria according to the manufacturer's instructions. Cover the tops with an airlock to allow CO_2 to escape.

17. Monitor the MLF using a paper chromatography assay according to the kit instructions.

18. When the MLF is complete, measure the residual sugar.

19. Make a fresh 10% solution potassium metabisulfite solution using the remaining 10 g of KMBS (see step 3) and add 2 ml of fresh solution per 1 gallon (3.8 L) of wine (0.5 ml per L of wine, equivalent to about 40 ppm addition).

20. Measure the pH and titratable acidity. Most important, you want a finished TA of about 6.5 g/L. The pH is secondary but should be around 3.7. Consider adding acid to adjust the TA before settling, but taste the wine first. Do not add acid if the wine is too tart.

21. Place the wine in a cool place to settle.

22. After 2 weeks, test for SO_2 and adjust as necessary to attain 0.8 ppm molecular SO_2.

23. In another 2 weeks, check the SO_2 again and adjust. Once the free SO_2 is adjusted, maintain it at this target level, checking every 2 months or so and before racking.

24. Rack the wine clean twice over the next 6 to 8 months. Consider using some oak chips for 1 to 2 weeks to add some oak flavors. Fine, as needed.

25. Once the wine is cleared (about 8 months), it is almost time to bottle. First, conduct bench trials to determine how much of the press fraction to integrate into the free run, and then proceed to blend.

26. Filter, if desired, and bottle. Maintain sanitary conditions while bottling.

Marquette

Yield: 5 gallons (19 L)

Marquette wines are often considered to have the closest resemblance to wines of *V. vinifera* that are made from a hybrid species. Red and black fruit characteristics of cherry and black currant are common. Other subtle flavors of blackberry, pepper, plum, tobacco, leather, and spice are also evident.

Ingredients

125 pounds (57 kg) fresh Marquette fruit

20 grams potassium metabisulfite (KMBS), divided

Distilled water

5 grams Fermaid K or equivalent yeast nutrient

Sugar, as needed

Tartaric acid (addition rate based on acid testing results), as needed

6 grams Go-Ferm or equivalent yeast starter

5 grams Lalvin D254 yeast or Premier Cuvée

5 grams diammonium phosphate (DAP)

Malolactic fermentation starter culture (Chr. Hansen or equivalent)

Potassium carbonate, as needed

Step by Step

1. Clean and sanitize all your winemaking tools, supplies, and equipment.

2. Crush and destem the grapes.

3. Make a 10% potassium metabisulfite solution by dissolving 10 g of KMBS into about 75 ml of distilled water; when dissolved, add up to 100 ml total of distilled water.

4. Transfer the must to your fermenter. During the transfer, add 15 ml of the solution (equivalent to about 50 ppm SO_2). Mix well.

5. Take a sample to test for Brix, acidity, and pH. Record the results and keep them handy.

6. Layer the headspace with inert gas and keep covered. Keep the mixture in a cool place overnight.

7. The next day, suspend the Fermaid K in about 20 ml of distilled water, mix well, and add it to the must. Now is the time to make any adjustments to Brix and acidity, if needed.

8. Prepare the yeast. Heat about 50 ml of non-chlorinated water to 110°F (43°C). Mix in the Go-Ferm. Measure the temperature. When the temperature drops to 104°F (40°C)—do not exceed this temperature as it will kill the yeast—sprinkle the yeast on the water's surface and gently mix so no clumps remain. Let sit for 15 minutes, undisturbed. Measure the temperature of the yeast suspension, then measure the temperature of the juice. You do not want to add the yeast to cool juice if the temperature difference exceeds 15°F (8°C). Acclimate your yeast by adding about 10 ml of cold juice to the yeast suspension. Wait 15 minutes, then measure the temperature again. Do this until you are within the specified temperature range. When the yeast is ready, add it to the top of the must. Do not mix it yet.

9. You should see signs of fermentation within 1 to 2 days, appearing as some foaming on the must surface, and it will seem as though the berries are rising out of the medium. This is called the cap rise.

10. Push the grapes back into the juice to promote color and tannin extraction. This is called punching down and should be done at least once a day, but three times is preferred. Use a sanitized utensil.

11. Monitor the Brix and temperature twice daily during peak fermentation (21 to 0°Brix). Keep the temperature between 80°F and 85°F (27°C and 29°C).

12. At about 19°Brix, sprinkle in the DAP and punchdown.

13. When the Brix reaches 0 (6 to 10 days), transfer to your press and press the cake dry, collecting the free-run juice in a 7.9-gallon (30-L) bucket. Keep the free-run wine separate from the press portion for now and label the vessels. Your press fraction may be only a gallon or two (up to 8 L).

14. After settling for a day, transfer the wine to a carboy. Make sure you do not have any headspace. Place an airlock on the vessel(s). The fermentation may perk up a little as the primary completes. When activity starts to slow, measure the residual sugar using a Clinitest kit, following the kit instructions. The wine is considered dry if the residual sugar is less than 1 g/L.

15. Inoculate the wine with malolactic bacteria according to the manufacturer's instructions. Cover the tops with an airlock to allow CO_2 to escape.

16. Monitor MLF using a paper chromatography assay according to the kit instructions.

17. When MLF is complete, make a fresh 10% potassium metabisulfite solution using the remaining 10 g of KMBS (see step 3) and add 2 ml of fresh solution per 1 gallon (3.8 L) of wine (0.5 ml per L of wine, equivalent to about 40 ppm addition).

18. Measure the pH and titratable acidity. You want a finished TA of between 6.5 and 7.5 g/L. If the MLF has not reduced the acidity to this range, consider setting up a de-acidification bench trial using potassium carbonate.

19. Place the wine in a cool place to settle.

20. After 2 weeks, test for SO_2 and adjust as necessary to attain 0.8 ppm molecular SO_2.

21. In another 2 weeks, check the SO_2 again and adjust. Once the free SO_2 is adjusted, maintain it at this target level, checking every 2 months or so and before racking.

22. Rack the wine clean twice over the next 6 to 8 months to clarify. During this period, consider using some oak chips to add oak flavors. The amount of oak is based on preference, but sample your wine frequently as you don't want to overoak it. Marquette is often quite capable of a good oaking regimen.

23. Once the wine is cleared, it is time to bottle (about 8 months after fermentation is complete).

24. Make the project fun by having a blending party to integrate the press fraction back into the free run. You may not need it all; use your judgment and make what you like.

25. If all has gone well to this point, given the quantity made, the wine can probably be bottled without filtration. Maintain sanitary conditions while bottling.

Norton

Yield: 5 gallons (19 L)

The distinctive "foxy" character present in other North American grape varieties is not as prominent in Norton, which was one of the reasons it held great favor as a commercially viable wine among grape growers.

Ingredients

125 pounds (57 kg) fresh Norton fruit

20 grams potassium metabisulfite (KMBS), divided

Distilled water

5 grams Fermaid K or equivalent yeast nutrient

6 grams Go-Ferm or equivalent yeast starter

5 grams Lalvin ICV D80 yeast

5 grams diammonium phosphate (DAP)

Malolactic fermentation starter culture (Chr. Hansen or equivalent)

Egg whites, as needed

Step by Step

1. Clean and sanitize all your winemaking tools, supplies, and equipment.

2. Crush and destem the grapes.

3. Make a 10% potassium metabisulfite solution by dissolving 10 g of KMBS into about 75 ml of distilled water; when dissolved, add up to 100 ml total of distilled water.

4. Transfer the must to your fermenter. During the transfer, add 15 ml of the solution (equivalent to about 50 ppm SO_2). Mix well.

5. Layer the headspace with inert gas and keep covered. Keep the mixture in a cool place overnight.

6. The next day, suspend the Fermaid K in about 20 ml of distilled water, mix well, and add it to the must.

7. Prepare the yeast. Heat about 50 ml of non-chlorinated water to 110°F (43°C). Mix in the Go-Ferm. Measure the temperature. When the temperature drops to 104°F (40°C)—do not exceed this temperature as it will kill the yeast—sprinkle the yeast on the water's surface and gently mix so no clumps remain. Let sit for 15 minutes, undisturbed. Measure the temperature of the yeast suspension, then measure the temperature of the juice. You do not want to add the yeast to cool juice if the temperature difference exceeds 15°F (8°C). Acclimate your yeast by adding about 10 ml of cold juice to the yeast suspension. Wait 15 minutes, then measure the temperature again. Do this until you are within the specified temperature range. When the yeast is ready, add it to the fermenter and mix.

8. You should see signs of fermentation within 1 to 2 days, appearing as some foaming on the must surface, and it will seem as though the berries are rising out of the medium. This is called the cap rise.

9. Push the grapes back into the juice to promote color and tannin extraction. This is called punching down and should be done at least once a day, but twice is preferred. Use a sanitized utensil.

10. Monitor the Brix and temperature twice daily during peak fermentation (10 to 21°Brix). Morning and evening are best and more often if the temperature shows any indication of exceeding 86°F (30°C), in which case add frozen water bottles to the fermenter. Mix the must. Wait 15 minutes, mix and check the temperature again. Do this as often as it takes to keep the temperature between 81°F and 86°F (27°C and 30°C).

11. At about 19°Brix, sprinkle in the DAP and punchdown.

12. When the Brix reaches 0 (5 to 7 days), transfer to your press and press the cake dry, collecting the free-run juice in a 7.9-gallon (30-L) bucket. Keep the free-run wine separate from the press portion for now and label the vessels. Your press fraction may be only a gallon or two (up to 8 L).

13. After settling for a day, transfer the wine to a carboy. Make sure you do not have any headspace. Place an airlock on the vessel(s).

14. Inoculate the wine with malolactic bacteria according to the manufacturer's instructions. Cover the vessel(s) with an airlock to allow CO_2 to escape.

15. Monitor MLF using a paper chromatography assay according to the kit instructions.

16. When MLF is complete, make a fresh 10% potassium metabisulfite solution using the remaining 10 g of KMBS (see step 3) and add 2 ml of fresh solution per 1 gallon (3.8 L) of wine (0.5 ml per L of wine, equivalent to about 40 ppm addition). Place the wine in a cool place to settle.

17. After 2 weeks, test for SO_2 and adjust as necessary to attain 0.8 ppm molecular SO_2.

18. In another 2 weeks, check the SO_2 again and adjust. Once the free SO_2 is adjusted, maintain it at this target level, checking every 2 months or so and before racking.

19. Rack the wine clean twice over the next 6 to 8 months to clarify. Consider adding oak chips to your press fractions, or the entire lot, depending on your goal for the wine.

20. Once the wine is cleared, it is time to bottle (about 8 months after fermentation is complete).

21. Make the project fun by having a blending party to integrate the press fraction back into the free

run. You may not need it all; use your judgment and make what you like. Fining with egg whites may be necessary to tame the tannins.

22. If all has gone well to this point, given the quantity made, the wine can probably be bottled without filtration. Maintain sanitary conditions while bottling.

Cinsault Rosé

Yield: 5 gallons (19 L)

This recipe utilizes the Blanc de Noir method to produce a rosé wine. Other wine grape varieties to try with this technique include Grenache, Mouvèdre, Pinot Noir, and Sangiovese to name a few.

Ingredients

125 pounds (57 kg) fresh Cinsault fruit

20 grams potassium metabisulfite (KMBS), divided

Distilled water

Rice hulls, as needed

Dry ice, as needed

Tartaric acid (addition rate based on acid testing results)

6 grams Go-Ferm or equivalent yeast starter

5 grams Lalvin 71B yeast or Red Star Premier Cuvee

10 grams Fermaid K or equivalent yeast nutrient

10 grams diammonium phosphate (DAP)

Step by Step

1. Clean and sanitize all your winemaking tools, supplies, and equipment.

2. Crush and destem the grapes.

3. Make a 10% potassium metabisulfite solution by dissolving 10 g of KMBS into about 75 ml of distilled water; when dissolved, add up to 100 ml total of distilled water.

4. Transfer the must to a 15-gallon (57-L) fermenter bucket. During the transfer, add 15 ml of the solution (equivalent to about 50 ppm SO_2). Mix well.

5. Layer the headspace with inert gas and monitor every 4 to 6 hours for color development. It will be time to press the must when a rosé color is achieved. The maximum time you'll want to leave the juice on the skins is 24 hours. Enzymes could be used to aid color extraction.

6. Measure the volume of the must and stir in the rice hulls—the goal is 30% rice hulls in the slurry. The rice hulls aid in pressing by creating juice channels. Your juice yields will increase significantly with their use.

7. For pressing, have dry ice chunks on hand. You'll want to see visible gassing, viewed as "smoke," bubbling when the must is pressed. Move the must/rice hull slurry directly to the press and press to a 7.9-gallon (30-L) bucket. The dry ice chunks should be in the bucket.

8. While pressing the juice to the bucket, add 8 ml of the KMBS solution (equivalent to about 20 mg/L [ppm] SO_2). Test the juice for acidity. Adjust with tartaric acid, as needed. You'll want to be around 6.5 to 7.5 g/L. Move the juice to the refrigerator.

9. Let the juice settle at least overnight. Layer the headspace with inert gas or add more dry ice. Keep covered.

10. When sufficiently settled, rack the juice off the solids into a 6-gallon (23-L) carboy.

11. Prepare the yeast. Heat about 50 ml of non-chlorinated water to 110°F (43°C). Mix in the Go-Ferm. Measure the temperature. When the temperature drops to 104°F (40°C)—do not exceed this temperature as it will kill the yeast—sprinkle the yeast on the water's surface and gently mix so no clumps remain. Let sit for 15 minutes, undisturbed. Measure the temperature of the yeast suspension, then measure the temperature of the juice. You do not want to add the yeast to cool juice if the temperature difference exceeds 15°F (8°C). Acclimate your yeast by adding about 10 ml of cold juice to the yeast suspension. Wait 15 minutes, then measure the temperature again. Do this until you are within the specified temperature range. When the yeast is ready, add it to the fermenter and mix.

12. Suspend the Fermaid K in about 20 ml of distilled water, mix well, and add it to the must.

13. Initiate the fermentation at room temperature (65°F to 68°F [18°C to 20°C]). Once fermentation is noticed (about 24 hours), move the mixture to a location where the temperature can be maintained at 55°F (13°C).

14. Two days after fermentation starts, dissolve the DAP in as little distilled water as needed to go completely into solution (usually about 20 ml), and add it to the carboy.

15. Normally you would monitor the progress of the fermentation by measuring Brix. One of the biggest problems with making rosé or white wines at home is maintaining a clean fermentation. Entering the carboy to measure the sugar is a prime way to infect the fermentation with undesirable microbes. So at this point, the presence of noticeable fermentation is good enough. If your airlock becomes dirty by foaming over, remove, clean, and sanitize it, and replace it as quickly and cleanly as possible.

16. Leave the mixture alone until bubbles in the airlock are about one bubble per minute, usually 2 to 3 weeks.

17. Measure the Brix. The wine is considered dry, or nearly dry, when the Brix reaches –1.5 or less.

18. When the fermentation is complete, make a fresh 10% potassium metabisulfite solution using the remaining 10 g of KMBS (see step 3) and add 3 ml of fresh solution per 1 gallon (3.8 L) of wine.

19. Transfer the wine off the lees to a carboy and lower the temperature to 38°F to 40°F (3°C to 4°C). Make sure there is no headspace. If you have leftover wine, you might as well have this for dinner.

20. After 2 weeks, test for pH and SO_2 and adjust as necessary to attain 0.8 ppm molecular SO_2.

21. In another 2 weeks, check the SO_2 again before the next racking, and adjust while racking. This is done at 4 to 6 weeks after the first SO_2 addition. Once the free SO_2 is adjusted, maintain it at this target level, checking every 3 to 4 weeks.

22. Fine and/or filter, if desired.

23. At about 3 months, you are ready to bottle. Maintain sanitary conditions while bottling.

Country Wines

Blueberry-Blackberry Wine

Yield: 5 gallons (19 L)

This wine, utilizing blueberries and blackberries, offers the best of both fruits. You will want more blueberries than blackberries as blackberries have stronger flavors and can overpower the blueberry quickly. A 60/40 blend results in a wine that expresses both beautifully.

Ingredients

13 pounds (5.9 kg) fresh blueberries, frozen

10 pounds (4.5 kg) fresh blackberries, frozen

9 pounds (4.1 kg) table sugar, plus more to backsweeten

4 gallons (15 L) water, plus more for the simple syrup, and as needed

17 grams pectic enzyme

13 grams acid blend

2.5 grams wine tannin

7 grams Fermaid K or equivalent yeast nutrient

6 grams Go-Ferm or equivalent yeast starter

5 grams Lalvin EC-1118 yeast

5 Campden tablets, plus more as needed to adjust SO_2 levels

Potassium metabisulfite (KMBS), as needed

2.5 teaspoons potassium sorbate

Step by Step

1. Clean and sanitize all your winemaking tools, supplies, and equipment.

2. Even when picking your own berries, it's best to freeze them since they don't all ripen at the same time. Freezing the berries has the added benefit of breaking down the cell walls so they give up their juice much more quickly.

3. Thaw the berries. Place the thawed berries in a muslin bag and add them to a fermenter. Add about 4 gallons (16 L) of water to bring the total volume in the fermenter up to 5 gallons (19 L).

4. Make a simple syrup with the sugar and as little water as necessary, adding water and stirring until the sugar dissolves. Add enough of the syrup to the mixture to bring the specific gravity to 1.092 (about 9 pounds [4.1 kg]).

5. With the must in the mid-70s°F (about 32°C), add the pectic enzyme, acid blend, wine tannin, and yeast nutrients. Let the mixture soak for 24 hours. Blueberries can be difficult to get a good fermentation going with as their skins contain enzymes that seem to inhibit fermentation. Yeast nutrient is a must when fermenting blueberries.

6. Prepare the yeast. Heat about 50 ml of non-chlorinated water to 110°F (43°C). Mix in the Go-Ferm. Measure the temperature. When the temperature drops to 104°F (40°C)—do not exceed this temperature as it will kill the yeast—sprinkle the yeast on the water's surface and gently mix so no clumps remain. Let sit for 15 minutes, undisturbed. Measure the temperature of the yeast suspension, then measure the temperature of the juice. You do not want to add the yeast to cool juice if the temperature difference exceeds 15°F (8°C). Acclimate your yeast by adding about 10 ml of cold juice to the yeast suspension. Wait 15 minutes, then measure the temperature again. Do this until you are within the specified temperature range. When the yeast is ready, add it to the fermenter and mix.

7. Once fermentation is well under way (24 to 48 hours), move the must to a slightly cooler spot, about 67°F (19°C). Allow the fermentation to complete.

8. Remove the berries, pressing the muslin bags lightly to extract any remaining juice. Let the wine sit for a few hours to allow any sediment stirred up by the berry removal to settle to the bottom. Rack the wine off the sediment and add 5 Campden tablets. Let sit for 1 month to clear.

9. After a month, rack off any remaining dead yeast or sediments. Test the SO_2 and add Campden or potassium metabisulfite to bring the wine to 30 ppm free. Degas the wine to help further clarify it.

10. After another month (or when the wine is totally clear), perform a final racking. Test for SO_2 and add Campden or potassium metabisulfite to bring it back to 30 ppm free. Add the potassium sorbate and let sit for 24 hours.

11. Fruit/berry wines really need a little sweetness to bring out the flavor of the fruit. Do bench trials to decide what sweetness level tastes best with the berries to your palate (we have found backsweetening with simple syrup to bring the specific gravity back up to 1.014 is a good starting point). It is important to backsweeten in stages and taste/remeasure along the way. The perception of sweetness can climb quickly and it is always easier to add more sugar than compensate for too much sweetness.

12. Bottle the wine once it tastes the way you like. Maintain sanitary conditions while bottling.

Country Strawberry Wine

Yield: 5 gallons (19 L)

Most strawberry wine recipes call for between 12.5 and 25 pounds (5.7 and 11.3 kg) of strawberries per 5-gallon (19-L) batch. You can concoct your own recipe by making a few logical adjustments. Choose an amount of strawberries between 12.5 and 25 pounds (5.7 and 11.3 kg); adjust the sugar level to produce the desired potential alcohol (20°Brix to result in a wine of about 11 percent ABV is a good starting point); use a titration kit to adjust the acid level to 0.6 percent tartaric. The wine tannin is optional. Add between 0 and 1 tsp. based on the amount of strawberries used. The more strawberries used, the less tannin required. The potassium metabisulfite should be dosed at roughly 1/16 teaspoon for every 8 pounds (3.6 kg) of strawberries.

Ingredients

25 pounds (11.3 kg) fresh or frozen strawberries

Potassium metabisulfite (KMBS), as needed

Acid blend, as needed

Pectic enzyme, as needed

1 teaspoon wine tannin (optional)

12 pounds (5.4 kg) sugar, plus more to backsweeten (optional)

6 grams Go-Ferm or equivalent yeast starter

5 grams Lalvin D-47 yeast or Red Star Pasteur Red yeast

5 teaspoons yeast nutrient

Step by Step

1. Clean and sanitize all your winemaking tools, supplies, and equipment.

2. If the strawberries are fresh, lightly rinse them with water and let drain. Remove the stems and leaves. Discard any questionable berries and chop off any unripened areas you may find. Then coarsely chop the berries. If the strawberries have been frozen, thaw completely, then mash them.

3. Place the strawberries into a primary fermenter, then add enough water to barely cover them.

4. Add the potassium metabisulfite, acid blend, and wine tannin, as needed (see headnote).

5. Add the pectic enzyme according to the manufacturer's instructions based on the total batch size (which is greater than the amount you are currently working with). This will allow the fruit's pectin to break down faster than normal. All fruits, including grapes, contain pectin but strawberries have an abundance of it. If it's not broken down, your resulting wine will end up with a permanent pectin haze. Pectic enzymes will help the yeast complete this process.

6. Cover the mixture with a lid or a light towel and let sit for 24 hours.

7. Add water to equal 5 gallons (19 L).

8. Stir in the sugar until completely dissolved.

9. Prepare the yeast. Heat about 50 ml of non-chlorinated water to 110°F (43°C). Mix in the Go-Ferm. Measure the temperature. When the temperature drops to 104°F (40°C)—do not exceed this temperature as it will kill the yeast—sprinkle the yeast on the water's surface and gently mix so no clumps remain. Let sit for 15 minutes, undisturbed. Measure the temperature of the yeast suspension, then measure the temperature of the juice. You do not want to add the yeast to cool juice if the temperature difference exceeds 15°F (8°C). Acclimate your yeast by adding about 10 ml of cold juice to the yeast suspension. Wait 15 minutes, then measure the temperature again. Do this until you are within the specified temperature range. When the yeast is ready, add it to the fermenter and mix.

10. Re-cover with the lid or a towel and allow the wine to ferment.

11. On or around the seventh day of a normal fermentation, the activity should start to decrease. The sugar level should be between 6 and 9°Brix. At this point, you're ready to rack your must into a secondary container. Leave as much of the pulp and sediment behind as possible.

12. Attach an airlock and let the wine ferment until it has completely stopped, 4 to 6 weeks.

13. Rack one more time into a clean secondary container, reattach the airlock, and let stand until the wine is completely clear. This will usually take an additional week or two. Make an SO_2 addition to bring level up to 35 ppm free.

14. If everything has gone as planned, the wine should be dry at this point. If you prefer your wine a little sweeter, this is the time to backsweeten to taste. Also consider a little strawberry extract if the fruit character is lacking. You can use anything from table sugar to honey, but remember that anytime you add sugar to a finished wine, you must add a stabilizer, such as a combination of potassium metabisulfite and potassium sorbate, or filter the wine using sterile filter pads to prevent refermentation.

Dandelion Wine

Yield: 1 gallon (3.8 L)

This recipe makes a light wine with a similarity to some Sauternes—that is, an aromatic white wine with a delicate flavor and light color. It will produce a fairly alcoholic wine, starting with a Brix of about 24. If a lighter wine is desired, the sugar may be reduced accordingly.

Ingredients

8 cups (60 g) loosely packed fresh dandelion petals

2.5 pounds (1.1 kg) sugar

1 pound (454 g) raisins, chopped

20 grams acid blend

1/4 teaspoon potassium metabisulfite

1/4 teaspoon wine tannin

1 gallon (3.8 L) hot water

6 grams Go-Ferm or equivalent yeast starter

5 grams Lalvin EC-1118 yeast

1 gram yeast hulls

1.5 grams diammonium phosphate (DAP)

Kieselsol, as needed

Chitin, as needed

1/4 teaspoon ascorbic acid

Step by Step

1. Clean and sanitize all your winemaking tools, supplies, and equipment.

2. In a primary fermenter, combine the dandelion petals, sugar, raisins, acid blend, potassium metabisulfite, and wine tannin. Pour in the hot water and stir with a sanitized spoon to dissolve the sugar.

3. Let cool naturally to room temperature, but to no less than 75°F (24°C).

4. Prepare the yeast. Heat about 50 ml of non-chlorinated water to 110°F (43°C). Mix in the Go-Ferm. Measure the temperature. When the temperature drops to 104°F (40°C)—do not exceed this temperature as it will kill the yeast—sprinkle the yeast on the water's surface and gently mix so no clumps remain. Let sit for 15 minutes, undisturbed. Measure the temperature of the yeast suspension, then measure the temperature of the juice. You do not want to add the yeast to cool juice if the temperature difference exceeds 15°F (8°C). Acclimate your yeast by adding about 10 ml of cold juice to the yeast suspension. Wait 15 minutes, then measure the temperature again. Do this until you are within the specified temperature range. When the yeast is ready, add it as well as the yeast hulls to the fermenter and mix.

5. Two days after fermentation starts, dissolve the DAP in as little distilled water as needed to go completely into solution (usually about 20 ml). Add the DAP solution directly to the carboy.

6. Three days after pitching your yeast, strain off into a closed fermenter fitted with an airlock, leaving the petals and raisin pulp behind.

7. When fermentation is complete (about 3 weeks) and the Brix has dropped below 0, rack the wine to a sanitized fermenter with an airlock. Make sure there is no empty headspace.

8. The second racking should be performed when the wine has thrown a deposit and is beginning to clear (after about 3 months).

9. When the wine is clear and stable, fine, if desired. Due to the virtually nonexistent protein level, fining is not usually necessary. If, however, the wine does not clear spontaneously, kieselsol—followed in 24 hours by chitin—is recommended. Follow the package directions and do not overfine.

10. Add ascorbic acid and potassium metabisulfite as an antioxidant and bottle. Maintain sanitary conditions while bottling. The wine may be slightly sweetened to about 1% residual sugar if a stabilizer, such as potassium sorbate, is also added to prevent refermentation in the bottle.

Cherry Port-Style Wine

Yield: 6 gallons (23 L)

By using fruit purée, the laborious task of pitting and processing all the fruit is complete. Aseptic fruit juice packs can also be used for this recipe.

Ingredients

10 pounds (4.5 kg) sugar, plus more as needed

Distilled water

13 grams pectic enzyme

21 grams yeast nutrient

30 grams acid blend

1 teaspoon grape tannin

6 (49-ounce, or 1.4-L) cans sweet cherry purée

10 grams Go-Ferm or equivalent yeast starter

8 grams Vintner's Harvest VR21 yeast

2.9 quarts (2.7 L) 190-proof Everclear

3.5 grams potassium sorbate

6.6 grams potassium metabisulfite (KMBS)

43 grams isinglass

Step by Step

1. Clean and sanitize all your winemaking tools, supplies, and equipment.

2. In a primary fermenter, combine 10 pounds (4.5 kg) of sugar and 2 gallons (7.6 L) of water. Stir to dissolve the sugar.

3. Add the pectic enzyme, yeast nutrient, acid blend, and grape tannin.

4. Add the cherry puree, then fill the fermenter with water to a total volume of 6 gallons (23 L). Stir thoroughly to dissolve and mix all the ingredients.

5. Check the initial specific gravity of the wine. If it is not at least 1.100, add sugar, as need needed, to bring it up to 1.100.

6. Prepare the yeast. Heat about 50 ml of non-chlorinated water to 110°F (43°C). Mix in the Go-Ferm. Measure the temperature. When the temperature drops to 104°F (40°C)—do not exceed this temperature as it will kill the yeast—sprinkle the yeast on the water's surface and gently mix so no clumps remain. Let sit for 15 minutes, undisturbed. Measure the temperature of the yeast suspension, then measure the temperature of the juice. You do not want to add the yeast to cool juice if the temperature difference exceeds 15°F (8°C). Acclimate your yeast by adding about 10 ml of cold juice to the yeast suspension. Wait 15 minutes, then measure the temperature again. Do this until you are within the specified temperature range. When the yeast is ready, add it to the fermenter and mix.

7. During primary fermentation, punchdown the cap and measure the specific gravity at least twice a day to keep close track of the fermentation process.

8. Once the specific gravity of the juice reaches 1.040, transfer sanitized 6-gallon (23-L) carboy containing the Everclear.

9. Over the next 3 days, stir the wine thoroughly multiple times a day to degas as much as possible.

10. Add the potassium sorbate and potassium metabisulfite to the wine and stir to dissolve. Note that fermentation will typically not stop completely for at least 12 hours, so make sure that the carboy is fitted with an airlock to prevent a buildup of gas pressure inside it.

11. After the wine has been degassed and stabilized, add the isinglass and stir thoroughly. Let the wine stand until clear, and then rack it away from the lees as many times as needed.

12. Depending on the volume of lees, it may be necessary to transfer the wine to a 5-gallon (19-L) carboy to limit oxygen exposure during clarification.

13. Once the wine has been clarified, bottle as usual, or in 375-ml bottles. Maintain sanitary conditions while bottling.

14. The wine will be at its best if allowed to age in the bottle for 6 months or more.

Plum Dessert Wine

Yield: 1 gallon (3.8 L)

When picked at peak ripeness, these plums can make a magnificent sweet wine of about 15% ABV that is perfect to serve during the holiday season.

Ingredients

10 grams Campden powder

Distilled water

8 pounds (3.6 kg) Damson plums, fully ripe but with no rot

2.5 pounds (1.1 kg) fructose or granulated sugar, for chaptalization, plus more for backsweetening

2.5 grams Fermaid K or equivalent yeast nutrient

6 grams Go-Ferm or equivalent yeast starter

5 grams Red Star Côte des Blancs yeast (enough for up to 6 gallons [23 L] of wine)

1 gram diammonium phosphate (DAP)

Campden tablets, as needed

1 gram bentonite

0.5 gram gelatin

1 gram potassium sorbate

Step by Step

1. Clean and sanitize all your winemaking tools, supplies, and equipment.

2. Make a 10% sulfite solution by dissolving the Campden powder in enough distilled water to make 100 ml. Store in a tightly sealed container.

3. Slice the plums and discard the pits. Stone fruits pits contain trace amounts of cyanide, and though it is unlikely to concentrate to dangerous levels in your wine, don't take chances.

4. Place the plum flesh (including the skins) into mesh bags, filling them loosely (maximum half full). Tie the bags closed and place them in your fermentation bucket along with any juice.

5. Dissolve 2.5 pounds (1.1 kg) of sugar in 5 pints (2.3 L) of water. Mix in the Fermaid K and 3 ml of the 10% sulfite solution. Pour this mixture over the fruit in the bucket and stir to make sure the sugar water and juice are mixed.

6. Prepare the yeast. Heat about 50 ml of non-chlorinated water to 110°F (43°C). Mix in the Go-Ferm. Measure the temperature. When the temperature drops to 104°F (40°C)—do not exceed this temperature as it will kill the yeast—sprinkle the yeast on the water's surface and gently mix so no clumps remain. Let sit for 15 minutes, then add 15 ml of juice from the bucket. This will acclimate the yeast to the temperature of your must. Let sit for another 15 minutes, then measure the temperature of the yeast and the temperature of the must. If the difference is more than 15°F (8°C), add another 15 ml of juice. Once the temperature difference is within 15°F (8°C), add the yeast to the fermenter.

7. Seal the lid on the bucket and affix an airlock.

8. Monitor to determine when fermentation starts. When it does, punchdown the must at least once per day, but preferably twice.

9. Two or 3 days after fermentation starts, dissolve the DAP in about 20 ml of distilled water and mix it into the fermentation bucket.

10. Monitor fermentation. When SG = 1.010 or less, "press." This means remove the mesh bags of fruit from the bucket, allowing as much of the liquid to drip out into the bucket as possible, and then gently squeeze the bags to get more juice but as little of the solids as possible. Reseal the bucket and continue to monitor the fermentation.

11. When fermentation finishes (SG = 0.998 or less, and stays the same for at least two days), rack the wine to a sanitized jug. Use extra jars, if needed, to handle more volume. Measure the pH and sulfite levels, then add an appropriate amount of 10% sulfite solution using the sulfite calculator at www.winemakermag.com/

sulfitecalculator (usually about 55 ppm/1 Campden tablet per 1 gallon [3.8 L]). Let rest undisturbed for 4 to 6 weeks.

12. Rack the wine again off the fine lees. Let rest for another 4 to 6 weeks.

13. Rack the wine off any sediment, then dissolve the bentonite in 5 times its weight of water. Mix the bentonite solution into the wine and allow it to settle for 1 week.

14. Rack the wine off the bentonite.

15. Prepare the gelatin. Mix the gelatin in warm water until dissolved and then stir the mixture into the wine. Let settle for 1 week.

16. Rack the wine off the gelatin.

17. Stabilize. Dissolve the potassium sorbate in 10 times its weigh of water. Add equal amounts of dissolved potassium sorbate solution and 10% sulfite solution to the wine and gently mix. Let rest undisturbed for at least 2 days.

18. Do bench test trials to determine the proper level of backsweetening sugar to add. An addition of 14 ounces per gallon (3.8 L; about 100 g/L) is a good starting point, but depending on how ripe the fruit is, the perfect amount for your wine could vary. Gently mix the backsweetening sugar into the wine until it is fully dissolved.

19. Filter, if desired, then the wine is ready to bottle. Maintain sanitary conditions while bottling. The wine will be good to drink as soon as it is bottled, but it will improve if allowed to cellar for 4 to 6 months. Provided it was sulfited properly, a good quality cork was used, and it is stored in a cool place, it should remain at peak condition for at least 3 to 5 years before it starts to show signs of decline.

Resources

Publications

From Vines to Wines: The Complete Guide to Growing Grapes & Making Your Own Wine by Jeff Cox

Home Winemaking: The Simple Way to Make Delicious Wine by Jack Keller

Modern Home Winemaking: A Guide to Making Consistently Great Wines by Daniel Pambianchi

The Best of WineMaker *25 Classic Wine Styles* by Chik Brenneman

The Best of WineMaker *Guide to Growing Grapes* by Wes Hagen

The Best of WineMaker *Guide to Wine Kits* by Tim Vandergrift

The Home Winemaker's Companion: Secrets, Recipes, and Know-How for Making 115 Great-Tasting Wines by Gene Spaziani and Ed Halloran

The Oxford Companion to Wine by Jancis Robinson and Julia Harding

The Wine Maker's Answer Book: Solutions to Every Problem; Answers to Every Question by Alison Crowe

Online

MoreWine! Manuals: morewinemaking.com/content/winemanuals
A large collection of high-quality, free .pdf manuals and winemaking instructions developed by the experts at *MoreWine!*

Musto Wine Grape: juicegrape.com
In addition to selling grapes and supplies, a plethora of educational information is available in their blog and (for purchase) winemaking videos at winemakinginstructions.com

The Home Winemaking Channel: youtube.com/@TheHomeWinemakingChannel
This YouTube channel by Rick Haibach covers home winemaking tips, tricks, reviews, and general information for the novice to the enthusiast!

WineMaker magazine: winemakermag.com
The online homepage for *WineMaker* magazine, featuring years of *WineMaker* articles, recipes, resource guides, a sulfite calculator, and more.

Acknowledgments

We would like to thank all of the great *WineMaker* staff who have contributed to our content over the years, as well as the many fantastic freelance writers and technical editors who have made *WineMaker* great, including:

❖ Jenne Baldwin-Eaton

❖ Dwayne Bershaw

❖ Andrew K. Boal

❖ Chik Brenneman

❖ David Cohen

❖ Chris Colby

❖ Alison Crowe

❖ Michael Fairbrother

❖ Florencia Gomez

❖ Wes Hagen

❖ Pat Henderson

❖ Michael Jones

❖ Ed Kraus

❖ Maureen Macdonald

❖ Christiana McDougal

❖ Christina Musto-Quick

❖ Daniel Pambianchi

❖ Betsy Parks

❖ Bob Peak

❖ Phil Plummer

❖ Dominick Profaci

❖ Andrew Reudink

❖ Larry Roux

❖ Alex Russan

❖ Jeff Shoemaker

❖ Ken Stafford

❖ Leah Stafford

❖ Jef Stebben

❖ Gail Tufford

❖ Danny Wood

We would also like to extend our gratitude to Musto Wine Grape Company in Hartford, Connecticut, United States of America, who allowed us to use their equipment and facility to shoot the majority of the photography in this book. The expertise and hospitality provided by their staff was exceptional.

About the Authors

WineMaker, launched in 1998, is the largest-circulation magazine for people interested in making wine at home. Every issue includes expert advice, how-to projects, and recipes to help you craft world-class wine. *WineMaker* publishes six issues annually from offices in Manchester Center, Vermont. The magazine's online home, winemakermag.com, offers a selection of the magazine's content as well as additional features to help the home winemaker.

Editor Dawson Raspuzzi joined *WineMaker* in 2013. He is a 2007 graduate of the journalism program at Castleton University in Castleton, Vermont, and lives with his wife and three children in southern Vermont.

Assistant Editor Dave Green joined *WineMaker* in 2007. He is a 2001 graduate of Colby College in Waterville, Maine, with a BA in biology. He lives with his two teenage children and became an Intro Level Sommelier to pass time during the pandemic.

Index